THE LAWYER–JUDGE BIAS IN THE AMERICAN LEGAL SYSTEM

Virtually all American judges are former lawyers. This book argues that these lawyer-judges instinctively favor the legal profession in their decisions and that this bias has far-reaching and deleterious effects on American law. There are many reasons for this bias, some obvious and some subtle. Fundamentally, it occurs because – regardless of political affiliation, race, or gender – all American judges share a single characteristic: a career as a lawyer. This shared background results in the lawyer–judge bias. The book begins with a theoretical explanation of why judges naturally favor the interests of the legal profession and follows with case law examples from diverse areas, including legal ethics, criminal procedure, constitutional law, torts, evidence, and the business of law. The book closes with a case study of the Enron fiasco, an argument that the lawyer–judge bias has contributed to the overweening complexity of American law, and suggestions of some possible solutions.

Benjamin H. Barton is the Director of Clinical Programs and Professor of Law at The University of Tennessee College of Law. His articles have been published in the *Michigan Law Review, California Law Review*, and *The Journal of Empirical Legal Studies* and discussed in *Time* magazine, the *New York Times*, and the *Wall Street Journal* law blog, among others. Barton has been twice named the Outstanding Faculty Advisor for UT Pro Bono and has received the Marilyn V. Yarbrough Faculty Award for Writing Excellence. He is the winner of the 2010 LSAC Philip D. Shelton Award for outstanding research in legal education.

The Lawyer–Judge Bias in the American Legal System

Benjamin H. Barton

The University of Tennessee College of Law

CAMBRIDGE
UNIVERSITY PRESS

CAMBRIDGE UNIVERSITY PRESS
Cambridge, New York, Melbourne, Madrid, Cape Town, Singapore,
São Paulo, Delhi, Dubai, Tokyo, Mexico City

Cambridge University Press
32 Avenue of the Americas, New York, NY 10013-2473, USA

www.cambridge.org
Information on this title: www.cambridge.org/9781107004757

First published 2011

Printed in the United States of America

A catalog record for this publication is available from the British Library.

Library of Congress Cataloging in Publication data

Barton, Benjamin H., 1969–
The lawyer–judge bias in the American legal system / Benjamin H. Barton.
p. cm.
Includes bibliographical references and index.
ISBN 978-1-107-00475-7 (hardback)
1. Judges – Selection and appointment – United States. 2. Lawyers – United States.
I. Title.
KF8776.B37 2011
347.73′14–dc22 2010035957

ISBN 978-1-107-00475-7 Hardback

Contents

Acknowledgments

I could not have finished this book without a great deal of help along the way. The book is dedicated to Indya, my wife, best friend, ardent supporter, and most faithful editor. My daughters Dahlia and Georgia were patient and kind while I worked nights and weekends, and dubbed the book "Judges ♥ Lawyers." My extended family was also there for me throughout, so thanks to Bill, Mary-Claire, Jake, Jenny, Louis, and Claire.

Special thanks are also due to several friends and colleagues. Charles Wolfram greatly improved the book with his time, wisdom, and encyclopedic knowledge. Brannon Denning read multiple drafts and sharpened its contents immeasurably. Jeff Hirsch and Glenn Reynolds sat through many lunches and chats in which we worked through the ideas found herein. I am also extremely grateful for comments from Dwight Aarons, Doug Blaze, Judy Cornett, Tom Davies, Joan Heminway, Jennifer Hendricks, Joseph King, George Kuney, Alex Long, Carl Pierce, Tom Plank, Mae Quinn, Paula Schaefer, Greg Stein, Maurice Stucke, and Penny White. I am also thankful for the supportive and collegial atmosphere at The University of Tennessee College of Law. Last, but not least, John Berger of Cambridge University Press guided me through this process with kindness and patience.

This book draws on previously published articles: "Do Judges Systematically Favor the Interests of the Legal Profession?" 59 *Alabama Law Review* 1 (2007); "The ABA, the Rules, and Professionalism: The

Mechanics of Self-Defeat and a Call for a Return to the Ethical, Moral, and Practical Approach of the Canons," 83 *North Carolina Law Review* 411 (2005); "An Institutional Analysis of Lawyer Regulation – Who Should Control Lawyer Regulation, Courts, Legislatures, or the Market?" 37 *Georgia Law Review* 1167 (2003); "Why Do We Regulate Lawyers? An Economic Analysis of the Justifications for Entry and Conduct Regulation," 33 *Arizona State Law Journal* 429 (2001); and "The Lawyer-Judge Hypothesis," in *The Pursuit of Justice: Law and Economics of Legal Systems* (Edward J. Lopez, ed., 2010).

Thanks to the *American Bar Association Journal* for allowing me to use the photograph on the cover. The original publication of the photo can be found at 11 *A.B.A. J.* 371 (1923). It is a photo of the Executive Committee of the American Bar Association in 1923. That year's executive committee included a future Chief Justice of the U.S. Supreme Court (Charles Evan Hughes), a co-founder of the American Law Institute (Cordenio Severance), a former Congressman from Michigan (John Corliss), as well as other judges, prominent attorneys, and high-level politicians. The photo well captures the power and prestige of the American Bar Association and suggests the genesis of the lawyer–judge bias.

1 An Ambient Bias

> When I refer to the secret life of judges, I am speaking of an inner turn of mind that favors, empowers, and enables our profession and our brothers and sisters at the bar. It is secret, because it is unobserved and therefore unrestrained – by the judges themselves or by the legal community that so closely surrounds and nurtures us. It is an ambient bias.
>
> – The Honorable Dennis Jacobs, Chief Judge, U.S. Court of Appeals for the Second Circuit[1]

THIS QUOTE COMES FROM A SPEECH, "THE SECRET LIFE OF Judges," that Dennis Jacobs recently gave at the Fordham Law School. Judge Jacobs's remarks are exceptionally frank for any sitting judge, and are particularly startling from the chief judge of the Second Circuit. It is quite unusual for any judge or lawyer to discuss a bias in favor of the legal profession; it is a criticism that cuts too close to the bone. If and when cases crop up that favor the legal profession, lawyers, judges, and law professors are quick to explain them away as correct decisions that reflect the unique position of lawyers in the American justice system or as anomalies. This may explain why relatively little has been written about what I call the lawyer–judge bias.

The lawyer–judge bias has also stayed largely hidden because of a national blind spot for judges. American lawyers have always been

[1] Dennis Jacobs, "The Secret Life of Judges," 75 *Fordham L. Rev.* 2855, 2856 (2007).

relatively unpopular, especially in recent years. In comparison, judges are held in relatively high esteem.[2] This raises a somewhat puzzling conundrum: Why does the public trust and admire lawyer-judges more than lawyers?

This gap in public perception is part of a much greater gap in our understanding of the American judiciary. The idea that all judges should be lawyers has become so ingrained in our national consciousness that it has become like wallpaper, barely noticed or discussed. In some circles, lawyers are seen as dishonest sharks who will do anything to win a case. Lawyer-judges are seen as measured arbiters of the law and facts.

I do not seek to convince readers that lawyer-judges are as bad as lawyers are perceived to be, nor do I aim to prove that lawyers are particularly maleficent. Instead I seek to demonstrate that lawyer-judges instinctively favor the legal profession in their decisions and actions and that this bias has powerful and far-reaching effects on our country. In this book I gather judicial decisions from diverse areas of the law and boil them down to a simple proposition I call the lawyer–judge bias: when given the chance, judges favor the interests of the legal profession over the public. The lawyer–judge bias hypothesis addresses the interests of the legal profession as a whole, not any particular lawyer representing any particular client, or even a particular subset of lawyers (such as prosecutors or defense lawyers). Those biases may exist, but I am addressing only a broader bias in favor of the interests of the entire profession.[3]

[2] Opinion polls show that the public holds the judiciary in much higher esteem than the legal profession. See Gallup, "Honesty/Ethics in Professions," available at http://www.gallup.com/poll/1654/honesty-ethics-professions.aspx. In recent years judges have polled ahead of lawyers, senators, governors, and other state and local officeholders, but behind clergy, doctors, and nurses.

[3] In this book I use the expressed desires of bar associations as a proxy for what the profession as a whole would prefer. If it strikes you as overreaching to refer to the "interests of the legal profession" or you think those interests are too multiple to be so reduced, please add the modifier "as expressed by bar associations" whenever the interests of the profession as a whole are at issue.

There are many reasons for this bias, some obvious and some subtle. At bottom, it occurs because regardless of political affiliation, judicial philosophy, race, gender, or religion, every American judge shares a single characteristic: every American judge is a former lawyer.[4] This shared background has powerful effects on the shape and structure of American law and has created the lawyer–judge bias.

Sahyers v. Prugh, Holliday & Karatinos, P.L.

It is helpful to choose a single emblematic case as an introduction, and we begin with *Sahyers v. Prugh, Holliday & Karatinos, P.L.*,[5] a 2009 case in the U.S. Court of Appeals for the Eleventh Circuit.[6] Subsequent chapters cover better-known cases, those with broader implications and others with more famous players. I choose *Sahyers* here, however, because it is narrow in scope but manages to encompass many of the underlying themes of the book. It offers a special benefit to the legal profession, largely on the basis of the judicial sympathy and empathy for fellow lawyers. It does so despite long-standing statutory and case law that suggests the opposite result. It justifies the decision because lawyers are "officers of the court" – that is, because lawyers are special and deserve special treatment. Finally, the court claims that it does all this not to benefit lawyers, but to benefit what the court ironically calls "the public interest."

One of the reasons *Sahyers* is such a great lawyer–judge bias case is that in most ways it is a very ordinary case. Plaintiff Christene Sahyers

[4] There are still some justices of the peace and magistrate-level judges who are not lawyers, but the vast majority of trial judges, and all appellate judges, are former lawyers. See Doris Marie Provine, *Judging Credentials: Nonlawyer Judges and the Politics of Professionalism* (Chicago: University of Chicago Press, 1986).

[5] *Sahyers v. Prugh, Holliday & Karatinos, P.L.*, 560 F.3d 1241 (11th Cir. 2009). Unless noted separately, all the facts and law that follow come from this decision.

[6] Please note that I have been involved with advising plaintiff's counsel in this case and am helping pro bono on a petition for certiorari to the U.S. Supreme Court.

worked as a paralegal at the law firm of Prugh, Holliday & Karatinos. She claimed that during her employment she worked unpaid overtime. This fact is not surprising: according to a survey taken by the National Federation of Paralegal Associations, more than 35 percent of paralegals are classified as "exempt" employees and are not subject to overtime rules, despite the fact that very few paralegals fit the legal definition of "exempt."[7]

After Ms. Sahyers left the law firm's employ she hired a lawyer and sued the firm in federal court for failure to pay overtime wages for hours she worked in excess of 40 per week, in violation of the Fair Labor Standards Act (FLSA).[8] Before filing suit, Sahyer's lawyer did not contact Prugh, Holliday for settlement negotiations or to warn the firm about the lawsuit. There was nothing unusual about this: the FLSA does not require any warning or contact before a lawsuit is filed,[9] and every day all over America there are defendants who first learn about a lawsuit when they are served with a complaint.

The complaint set forward no particular amount of damages and no specific amount of hours of overtime. This was also quite typical. The American legal system generally allows "notice pleading": a plaintiff's complaint must set forth only sufficient details to put the defendant on notice of the claim, not enough details to flesh out every part of the claim.

Prugh, Holliday answered the complaint and denied the allegations. The parties continued on to discovery, the part of a lawsuit in which the parties request information from each other about their claims.

[7] See National Federation of Paralegal Associations, "Paralegal Compensation & Benefits Survey Report, Sept. 2006," available at: http://www.paralegals.org/display common.cfm?an=1&subarticlenbr=926. See 29 CFR §§541.100–541.300 (2009) for the exemptions that might fit paralegals.

[8] 29 USC §§201–219 (2009).

[9] *Barrentine v. Arkansas-Best Freight System*, 450 U.S. 728, 738 (1981) held that the FLSA wage provision "permits an aggrieved employee to bring his statutory wage and hour claim 'in any Federal or State court of competent jurisdiction.' No exhaustion requirement or other procedural barriers are set up."

Prugh, Holliday requested an accounting of the total number of unpaid overtime hours and the evidence supporting that calculation. The plaintiff objected to this request. Discovery disputes are likewise endemic to the American legal system; this case was no different.

After discovery closed, Prugh, Holliday filed an offer of judgment under Federal Rule of Civil Procedure 68 for $3,500 plus any attorney's fees and costs to which the district court determined the plaintiff was entitled. Rule 68 allows a defendant to make a settlement offer before trial. If the plaintiff rejects the offer and receives less than the amount offered at trial, the plaintiff must pay the defendant's costs from the time of the Rule 68 filing.[10] As is typical, Prugh, Holliday denied all liability in the Rule 68 offer.

Sahyers accepted the Rule 68 offer. The district court entered judgment in favor of Sahyers and, as is customary in an FLSA case, allowed Sahyers and her attorney a chance to file a motion for fees and costs. The FLSA requires judges to award "a reasonable attorney's fee" and costs to successful parties.[11] The purpose of awarding attorney's fees is to encourage employees to act as "private attorneys general" and enforce the FLSA when the Department of Labor cannot. It also encourages attorneys to represent employees despite the relatively small amount of damages generally in question.[12] In short, the fees provision is an incentive to draw lawyers into taking these cases, despite the fact that the total damages on fifty hours of lost overtime might be too little to otherwise interest a lawyer. Although many other statutory fee-shifting provisions are left to a judge's discretion, the FLSA is mandatory. If a plaintiff wins, the court must allow a reasonable attorney's fee.[13]

[10] Federal Rule of Civil Procedure 68 (2008).

[11] 29 USC §216(b) (2008).

[12] See *Jones v. Central Soya Co., Inc.*, 748 F.2d 586, 592–93 (11th Cir. 1984); *United Slate, Tile and Composition Roofers, Damp and Waterproof Workers Association, Local 307 v. G & M Roofing & Sheet Metal Co.*, 732 F.2d 495, 501–02 (6th Cir. 1984).

[13] See *Shelton v. Erwin*, 830 F.2d 182, 184 (11th Cir. 1987).

Sahyers's lawyer filed for $13,800 in attorney's fees and $1,840.70 in costs. Up to this point in the story, *Sahyers v. Prugh, Holliday & Karatinos* was a perfectly typical FLSA lawsuit. What comes next was quite unusual.

First, the district court scheduled oral argument on the fee request at its own motion. Usually the issuance of legal fees in an FLSA action is pretty straightforward. A court must award fees to the prevailing party. The court determines a reasonable fee by calculating the "lodestar" – the product of the number of hours reasonably expended and the customary fee charged in the community for similar services. The court may then adjust the lodestar based on a limited number of factors,[14] which deal with the difficulty of the case, awards in similar cases, and other related issues.[15] None of the factors covers civility during the lawsuit or whether the plaintiff contacted the defendant before filing the case.

Nevertheless, at the oral argument, "the district court asked Plaintiff's lawyer, among other things, to respond to Defendants' contention that he afforded Defendants no notice of Plaintiff's claim before filing suit. Plaintiff's lawyer admitted that the allegation was true."[16] It is hard to get much of a sense of pique from a written order, but it is clear that the district judge was greatly aggrieved by Sahyers's lawyer's failure to call his fellow lawyers before filing suit:

> At no time prior to filing this lawsuit did Plaintiff make a written demand to Defendants for payment of the overtime compensation

[14] *Hensley v. Eckerhart*, 461 U.S. 424, 429–30 (1983).

[15] The factors are (1) the time and labor required; (2) the novelty and difficulty of the questions; (3) the skill requisite to perform the legal service properly; (4) the preclusion of other employment by the attorney owing to the acceptance of the case; (5) the customary fee; (6) whether the fee is fixed or contingent; (7) time limitations imposed by the client or the circumstances; (8) the amount involved and the results obtained; (9) the experience, reputation, and ability of the attorneys; (10) the "undesirability" of the case; (11) the nature and length of the professional relationship and the client; and (12) awards in similar cases. *Johnson v. Georgia Highway Exp., Inc.*, 488 F.2d 714, 717–19 (5th Cir. 1974).

[16] *Sahyers*, 560 F.3d at 1244.

> she now seeks. Furthermore, Plaintiff's attorney did not send Defendants a pre-suit demand letter prior to filing this lawsuit. This Court is not ruling that a pre-suit letter is always required, but in this case, the Plaintiff's lawyer did not even make a phone call to try to resolve the issue before filing suit. The Defendant is a law firm. Prior to filing suit in this local area, it is still reasonable to pick up the phone and call another lawyer so it won't be necessary to file suit. The defense proffered by Plaintiff's lawyer for not doing so is that his client instructed him to file suit first and ask Questions [*sic*] later.
>
> Absent any pre-suit demand, a defendant who unknowingly failed to compensate an employee for overtime would have no opportunity to voluntarily do so outside of litigation. As a result, such a defendant would be subject to additional litigation expenses and attorney's fees despite its good faith desire to properly compensate the employee. Furthermore, additional judicial time and resources would be spent on unnecessary litigation.[17]

The judge went on to rule that Sahyers had indeed prevailed on her suit, but that "there are some cases in which a reasonable fee is no fee," and he rewarded Sahyers no attorney's fees or costs whatsoever.[18]

There are several striking aspects to this decision. The decision is in clear conflict with the FLSA and prior case law. The FLSA does not require any presuit activities. There is no letter requirement. There is no phone call requirement. This is not an oversight on Congress's part: when Congress wants a presuit procedure, it knows how to require it. Humorously, Congress did create a presuit notice requirement for FLSA suits by employees of Congress.[19] The district court itself recognized this by stating, "This Court is not ruling that a presuit letter is always required."

Moreover, the FLSA requires a court to award a reasonable attorney's fee to a successful plaintiff. There is forty-odd years of case law on how to determine those fees; whether the defendant is a law firm or

[17] District court's written order, quoted in appellant's brief, 2008 WL 2336850.

[18] Id.

[19] 42 USCA §2000e-16a et seq. (2008).

whether it would have been more considerate to contact the employer ahead of time are not on the list of factors that courts must use to calculate fees.

The court also seems much more worried about the poor defendant law firm that "unknowingly" fails to pay overtime than it is about the paralegal who was illegally uncompensated for her overtime. The FLSA, like many other statutes, has no requirement that the failure to pay overtime be intentional. There is a good reason that the statute does not require intent: every employer claims that it "unknowingly" failed to pay overtime. Nevertheless, in this judge's opinion, it is the plaintiff's lawyer, who had the temerity to sue another local law firm, who is the villain.

The district court's palpable sympathy for the law firm is somewhat startling. After all, it is the law firm, not the plaintiff, that violated the law. Of course the reason for this sympathy is not a general worry about unsavvy employers, or even the more reasonable worry about unnecessary litigation. To the contrary, the reason for the concern is that the "Defendant is a law firm. Prior to filing suit in this local area, it is still reasonable to pick up the phone and call another lawyer so it won't be necessary to file suit."

For critics of the American legal system, the aforementioned sentences will strike a particular chord. The experience of Prugh, Holliday in the American civil justice system is extremely typical. In comparison with the more high-profile cases of innocent defendants ruined or bankrupted defending themselves, this case seems mild indeed.[20] However, it took a case in which a law firm suffered the indignity of a lawsuit and a lengthy discovery and settlement process to really irk this judge.

Unsurprisingly, Sahyers's lawyer decided to appeal to the U.S. Court of Appeals for the Eleventh Circuit. The argument was pretty straightforward: Sahyers was the successful party, the statute requires an award of fees to a successful party, there is no presuit notice requirement in the

[20] Philip Howard's three books are packed with such examples. See, e.g., Philip K. Howard, *Life Without Lawyers* (New York: W. W. Norton, 2009), 68–92.

FLSA, and "judicially created exemptions from laws of general applicability only for lawyers are wrong."[21] The National Employment Lawyers Association filed an amicus brief in support, basically making the same arguments.[22]

The defendants countered that Sahyers was not a successful party in the suit (despite her receipt of a Rule 68 settlement) and that it was allowable to lower attorney's fees if a case involved a "nuisance settlement" or unnecessary legal fees; they included several references to the "special circumstances" involved in a suit against a law firm.[23] Notably, Prugh, Holliday did not argue that a special rule should apply to law firms, or that a presuit notice requirement was appropriate, nor did Prugh, Holliday argue that the federal courts have special "inherent authority" over the legal profession that allows a court to disregard settled FLSA law when it comes to a suit against a law firm if it does not like the behavior of one of the parties' lawyers. Nevertheless, the Eleventh Circuit's decision held exactly that.

First, it is important to note what the Eleventh Circuit did *not* hold. The Eleventh Circuit did not hold that Sahyers was an unsuccessful party in the underlying lawsuit or that Rule 68 settlements are somehow different from other settlements.[24] The court also did not hold that despite Sahyers's status as a successful party, the district court could choose not to award a reasonable attorney's fee. To the contrary, the very first sentence of the court's legal discussion conceded, "In general, a prevailing FLSA plaintiff is entitled to an award of some reasonable attorney's fees and costs."[25]

The Eleventh Circuit did not, however, apply the "lodestar" test for determining attorney's fees, nor did it discuss why the district court should or should not have used that well-established test. Instead, the

[21] Appellant's brief, available at 2008 WL 2336850.
[22] Brief of amicus curiae, available at 2008 WL 3980717.
[23] Appellee's brief, available at 2008 WL 3980718.
[24] *Sahyers*, 560 F.3d at 1244.
[25] Id.

court created a brand-new defense of the district court's brand-new exception to settled law on FLSA attorney's fees: "The district court, in substance, based this exception on its inherent powers to supervise the conduct of the lawyers who come before it and to keep in proper condition the legal community of which the courts are a leading part."[26]

Before we flesh this argument out, note the phrase "in substance." In fact, the district court never mentioned inherent authority or supervising the legal profession in its opinion at all. The district court judge was clearly annoyed that one lawyer had failed to show the requisite consideration to another lawyer, but he certainly never said, "As a judge I am in charge of relations between lawyers and under my inherent authority I am going to punish one of my wayward brethren." Nevertheless, the Eleventh Circuit decided to treat the case as an inherent authority case, despite the fact that neither the district court's opinion, the briefs of the parties, nor the amicus curiae had done so.

We will spend much more time on the "inherent authority" of courts to govern lawyers later, so I offer only a brief explanation here. Federal courts have "inherent powers" that are not granted by rule or statute: "Courts of justice are universally acknowledged to be vested, by their very creation, with power to impose silence, respect, and decorum, in their presence, and submission to their lawful mandates."[27] The federal courts' powers include the right "to control admission to its bar and to discipline attorneys who appear before it."[28] A judge's ability to hold persons in the courtroom in contempt is also an inherent power. The Supreme Court has noted that these powers are limited and are to be "exercised with restraint and discretion."[29]

The Eleventh Circuit noted this traditional statement of a federal court's "inherent authority" before launching into a much broader statement of these powers. I will spend a little time on what comes next in the

[26] Id.
[27] *Chambers v. NASCO, Inc.*, 501 U.S. 32, 43 (1991).
[28] *Chambers*, 501 U.S. at 43.
[29] Id. at 44.

opinion, because it raises several themes that we will see throughout the cases discussed in this book.

First, the court claimed that part of its inherent authority "derives from a lawyer's role as an officer of the court."[30] The term "officer of the court" denotes the special role of lawyers in the justice system: "Membership in the bar is a privilege burdened with conditions. A lawyer is received into that ancient fellowship for something more than private gain. He becomes an officer of the court, and, like the court itself, an instrument or agency to advance the ends of justice."[31] In short, lawyers are so much more than mere craftspeople seeking pecuniary gain: they are part of an "ancient fellowship" seeking more than mere "private gain." Throughout this book you will see examples of courts using the term "officer of the court" to describe the legal profession, despite the fact that even if it was not always thus, it is certainly true now that law is a business first and foremost. A court's use of the term "officer of the court" and its hearkening to the halcyon days when law was a calling, not a business, almost always presages a decision that greatly favors the legal profession. This case is no exception.

Second, after the "officer of the court" reference, the court ties its favorable treatment of lawyers to an alleged public benefit: "We believe and defend the idea that maintaining a bar that promotes civility and collegiality is in the public interest and greatly advances judicial efficiency."[32] Thus, a rule that requires special treatment for a lawsuit against a law firm is appropriate because it promotes "civility and collegiality" and will eventually result in "judicial efficiency." Moreover, this benefit outweighs the public's interest in having courts follow the law as written or the public's interest in punishing employers that fail to pay overtime with the payment of attorney's fees.

Third, the Eleventh Circuit is unabashed in its willingness to create a decision that applies only to law firms. It baldly notes, "Defendants are

[30] *Sahyers*, 560 F.3d at 1244 and n. 4.

[31] Id.

[32] Id. at 1245 and n. 5.

lawyers and their law firm." That fact greatly affects the court's irritation that "the lawyer for Plaintiff made absolutely no effort – no phone call; no email; no letter – to inform them of Plaintiff's impending claim much less to resolve this dispute before filing suit. Plaintiff's lawyer slavishly followed his client's instructions and – without a word to Defendants in advance – just sued his fellow lawyers."[33] The Eleventh Circuit could have upheld the decision on either of the grounds suggested by Prugh, Holliday: that Sahyers was not a successful party or that there was evidence that the plaintiff's lawyer dragged his feet in pursuit of a higher fee. Instead, the court feels comfortable creating an extremely friendly, lawyers-only rule.

Last, the Eleventh Circuit makes clear that the precedential effect of its decision should be very limited – limited to law suits against law firms, in fact:

> We strongly caution against inferring too much from our decision today. These kinds of decisions are fact-intensive. We put aside cases in which lawyers are not parties. We do not say that pre-suit notice is usually required or even often required under the FLSA to receive an award of attorney's fees or costs. Nor do we now recommend that courts use their inherent powers to deny prevailing parties attorney's fees or costs. We declare no judicial duty. We create no presumptions.[34]

To review: There is no legal requirement to call or write a letter before filing a FLSA claim, unless one is suing a law firm. If so, "collegiality" requires special treatment. If a plaintiff's lawyer fails to be "civil" in this fashion, the FLSA's mandatory award of attorney's fees and costs will be ignored. If the suit is not against a law firm, though, please disregard this case altogether.

Sahyers's counsel then requested that the Eleventh Circuit rehear the case en banc. The Eleventh Circuit declined to rehear the case. Three

[33] Id. at 1245.
[34] Id. at 1246.

judges filed opinions – two dissents and one concurrence.[35] The dissents raised many of the complaints discussed here: the FLSA does not have an exception for lawyers and federal courts do not have the power (inherent or otherwise) to ignore plain congressional language "in the interest of promoting a professional courtesy."[36]

The concurring opinion wrote in support of the original opinion and added two additional wrinkles. First, the concurrence reiterated, "Courts have the inherent and main – if not exclusive – authority (along with the duty and responsibility) to supervise their Bar members" and "Courts ought to be highly reluctant to cede this traditional power."[37] As we shall see, courts have indeed jealously guarded this power.

The concurrence goes further, however. It has long been black-letter law that "[e]ven a sensible and efficient use of the supervisory power . . . is invalid if it conflicts with constitutional or statutory provisions."[38] The Supreme Court has warned that to hold otherwise "would confer on the judiciary discretionary power to disregard the considered limitations of the law it is charged with enforcing."[39]

The concurrence eludes this stricture on its inherent power by holding that if Congress means to abrogate a court's inherent powers it must do so "specifically, explicitly, and directly" in language that is "clear and plain."[40] Note how this requirement turns the inherent powers doctrine on its head. Now Congress must explicitly state "We hereby abrogate the inherent powers of federal courts" to prevent a federal court disregarding a statute's plain language. As a 2010 search of the U.S. Code shows no such language in any statute,[41] the Eleventh Circuit's decision

[35] *Sahyers v. Prugh, Holliday & Karatinos, P.L.*, 2010 WL 1488520.

[36] *Sahyers*, 2010 WL 1488520 at *4.

[37] Id. at 1–2.

[38] *Thomas v. Arn*, 474 U.S. 140, 148 (1985).

[39] *U.S. v. Payner*, 447 U.S. 727, 737 (1980).

[40] *Sahyers*, 2010 WL 1488520 at *2.

[41] A May 26, 2010 search of the Westlaw database "USC" for the terms "inherent power" /s court returns 29 documents, almost all of them from the Federal Rules of Civil or Criminal Procedure and none explicitly abrogating inherent authority.

essentially holds that it can use its inherent authority at will regardless of a contrary statute.

Sahyers is a small case that hardly caused a ripple of public interest, let alone outrage.[42] Nevertheless, the main purpose of this book is to demonstrate that this case is not an anomaly; it is part of a long-standing and deleterious trend I call the lawyer–judge bias.

This book lays out the lawyer–judge bias in several steps. In Chapter 2 I present a theoretical explanation of why lawyers and judges naturally work together to forward joint interests. I separate out the reasons that judges naturally favor lawyers into two groups, the conscious/crass reasons and the unconscious/subtle ones. I then use two prevailing analytical models to discuss these incentives. For the crass reasons I use public choice theory, which looks at the underlying incentives for any governmental actor to predict that actor's output. Simply put, for public choice theory one figures out what motivates judges, and then one tries to determine where those incentives lead.

A number of conscious factors might influence judges to favor the legal profession. Judges are all lawyers, many of their friends and colleagues are lawyers, and (whether they are elected or appointed) they likely have their jobs in large part because of the efforts of other lawyers on their behalf. Seen in this light, it is obvious that the judiciary would favor the interests of the individuals with whom they interact on a daily basis.

For the subtle reasons I use the new institutionalism, an analytical tool made famous by Nobel Prize winner Douglass North. In the new institutionalism, an "institution" is not a building or fixed social group but is a set of norms, thought patterns, and behaviors. An institution is a way of looking at and processing the world, a kind of über-heuristic. Legal thinking is a powerful institution. Law professors regularly brag that they teach law students to "think like a lawyer," a jarring and

42 *Sahyers* has, however, already been cited by courts both inside and outside the Eleventh Circuit. See *Sahyers*, 2010 WL 1488520 at *5 and n. 1.

grueling process that, when successful, actually creates a new way of analyzing and processing the world. This education is reinforced by years of practice. Judges tend to come from a very select group of individuals who have thrived within the institution of legal thought. As a result, judges take a particular set of deeply ingrained biases, thought processes, and views of the world with them to the bench. These institutions cannot help but color and control judicial thinking and outcomes. I argue that this "institutional," and largely unconscious, similarity between judges and lawyers is actually more important than the crass reasons for the lawyer–judge bias. The similarity of thought processes and natural sympathy of judges for lawyers leads inevitably to judicial output favoring lawyers.[43]

In Chapters 3 through 9 I offer a series of case law examples as evidence of the existence of an endemic judicial bias toward the interests of the legal profession. In so doing I hope to establish the accuracy of the theory and its far-reaching consequences. As a bonus, I also offer a single explanation for a series of puzzling legal anomalies.

Each chapter is organized around a specific area of the law. Chapter 3 discusses criminal procedure, Chapter 4 covers civil constitutional law, and so on. I do this for ease of reference for readers and also as a natural way to categorize the cases. This grouping should make skipping around or reading only chapters of interest more manageable.

[43] Although I regularly refer to "judges" and "lawyers" as monolithic groups, there is obviously a great deal of difference between a general practice lawyer in Montana and a Wall Street bankruptcy lawyer. Similarly, there is a vast gulf between a U.S. Supreme Court Justice and a sessions court judge in Tennessee. These differences are measured not only in their day-to-day existences, but also in their relative effect on American law. When this book refers to "lawyers," a skeptical reader may want to substitute the words "the majority of lawyers" or "the organized bar." "Judges" refers to all judges, but I will sometimes differentiate between "lawmaking judges," which includes the U.S. Supreme Court, state supreme courts, and federal and state appellate courts, and "law-applying judges." This is not to suggest that trial courts do not have substantial lawmaking power. The nature of precedent and judicial hierarchy, however, means that the lawmaking courts have the most power to shape and affect American law.

Each of the chapters asks challenging questions about American law. Chapter 3 covers criminal procedure and notices a series of anomalies that add up to an enormously lawyer-friendly system. For example, the famous *Miranda* warnings tell defendants that they have the right to remain silent and they have a right to a lawyer. Why is it, then, that an arrestee who asks for a lawyer is treated much more favorably than an arrestee who asks to remain silent? If one arrestee asks for a lawyer, all questioning must cease until the lawyer arrives. If another asks to remain silent, questioning can resume within a few hours. Why is the right to an appointed lawyer protected more aggressively than the right to a jury? A defendant facing any jail time at all gets a lawyer; in contrast, a jury is guaranteed only for cases with potential jail time of six months or longer. Nevertheless, at the time of the framing of the Constitution and the Bill of Rights, the right to a jury was considered much more important than the right to a lawyer and there was no right to appointed counsel whatsoever.

Chapter 4 examines a series of civil constitutional cases and asks why government-supported doctors are treated less favorably than government-supported lawyers in the restrictions allowed on their advice. The Supreme Court has held that Congress may limit the advice that government-supported doctors can give pregnant women, but has also held that Congress may not limit the legal advice of legal aid lawyers.

In Chapters 5 and 6 I ask why lawyers are the only American profession to be truly and completely self-regulated. State supreme courts govern the regulation of lawyers in every state in the union, often as a result of state supreme court decisions claiming an "inherent authority" to govern the legal profession. In contrast, state legislatures control the regulation of every other profession. Many of these state supreme courts have taken this regulatory authority and delegated it back to state bar associations. Predictably, this level of self-regulation has been exceptionally helpful to the legal profession and has often resulted in regulation by the lawyers, for the lawyers.

Chapter 7 considers torts and shows that a legal malpractice case is much harder to win than is a medical malpractice case. Moreover, the common law tort of malicious prosecution has been shaped so that it is much easier to sue a criminal complainant or civil plaintiff than to sue the lawyers who represented them.

Chapter 8 discusses the many advantages offered to lawyers in the law of evidence. Why is it that the attorney–client privilege is the oldest and most jealously protected of all the professional privileges? The attorney–client privilege has been protected at common law for more than three hundred years. It is an immensely powerful tool: as a general rule, a client can rest assured that whatever she tells the lawyer is protected by the privilege and virtually undiscoverable in court proceedings. In contrast, there was never a common law doctor–patient privilege. That privilege has been largely established by statute and is subject to many more exceptions than the attorney–client privilege. Other professionals, such as accountants, journalists, or members of the clergy, receive even less protection.

Chapter 9 covers the business of law. Why are clients barred from pursuing Consumer Protection Act claims against lawyers in many states? Why are lawyers granted special common law liens to help them collect against former clients? Unsurprisingly, special judge-created rules have made the business of law much easier to pursue.

Chapter 10 offers a high-profile, real-life example of the lawyer–judge bias: the treatment of the lawyers in the Enron fiasco. There were three main parties in the Enron affair: the executives, the accountants, and the lawyers. The Enron debacle cost Americans billions, sent multiple executives to jail, destroyed the largest energy company in the world, and completely extirpated Enron's outside auditor, Arthur Andersen. Nevertheless, Enron's primary outside counsel, the Houston law firm of Vinson & Elkins, walked away virtually unscathed despite its involvement in the creation of many of Enron's off-book subsidiaries. A combination of lenient lawyer regulation, smart lawyering, and understanding prosecutors meant that Arthur Andersen and Enron executives faced the full brunt of public antipathy, whereas the lawyers basically skated after a settlement payment to the bankruptcy estate. Moreover, each of the law firms involved is still open for business and quite profitable. None of the lawyers involved has even faced professional sanction for the Enron work and each is still currently practicing law.

These chapters cut a swath across almost every area of the law (professional responsibility, evidence, constitutional law, criminal procedure, employment law, and torts). Each has been explained away within its own boundaries, but they are all better understood as examples of the lawyer–judge bias. These are cases in which judges simply found a way to treat lawyers better than other litigants.

The point of Chapters 3 through 10 is to offer overwhelming evidence that the lawyer–judge bias exists and is pervasive. To some readers this may seem like overkill: when I describe my thesis to some, it seems patently obvious. Nevertheless, the theory has proven quite controversial within legal academia, the legal profession, and the judiciary as a whole, and I have encountered disagreement over almost every example in the book. The point of gathering all the evidence is to add length and breadth to the argument and to establish the existence of the lawyer–judge bias once and for all.

Chapter 11 offers a less direct and more controversial effect of the lawyer–judge bias: what Judge Richard Posner has called "the appalling complexity of American law."[44] Why are American law and procedure so complex? At least part of the answer lies in the relationship between lawyers and judges. A complex system works out better for lawyers and appellate judges, partly because complexity offers all parties more room to operate, partly because a complex system generates business for lawyers, and partly because many lawyers and judges simply enjoy the process of complex legal thought. Because complexity works for lawyers

[44] *Holmes v. Buss*, 506 F.3d 576 (7th Cir. 2007).

and judges, and they are the repeat players in the game, complexity is what we get, despite its great cost to litigants and the public.

Chapter 12 begins by noting that a trio of recent Supreme Court cases have shown some resistance to the lawyer–judge bias and expresses hope that this trend might continue. This chapter then discusses some of the ramifications and possible solutions to the lawyer–judge bias. Assuming that the theory and the evidence convince you, some hard questions remain: Is this a bad thing, and what, if anything, can be done about it? Most people react negatively to a bias among judges, so I will assume that the favorable treatment of the legal profession by the judiciary is unwelcome. That being said, any potential cure to this bias might be worse than the problem.

Nevertheless, Chapter 12 argues that it is not obvious that all judges should be lawyers. Like the rise of the common law itself, the rise of lawyer-judges in medieval England was a result of a series of serendipitous historical events and trends, and certainly not the result of careful consideration of who would best fill the role of the common law judge in the common law system. The same is true in America. Historically, nonlawyer judges were much more common, and although no nonlawyer has ever served on the Supreme Court, being a lawyer is not a constitutional requirement for the job. Nonlawyer judges are quite common throughout the world, and many countries train judges separately from lawyers.

Another – smaller-bore – solution is simply to make the public and the judiciary more aware of the lawyer–judge bias. Greater self-awareness alone may stem the unconscious judicial bias, and public awareness may offer shame as a check for conscious bias. Regardless of whether large-scale corrections are possible, or even necessary, it is important to bring the bias to light and hope that judges such as Judge Jacobs – whose observation about the "secret lives of judges" began this book – will lead to changes in the future decisions and behavior of American judges toward the legal profession.

2 The Theory

> We propose the general hypothesis: every industry or occupation that has enough political power to utilize the state will seek to control entry. . . . Crudely put, the butter producers wish to suppress margarine and encourage the production of bread.
>
> – George Stigler[1]

> Institutions are the rules of the game in a society or, more formally, are the humanly devised constraints that shape human interaction.
>
> – Douglass North[2]

THERE WAS A TIME WHEN JUDGES WERE VIEWED AS INFALlible, their decisions a natural and required result of an immutable divine or customary law. Judges did not weigh the law, equities, and facts to reach a decision; instead, they simply and correctly applied fixed principles of law without error or uncertainty. Judicial authority and decision making were very much intertwined with religious authority; there was a general sense that infallibility flowed naturally from judges, whose authority and wisdom came directly from God and the monarch.[3]

1 George J. Stigler, "The Theory of Economic Regulation," 2 *Bell J. Econ. & Mgmt. Sci.* 4–6 (1971).

2 Douglass C. North, *Institutions, Institutional Change, and Economic Performance* (Cambridge: Cambridge University Press, 1990), 3.

3 See Brian Z. Tamanaha, *Law as a Means to an End: The Threat to the Rule of Law* (Cambridge: Cambridge University Press, 2006), 11–23.

Since that time, it has become clear that law is a human creation, and that the judges who interpret and create that law are fallible. Nevertheless, some of the trappings of judicial majesty and infallibility remain. The Supreme Court meets in a massive stone building that resembles an ancient Greek temple. Judges wear robes and carry gavels. Bailiffs call "all rise" when judges enter the court, and judges are still called "Your Honor."

These trappings are meant to impart gravity and importance to participants and viewers. Perhaps in part because of these trappings, American judges tend to get the benefit of the doubt from scholars and the public alike. For example, Richard Posner and other scholars of economics and the law have argued that common law judicial decision makers are more likely than legislatures to create efficiency-maximizing rules of law.[4] Similarly, opinion polls show that the public holds the judiciary in much higher esteem than it does the legal profession itself.[5]

Nevertheless, from the legal realist movement of the late nineteenth and early twentieth centuries to the present day, there have been scholars and jurists who have recognized that judges are people too. Judges are driven by the same combination of incentives, experiences, and cognitive biases as the rest of us. Recently, scholars have begun to systematically analyze how human foibles, biases, and cognitive limitations affect both judging and the law as a whole.

Political scientists study the "attitudinal model," which argues that political ideology is the single best predictor of judicial decisions.[6] Cognitive psychologists study the influence of judicial heuristics.[7] Economists

[4] See Richard Posner, *Economic Analysis of Law* (New York: Aspen Publishers, 2003), 532.

[5] See Gallup, "Honesty/Ethics in Professions," available at http://www.gallup.com/poll/1654/honesty-ethics-professions.aspx. In recent years, judges polled ahead of lawyers, senators, governors, and other state and local officeholders, but behind clergy, doctors, and nurses.

[6] See, e.g., Jeffrey A. Segal and Harold J. Spaeth, *The Supreme Court and the Attitudinal Model* (Cambridge: Cambridge University Press, 1993).

[7] *Heuristics* are ingrained thought processes and shortcuts to decision making. See, e.g., Stephen M. Bainbridge and G. Mitu Gulati, "How Do Judges Maximize? (The Same

examine the myriad incentives that influence judicial behavior.[8] It is a sign of the power of the judicial myth that it has taken this long for scholars and the public to recognize that judges are not law machines.

One helpful attribute of the lawyer–judge bias is that it singles out specific areas of the law in which judicial incentives have had discernable and predictable effects. Although some empirical studies have suggested ways in which these various incentives play out in practice, scholars have had a hard time translating these incentives into substantive law – that is, finding areas of the law in which they apply sufficiently to have a predictive value. In this way, the existing studies have suffered from a "missing link" problem – they have established that judges take certain shortcuts in deciding all cases, but they have not demonstrated a rule that predicts an outcome in any particular type of case. The lawyer–judge hypothesis bridges this gap by establishing predictable legal results from judicial attitudes and incentives.

This book uses public choice theory and the new institutionalism to discuss why we would expect judicial incentives and proclivities to lead to decisions that favor the legal profession. Public choice theory helps illuminate the conscious, crass considerations, and the new institutionalism explains the unconscious, subtle ones. I may have my own biases, but I think the subtle explanations better explain lawyer–judge bias than the crass ones do.

Conscious, Crass Considerations

Public choice theory is the application of economic analysis to noneconomic, governmental behavior. As a general rule, early political scientists assumed that government actors were motivated primarily by a desire to serve the public good. In contrast, public choice assumes that

Way Everybody Else Does – Boundedly): Rules of Thumb in Securities Fraud Opinions," 51 *Emory L.J.* 83 (2002).

[8] See, e.g., Richard A. Posner, "What Do Judges and Justices Maximize? (The Same Thing Everybody Else Does)," 3 *Sup. Ct. Econ. Rev.* 1 (1993).

government actors behave according to the assumptions of classical economics – that is, they are rational and self-interested, and they seek to maximize their own welfare, happiness, and utility.

This has two very important results. The first is to analyze government action on an individual basis rather than through monolithic discussions of the government as a whole. The second is that it recognizes that government outputs are the result of the rational, self-interested actions of the people who run the government.

Although the public choice assumptions about human behavior seem fairly straightforward, they actually represent a sea change in the way in which we view the government and form the basis of much modern libertarian thought. If it is true that the individuals in the government are more interested in their own benefit than that of the public, perhaps we should limit the scope of the government or consider governmental structures that encourage public-mindedness.

Nevertheless, just as classical economics has had to digest the findings of cognitive psychologists and others who have shown that the assumption of rational self-interest is often wrong in practice, the public choice assumptions have occasionally wilted in various real-life scenarios.[9] Although the theory cannot explain every governmental action, James Q. Wilson has aptly noted that the "virtues of the economic perspective" are clear; "it offers an elegant and parsimonious way of explaining a great deal of human behavior."[10]

Interest group theory is a subset of public choice theory. It starts with the assumption of rational, self-interested bureaucrats and politicians

[9] For example, strict adherence to the public choice behavioral assumptions makes voting difficult to explain because the odds of any individual vote making a difference in an election is quite small, especially when compared with the time and effort involved in voting. Critics of public choice have wondered about the usefulness of a theory that has difficulty explaining such a critical element of democratic governance. See Donald P. Green and Ian Shapiro, *Pathologies of Rational Choice Theory: A Critique of Applications in Political Science* (New Haven, CT: Yale University Press, 1994).

[10] James Q. Wilson, "The Politics of Regulation," in *The Politics of Regulation*, ed. James Q. Wilson (New York: Basic Books, 1980), 360.

and predicts that concentrated interest groups will have an outsized influence on governmental actions. In its most generic form this phenomenon is called *agency capture* – a situation in which a government agency serves the interests of the regulated in lieu of the interests of the public. The key insight is that government regulation is a product that can be purchased by an industry. Industry provides the items that legislators desire – campaign contributions, votes, and assistance through lobbying – and legislators and regulators deliver the helpful regulation (or deregulation) that industry desires.

The government is a uniquely powerful entity because it has the power to coerce private behavior through law. The state can seize money through taxation or enforce certain standards of industry or consumer behavior. These powers provide tremendous possibilities for an industry to increase its profitability through government action or inaction. These actions can take the form of direct purchases or payments (sometimes referred to as "pork barrel spending"), special tax treatment, deregulation of one industry, or overregulation of another industry. Thus, every industry or occupation that can will seek to use the state's assistance, through direct subsidies, price fixing, barriers to entry (e.g. entry requirements to law school or the bar exam), or suppression of competing industries (consider laws barring the unauthorized practice of law) and the encouragement of complementary products. As one of the founders of interest group theory, George Stigler, notes, "Crudely put, the butter producers wish to suppress margarine and encourage the production of bread."[11]

This process is made simpler because of the difficulties involved in organizing large groups of voters to oppose any particular piece of harmful legislation. As a general rule, concentrated groups with a large per capita stake in government action will regularly triumph over larger,

[11] George J. Stigler, "The Theory of Economic Regulation," 4–6. For a humorous look at just how hard the government made it for margarine producers in the twentieth century, see Ruth Dupre, "'If It's Yellow, It Must be Butter': Margarine Regulation in North America since 1886," 59 *J. Econ. Hist.* 353 (1999).

diffuse groups with little personally at stake, even if the aggregate cost to the large group dwarfs the gain to the small group. Large groups struggle to organize because of the high transaction costs for each individual, as well as the temptation to do nothing and get a free ride on the efforts of others. Economists call this the *problem of collective action*.[12]

Air pollution is a classic collective action problem. The cost to any individual of forcing the government to regulate polluting industries (either individually or by organizing a group) is huge and outweighs the cost of the pollution to that individual. The costs of air pollution are borne by everyone; in contrast, the benefits rest in the relatively small group of polluters. As a result, polluters lobby the government vociferously to lessen regulation, whereas any individual faces great organizational obstacles to any opposition. Assuming that the societal costs of air pollution are higher than the benefits to the polluters, society as a whole is worse off.

This is not to say that the power of concentrated interests is unlimited. As government regulation becomes too one-sided, the costs to the public rise and the chances of collective action in opposition to the special interest group increase dramatically. The existence of pro-environmental nonprofits and the creation of the Environmental Protection Agency are prime examples.

Public choice theory also predicts that agency capture can work on two levels, first with the legislature and later with the bureaucrats tasked with enforcing the legislation. Thus, even if legislation is passed to curtail an interest group, there is a chance that bureaucrats will subvert its purpose. Rational, self-interested bureaucrats will naturally seek to increase their influence and make their jobs easier. They accomplish these goals by catering to the entities they most frequently encounter and the parties that care most about the regulation – the regulated industries. This

[12] See Mancur Olson, *The Logic of Collective Action* (Cambridge, MA: Harvard Univ. Press, 1965).

makes their job easier because they please the repeat players in the system and silence those most likely to criticize any agency action.

Moreover, the bureaucrats themselves often come from the regulated industries, because the agencies have to hire experts as regulators. The regulatory bodies governing lawyers, for example, must be staffed by people knowledgeable about the legal profession – lawyers.

The application of public choice theory to judges, however, has come more slowly than its application to bureaucrats or legislators. Because courts are less open than legislatures to lobbying, some public choice theorists have assumed that interest group pressures affect judges less than they affect legislators.[13] Moreover, many judges have lifetime tenure and are assumed to have a fixed amount of work and a set salary, so the effects of self-interest are muted. Judicial behavior toward the legal profession, however, establishes that judges are hardly immune from self-interest or external pressures in their decision making, especially when those pressures come from the legal profession.

Many previous studies of judicial incentives focus on nonmonetary incentives, such as maximizing leisure time, prestige, or opportunities for further judicial promotion instead of salary effects, on the assumption that judicial decisions have no effect on salaries.[14] When the relationship between the legal profession and judges is considered, however, it becomes apparent that lawyers affect every aspect of a judge's job, up to and including the judge's ability to get and keep the job.

A brief study of judges – who they are, how they are trained, what their jobs are like, and salary effects – leads inexorably to the conclusion that judges will regularly favor the interests of lawyers over those of other litigants. For starters, many judges rely on lawyers to get and keep their jobs. Most state judges face some type of election (either contested

[13] See Frank B. Cross, "The Judiciary and Public Choice," 50 *Hastings L.J.* 355, 358–60 and nn. 15–17 (1999) for a list of public choice scholars favoring the judiciary over legislatures or bureaucrats.

[14] See Posner, "What Do Judges and Justices Maximize," at 20–21.

or retention), and lawyers provide most of the elected judiciary's campaign donations.[15] In elective states – including merit selection states with retention elections – bar associations frequently endorse judicial candidates and conduct and publish "bar polls" on the judges.[16] A judge who alienates her lawyer colleagues may soon be looking for other employment.

Similarly, a great many judges likely owe their initial appointment to the organized bar. Almost half of the states select judges through "merit plans." The definition of "merit" and the selection process itself are often driven by the organized bar.[17] Historically, the American Bar Association (ABA) has played an enormous role in the selection and vetting of federal judges.[18] The ABA has also advocated a "merit plan" in which the lawyers would be heavily involved in creating a list of potential nominees for any vacant federal judgeship as part of an effort to remove politics from judicial selection.[19]

Likewise, bar associations have lobbied tirelessly on behalf of the judiciary. The ABA has continually worked against judicial elections

[15] See David Barnhizer, "'On the Make': Campaign Funding and the Corrupting of the American Judiciary," 50 *Cath. U.L. Rev.* 361, 393 (2001).

[16] See James H. Guterman and Errol E. Meidinger, *In the Opinion of the Bar* (Chicago: American Juricature Society, 1977); Mark S. Cady and Jess R. Phelps, "Preserving the Delicate Balance Between Judicial Accountability and Independence: Merit Selection in the Post-White World," 17 *Cornell J.L. & Pub. Pol'y* 343, 376–78 (2008). For example, the Iowa Bar conducts a "plebiscite" requesting feedback about each judge up for election. The responses are then distributed to the state's voters. See http://www.iowabar.org/NEWSROOM.nsf/ and http://www.iowabar.org/NEWSROOM.nsf/2b85a4ea12f4bfac8625669d006e27ab/c18e0b83e1e62adb862574da006a8088/$FILE/2008%20Judicial%20Plebiscite.pdf.

[17] See Kelley Armitage, "Denial Ain't Just a River in Egypt: A Thorough Review of Judicial Elections, Merit Selection and the Role of State Judges in Society," 29 *Cap. U.L. Rev.* 625, 656 (2002); Charles R. Ashman, *The Finest Judges Money Can Buy* (Los Angeles: Nash Publishing, 1973), 242.

[18] See "The Role of the American Bar Association in the Judicial Selection Process," 101st Cong., 1st Sess. (1989). Recently, Republican administrations have relied more on the Federalist Society, which is also staffed by lawyers and law professors.

[19] See http://abajournal.com/files/118Revised.pdf.

and for lifetime judicial appointment.[20] Bar associations have also been among the most vocal proponents of higher judicial salaries.[21] The ABA has been advocating for higher judicial salaries for almost one hundred years.[22] The ABA has also lobbied for better judicial benefits and to improve the public perception of judges.[23] The comments to the Model Rules of Professional Conduct encourage lawyers "to continue traditional efforts to defend judges and courts unjustly criticized" in an effort "[t]o maintain the fair and independent administration of justice."[24] In short, lawyers have made every effort to curry favor with the bench.[25]

Almost all judges are former lawyers.[26] All American state supreme court justices are lawyers.[27] Most judges are members of bar associations.

[20] See ABA, *Justice in Jeopardy: Report of the ABA Commission on the 21st Century Judiciary* (Chicago: ABA, 2003), available at http://www.abanet.org/judind/jeopardy/pdf/report.pdf.

[21] See ABA and Federal Bar Association (FBA), *Federal Judicial Pay Erosion: A Report on the Need for Reform* (Washington, DC: ABA, 2001). State bars make similar efforts; see, e.g., Gerald M. Edenfield, "On the Merits, Judges Deserve Decent Pay Raise," *Atlanta Journal-Constitution*, May 28, 2008 (president of state bar describing lobbying effort for higher judicial salaries).

[22] In 1912, the ABA formed a committee to increase judicial salaries; see 35 ABA Rep. 36–37 (1912). The committee also gathered and disseminated the salaries of state judges, to induce raises in the low-salary states. See 54 ABA Rep. 58–59 (1931).

[23] For benefits, see, e.g., ABA National Conference of State Trial Judges, *A Survey of State Judicial Fringe Benefits* (Williamsburg, VA: ABA, 1994). For public opinion, see ABA, *Unfair Rapid Response to Unfair and Unjust Criticism of Judges*, available at http://www.abanet.org/judind/toolkit/impartialcourts/Rapid_Response_Pamphlet.pdf.

[24] Model Rule of Professional Conduct 8.2, comment 3 (2008).

[25] In another example, the ABA organized and helped draft the national code of judicial conduct. See Lisa L. Milford, *The Development of the ABA Judicial Code* (Chicago: ABA, 1992), 3–8.

[26] See Doris Provine, *Judging Credentials: Nonlawyer Judges and the Politics of Professionalism* (Chicago: University of Chicago Press, 1986).

[27] Forty-eight states explicitly require their supreme court justices to be lawyers. See Council of State Governments, *Qualifications of Judges of State Appellate Courts and General Trial Courts*, available at http://www.csg.org/pubs/Documents/QualificationsofJudgesofStateAppellateCourtsandGeneralTrialCourts.pdf. Although New Hampshire and Massachusetts do not require their justices to be lawyers (id.), all their current justices are. See Supreme Judicial Court of Massachusetts, Justices, available at http://www.state.ma.us/courts/courtsandjudges/courts/supremejudicialcourt/justices

Thirty-six states have what is called a *unified bar*, which means that all lawyers must be members of the state bar association to be licensed. In these thirty-six states the judges are ipso facto members of the state bar association. Thirty-two states explicitly require their supreme court justices to be members of the state bar.[28]

Another early-twentieth-century ABA project was the recruitment of judges into the membership. By 1915, the ABA could brag that 85 percent of the federal judiciary and 56 percent of state judges were members.[29] At present, more than four thousand American judges are members of the ABA.[30]

Of course, bar association membership and a career as a lawyer really only begin to describe the effects of judicial "membership" in the legal profession. Judges are lawyers first, both temporally and emotionally. Most judges have spent the bulk of their formative working years as lawyers. Their peer group, former colleagues, and many of their friends are likely to be lawyers. Each of these contacts and experiences works on both a conscious and a subconscious level. On a conscious level, no judge wants to be a pariah among her friends and colleagues, and most judges seek acceptance and admiration from those same people. Judges want to maximize their own prestige, which generally means their standing among other lawyers.[31]

It is worth contrasting the judicial ideal of independence with the judicial desire to be seen as an excellent judge. Judicial independence

.html; New Hampshire Judicial Branch, Supreme Court Justices and Clerks, available at http://www.state.nh.us/courts/aoc/nameadrs/suprjudg.htm. Likewise, forty-five states require all judges to be lawyers. See Council of State Governments, *Qualifications of Judges of State Appellate Courts.*

[28] Id.

[29] 40 ABA Rep. 30 (1915).

[30] See ABA, *Judicial Division*, available at http://www.abanet.org/jd/membership.html. In contrast, the largest judicial association, the American Judges Association, has only three thousand members. See American Judges Association, *About*, available at http://aja.ncsc.dni.us/htdocs/aboutaja.htm.

[31] Frederick Schauer, "Incentives, Reputation, and the Inglorious Determinants of Judicial Behavior," 68 *U. Cin. L. Rev*. 615, 627–31 (2000).

requires a disinterest in the opinions of the public at large: a judge applies the law regardless of whether it is popular or not.[32] In contrast, the desire to be seen as a "good judge" largely involves respect from the legal profession and other judges. Given that judges are told repeatedly to ignore public opinion and also that laypeople cannot fairly measure the quality of judicial decisions, a judge's desire for approval naturally focuses on the legal profession. This effect is further magnified because judicial salaries are fixed, making nonpecuniary factors, such as prestige within the profession, even more important for judicial job satisfaction.[33]

The powerful effect of repeat players in an iterated game must also be noted. Game theory draws a sharp distinction between one-time games and iterated games, games played over and over again with the same players. In one-time games the players have less incentive to cooperate – they are unlikely to ever meet the other players or replay the game, so the incentives are stacked toward self-interest and even cheating. In contrast, in an iterated game there are substantial benefits to cooperation, and the possibility of punishing errant behavior shifts the calculus for each player.[34]

From a judge's point of view, lawsuits are a combination of one-time and iterated games. The litigants are usually one-time players, whereas the lawyers tend to cycle through again and again. In appellate courts litigants are virtually invisible (except for giving statements of fact and being faces in the audience). Game theory thus predicts that judges will work much harder to cooperate with lawyers than with litigants.

Judges work in a remarkably insulated world – the litigants, witnesses, and jurors in a lawsuit are often the only members of the public a judge sees in a workday. The structure of the judiciary is a major

[32] Richard Posner's *How Judges Think* argues quite persuasively that judges cannot simply "apply the law" in most such circumstances, and that politics or personal preferences invariably come into play. See Richard A. Posner, *How Judges Think* (Cambridge, MA: Harvard University Press, 2008).

[33] Id. at 59.

[34] Robert Axelrod, *The Evolution of Cooperation* (New York: Basic Books, 1984).

contributor to this effect. American courts are designed to be independent, and American judges are supposed to be uniquely resistant to public pressures or lobbying. This is obviously true in the federal court system, in which life tenure is mandatory. The regular contact between judges and lawyers thus looms even larger in the judicial worldview and makes judges an easy target for lawyer lobbying.

This is true even for elected judges. Studies have shown that members of the public are unlikely to know who their state supreme court justices are.[35] Judicial elections tend to be of "low salience," meaning that voters do not have much interest in or knowledge about the candidates for judicial office. Voter turnout in judicial elections is low.[36] Voter apathy is partly a result of the behavior of the candidates. The judicial canon of ethics and professional norms discourages any campaign promises about future decisions in any specific area of the law; voters thus have little incentive to learn about any specific judicial candidate.[37]

A closer examination of the nuts and bolts of a judge's job also demonstrates how crucial lawyers are to the work of judging. In the advocacy system, most judges rely on the lawyers to do the great bulk of the work in trying, briefing, researching, and investigating cases. When the system is working properly, the judges decide cases based on the legal and factual work of the lawyers. In contrast, judges are often at their wits' end when dealing with pro se litigants or incompetent lawyers.[38] Judges and lawyers have a symbiotic relationship, and neither party is eager to disturb the other.[39]

[35] Deborah R. Hensler, "Do We Need an Empirical Research Agenda on Judicial Independence?," 72 *S. Cal. L. Rev.* 707, 721 (1999).

[36] Philip L. DuBois, "Voting Cues in Nonpartisan Trial Court Elections: A Multivariate Assessment," 18 *L. & Soc. Rev.* 395, 397 (1984); Richard L. Hasen, "'High Court Wrongly Elected': A Public Choice Model of Judging and Its Implications for the Voting Rights Act," 75 *N.C. L. Rev.* 1305, 1315–18 (1997).

[37] Model Code of Judicial Conduct Canon 5(3) (2008).

[38] See Jonathan D. Glater, "In a Downturn More Act as Their Own Lawyers," *New York Times*, April 9, 2009, A1.

[39] Chapters 5 and 6 argue that because judges and current lawyers both profit when entry tightens, this judicial incentive has led directly to higher barriers to entry, including the

On a more basic level, most judges probably do not want to face a courtroom of disgruntled lawyers on a regular basis, simply because of their ongoing working relationships. In sum, judges have a multitude of job-related reasons for seeking the favor of the lawyers who practice before them and of the legal profession as a whole. Most human beings react to incentives, and the incentives clearly favor a close (or inseparable) relationship between the bench and the bar.

Unconscious, Subtle Considerations

In the preceding section we considered the many conscious reasons for judges to favor lawyers. The subconscious reasons, however, are at least as important. Here the work of the new institutionalists is particularly instructive. Nobel prize winner Douglass North formally launched the new institutionalism with his book *Institutions, Institutional Change, and Economic Performance*, but many others have been involved.[40]

The central insight of the new institutionalism is that human behavior is bounded by "institutions" and these institutions are extremely important to the study of economics. North defines institutions broadly as "formal and informal rules that constrain individual behavior and shape human interaction. [They] are the framework within which human interaction takes place."[41] Institutions are a constellation of behaviors, rules, and norms that bind and constrain groups of individuals. In contrast,

requirement of three years of law school and an ever more difficult bar exam. Lawyers profit because of decreased competition and judges profit because the lawyers who appear before them are better qualified.

[40] North, *Institutions, Institutional Change, and Economic Performance*. Many consider Ronald Coase, "The Nature of the Firm," 4 *Economica* 386 (1937), the first work of new institutionalism. Oliver Williamson, "The New Institutional Economics: Taking Stock, Looking Ahead," 38 *Journal of Economic Literature* 595 (2000) and *Empirical Studies in Institutional Change*, eds. Lee J. Alston, Thrainn Eggertsson, and Douglass C. North (Cambridge: Cambridge University Press, 1996) offer excellent overviews of other seminal work in this area.

[41] North, *Institutions, Institutional Change and Economic Performance*, 4.

"organizations" are groups of people working together, such as a company, the judiciary, or a legislature.[42]

Classical economics, however, hews firmly to the assumptions described earlier for public choice theory: individuals are rational and self-interested and seek to maximize their own welfare, happiness, and utility. North's institutions help explain why different societies have developed so differently over time and why some economies have fared so much better than others. North argues that institutions – and the evolution of institutions over time – are a missing key ingredient to our understanding of human and societal behaviors.[43]

Institutions are a human response to what economists call "transaction costs." Every economic transaction has an obvious cost (the price of the goods), as well as a series of transaction costs: the costs of finding, evaluating, negotiating, and so on. Societies develop institutions to try to reduce uncertainty and clarify transactions. Different institutions have different effects on transaction costs; some are more efficient than others. These different institutions help explain why some economies flourish and others fail.[44]

Although institutions do evolve, they can be quite sticky. North notes that even as whole governments turn over through revolution or constitutional redesign, the great bulk of human interaction stays the same.[45]

The American practice of law is a great example of an institution. In any given community, lawyers are bound by formal rules – the terms of their state licensure, state and federal laws governing the practice

[42] Id. at 5.

[43] To anyone who is not an economist, the insight that people are not always perfectly rational and are often driven by custom, personal experiences, and various heuristics may seem patently obvious. Nevertheless, it is a key insight for economics, as economists struggle to translate their models of human behavior into a better understanding of actual human behavior. Likewise, my use of public choice theory and the new institutionalism also attempts to bridge law, economics, psychology, and sociology.

[44] Id. at 25–26.

[45] Id. at 89–91.

of law, and local rules of court – as well as a set of informal rules that range from the correct way to address a judge to the proper professional attire. When a lawyer from one state moves to another, she must learn much more than the differences in the written rules and law. The lawyer must learn the informal structures that bind and delineate the legal community.

As such, the new institutionalism offers an exceptionally helpful way to think about the deep ties that bind lawyers and judges. Judges respond to the world, and particularly to judicial decisions, as *lawyers*. As Charles Wolfram has noted, "in both England and America, there has never been any significant difference between judges and lawyers in their background, training, mutual set of expectations about the nature of the work that each would perform, professional ambitions, or professional culture."[46]

Unlike judges in civil law systems, American judges receive no special training or degree before becoming judges.[47] A lengthy period of legal practice certainly offers future judges a chance to observe a judge's job from the lawyer's point of view. Practice also trains in advocacy and legal reasoning. However, a judge's job is quite distinct from a lawyer's. This further establishes the shared professional identity between judges and lawyers: there is no real break between practice and judging, and any changes in thought processes or point of view occur in tandem with judging itself.

Lawyers and judges are further united by the powerful institution of Anglo-American legal thought, which is itself a result of more than five hundred years of legal education and the practice of law. Legal thinking is a powerful and constraining institution.[48] The goal of American

[46] Charles W. Wolfram, "Toward a History of the Legalization of American Legal Ethics – II, The Modern Era," 15 *Geo. J. Legal Ethics* 205, 211 (2002).

[47] Stephen McG. Bundy, "The Policy In Favor of Settlement in an Adversary System," 44 *Hastings L.J.* 1 and n. 21 (1992). The difference in civil law training for judges is discussed in greater detail in Chapter 12.

[48] Lynn Lopucki has made this point quite well: "Law is practiced mostly in communities. Those communities forge shared mental models of the law and process cases

law school is to teach students to "think like a lawyer," explicitly institutionalizing the process of legal analysis. There is no set definition for what constitutes "thinking like a lawyer," but there is general agreement on several points. "Thinking like a lawyer" requires a rigorous, logical approach to each situation. The initial task is to separate the legally operative facts from the useless facts. The legally operative facts consist of the facts that will prove crucial to a court's decision. For instance, in a breach of contract case the terms of the contract itself are always operative, the negotiations between the parties are sometimes operative, and the betrayal felt by the allegedly wronged party is generally not operative.

After the operative facts have been determined, the lawyer turns to analyzing, synthesizing, and interpreting the relevant law. This requires a lawyer to find what law may prove applicable from the vast thicket of potential precedents, statutes, regulations, and so forth. Often various sources of law are in conflict and several different categories of law might apply. For example, in a breach-of-contract case a lawyer might use the law of contracts for the economic breach issues and try a tort (personal injury) claim for the feelings of betrayal. Both statutes and case law will likely apply. As such, legal analysis continuously separates the wheat from the chaff to try to bring order from disorder.

A lawyer's main goal is to find a satisfactory legal analysis that brings a good result for her clients. The goal-oriented aspect of legal analysis is critical for any understanding of legal practice. Lawyers regularly start their analysis with a goal in mind, and then work backward through the process of sorting the facts and the law. This mode of thinking continues as lawyers become judges. Often the legal analysis that serves lawyers and clients so well unfortunately results in judges who work backward from results to reasoning, rather than the other way around.[49]

principally in accord with them." Lynn M. Lopucki, "Legal Culture, Legal Strategy, and the Law in Lawyers' Heads," 90 *NW U. L. Rev.* 1498, 1501–02 (1999).

[49] See, e.g., Charles B. Blackmar, "Judicial Activism," 42 *St. Louis U. L.J.* 753, 756 (1998).

Any lawyer will tell you that law school and legal practice change the way she views the world.[50] The previous description of legal analysis should ring a bell to the new institutionalists. Legal thought is an institution that allows lawyers and judges to talk about complicated factual and legal issues without reinventing the wheel for each case. The institution of legal thought includes formal and informal constraints, everything from how to address judges and prosecutors, to the order of legal arguments and the format of briefs, to rules of civil and criminal procedure. There is a vast amount to learn and understand in the practice of law, and it forms a powerful and binding institution.

The influence of legal thought in the judiciary is particularly strong because judges are typically individuals who thrived in law school and the practice of law. Judges approach their work with a prescribed set of heuristics, behaviors, and notions about the world. These institutions are precisely why judges succeeded as lawyers and contribute to their value as judges. Nevertheless, these same factors lead judges to overempathize with lawyers. On a subconscious level, when judges face a question that will affect the legal profession, judges naturally react in terms of how it will affect "us" more than "them."

Note that the "us" versus "them" dynamic is a natural holdover from practice – one thing that all lawyers share is complaints about clients. In the same way that judges carry a set of positive reactions to the legal professions, they carry a set of beliefs about other litigants based on their experiences with clients.

Of course, judges do not like to believe that they are biased. To the contrary, judges work hard on legal reasoning not only to convince the litigants and the public that their decision is correct and unbiased, but to convince themselves as well. Richard Posner's *How Judges Think* terms

[50] One persistent criticism of American law schools and legal thought is that they are quite dehumanizing. Lawyers and law students learn to divorce emotional responses to cases and facts and view them with a logical, critical eye focused on analysis. Shared dehumanization may be another binding result of legal thought.

this approach to legal questions "legalism."[51] Judges want to believe that there is a correct answer to most, if not all, legal questions and that their decisions are an inevitable result of that reasoning. To a certain extent, everything about judging, from the arguments of counsel to complex written decisions with ornate legal reasoning, is set up to give credence to the power of legalism and legal thought.

As Posner notes, however, there is a large body of cases in which there is no clearly right answer based on the law; in those cases judges, whether they admit it to themselves or to the public, are forced to turn to other modes of decision making, such as ideology or personal experience.[52] When a gray-area case arises that could affect the legal profession, the lawyer–judge bias predicts a decision that favors the legal profession. This book seeks to demonstrate that the case results described in the chapters to come cannot be explained through legalism, but rather only as a result of conscious and/or unconscious bias.

[51] Posner, *How Judges Think*, 41–56. Posner's analysis here is consonant with the writings of many other judge-scholars of the past, including Benjamin Cardozo and Oliver Wendell Holmes. See Benjamin N. Cardozo, *The Nature of the Judicial Process* (New Haven, CT: Yale University Press, 1921); Oliver Wendell Holmes, "The Path of the Law," 10 *Harv. L. Rev.* 457 (1897).

[52] Id. at 78–121.

3 Constitutional Criminal Procedure

> The right to be heard would be, in many cases, of little avail if it did not comprehend the right to be heard by counsel. Even the intelligent and educated layman has small and sometimes no skill in the science of law.... He requires the guiding hand of counsel at every step in the proceedings against him.
>
> – *Powell v. Alabama*[1]

> The Constitution says that everyone is entitled to an attorney of their choice. But the Constitution does not say that the lawyer has to be awake.
>
> – Judge Doug Shaver[2]

THE 1960S MARKED A DUE PROCESS REVOLUTION FOR criminal procedure, with the Supreme Court guaranteeing a set of rights to criminal defendants in both federal and state courts. Before the 1960s, the Court had applied many constitutional provisions in federal prosecutions, but not in state cases. In 1961, *Mapp v. Ohio* applied the exclusionary rule (which suppresses evidence that comes as a result of an unconstitutional search or seizure) to the states.[3] In 1963, *Gideon v. Wainwright* extended the Sixth Amendment

[1] *Powell v. Alabama*, 287 U.S. 45, 68–69 (1932).

[2] Bruce Shapiro, "Sleeping Lawyer Syndrome," *The Nation*, Apr. 7, 1997, at 27–29 (quoting Judge Doug Shaver).

[3] *Mapp v. Ohio*, 367 U.S. 643 (1961).

right to counsel to all indigent felony defendants.[4] The Court extended the Fifth Amendment privilege against self-incrimination to the states in 1964,[5] and it extended the Sixth Amendment right to confront and cross-examine witnesses to the states in 1965.[6] The year 1966 brought perhaps the most famous case of them all, *Miranda v. Arizona*.[7]

In the following decades, the Supreme Court has clarified, and often restricted, these rights. In the creation and development of these rights, the lawyer–judge bias has been a constant theme. This chapter covers three examples: the cases that follow *Miranda* favor a request for a lawyer over a request to remain silent; the right to an appointed lawyer is better protected than the right to a jury; and, despite the robust right to a lawyer, criminal defendants have little protection from ineffective lawyers. The overall thrust of these cases is to employ as many lawyers as possible in the defense of the indigent, but they offer little recourse to someone convicted partly or fully because of incompetent counsel.

I am certainly not arguing against the value or necessity of appointed counsel for the indigent – in fact, a large part of my academic career is in service as appointed counsel in criminal cases. I am also not arguing that all appointed counsel is incompetent. Instead, I am arguing that the structure of the Supreme Court decisions is much more favorable to lawyers than to the indigent and that despite the flowery language of *Miranda*, *Gideon*, and other cases, the lack of any protection against incompetent lawyering has created very predictable results: the lawyers get the business and many indigent defendants get little help.

Miranda v. Arizona

The cases listed in the preceding section served as a backdrop in 1966 when the Supreme Court revolutionized the law of police interrogations

[4] *Gideon v. Wainwright*, 372 U.S. 335 (1963).
[5] *Malloy v. Hogan*, 378 U.S. 1 (1964).
[6] *Pointer v. Texas*, 380 U.S. 400 (1965).
[7] *Miranda v. Arizona*, 384 U.S. 436 (1966).

with *Miranda v. Arizona*. *Miranda* required that police officers warn a suspect in custody, prior to interrogation, that he has the right to remain silent; the right to have counsel present at questioning; the right to have counsel appointed if he cannot afford one; and the caveat that anything the detainee says can be used against him in court.[8] If these warnings are not given prior to interrogations, statements taken in violation of *Miranda* generally cannot be introduced at trial.[9]

The impact of the various criminal procedure cases from the 1960s has been huge, but none of them has penetrated the American consciousness the way that *Miranda* has. Anyone who has watched a police movie or television program in the past forty years has heard the now familiar warnings, let alone all the suspects who have heard them. Reading of the rights has become an iconic and profound statement about the nature of the American justice system.

At the outset, consider the government-sponsored free advertising the Court granted the legal profession in *Miranda*. The very first thing a law enforcement officer must tell a suspect strongly suggests that whatever else the suspect does, it would be a good idea for her to hire a lawyer or get a free one appointed. In this case and others it is clear that the Court considers a lawyer the sine qua non for navigating the criminal justice system and requires the state to advise each person under custodial investigation to get a lawyer as soon as possible. The Court may well be right that this is a good idea, but including the suggestion in a mandatory set of warnings in a case aimed at protecting the right to remain silent, not the right to a lawyer, is a striking move.[10]

Moreover, the decision to include two rights – the right to remain silent and the right to an attorney – is intriguing. Criminal defendants

[8] *Miranda*, 384 U.S. at 467–71.

[9] *Miranda*, 384 U.S. at 479. There are, naturally, exceptions to this rule. See "Custodial Interrogations," 35 *Geo. L.J. Ann. Rev. Crim. Proc.* 162, 164 and n. 523 ("Exceptions to the Miranda rule include good faith, attenuation, independent source, and independent discovery.").

[10] The fact that *Miranda* is a Fifth Amendment right-to-silence case, and not a Sixth Amendment right-to-counsel case, will be discussed at length later.

have a large number of constitutional and procedural safeguards that might be useful to know at the time of arrest, including bond rights, the right to a jury, the right to a speedy trial, and so on. *Miranda* was, at heart, an interrogation/Fifth Amendment case involving the right to remain silent, so the inclusion of that right was obvious. The interesting choice was to include the right to a lawyer and exclude the other rights.

At the time of *Miranda*, the Court had several model warnings from which to select. The FBI gave arrestees a warning that was basically identical to the warning required by *Miranda*.[11] The Court also cited two additional warnings – the contemporary British and Uniform Code of Military Justice warnings – that included only the right not to answer questions and made no mention of lawyers. Accordingly, the Court certainly could have chosen to require a shorter warning focused solely on silence.[12]

All the same, the Court's opinion makes it absolutely clear that the presence of an attorney is a critical safeguard against coercive interrogation techniques, that defense attorneys play a crucial role in the criminal justice system and that, in the Court's opinion, the presence of lawyers at interrogations will have a number of salutary effects:

> The presence of counsel at the interrogation may serve several significant subsidiary functions as well. If the accused decides to talk to his interrogators, the assistance of counsel can mitigate the dangers of untrustworthiness. With a lawyer present the likelihood that the police will practice coercion is reduced, and if coercion is nevertheless exercised the lawyer can testify to it in court. The presence of a lawyer can also help to guarantee that the accused gives a fully accurate statement to the police and that the statement is rightly reported by the prosecution at trial.[13]
>
> If the individual desires to exercise his privilege, he has the right to do so. This is not for the authorities to decide. An attorney may advise

[11] *Miranda*, 384 U.S. at 483–86.

[12] Id. at 487–89 and n. 57.

[13] Id. at 470.

> his client not to talk to police until he has had an opportunity to investigate the case, or he may wish to be present with his client during any police questioning. In doing so an attorney is merely exercising the good professional judgment he has been taught. This is not cause for considering the attorney a menace to law enforcement. He is merely carrying out what he is sworn to do under his oath – to protect to the extent of his ability the rights of his client. In fulfilling this responsibility the attorney plays a vital role in the administration of criminal justice under our Constitution.[14]

The Court also states that the lawyer portion of the warning "is an absolute prerequisite to interrogation."[15]

In short, the Court's opinion shows an extraordinary sensitivity for, and confidence in, the role of lawyers in the criminal justice system. Would nonlawyers share the Justices' view that a lawyer is *the* critical safeguard or that criminal defense lawyers do, indeed, play the helpful role the Court envisions within the contemporary justice system? The point is not whether the Court is right or wrong on the merits, but to note the Court's strong belief in the legal profession and how that plays itself out in the decision and the required warnings. Furthermore, it is the later cases that have expanded (and shrunk) *Miranda* that really highlight the lawyer–judge bias.

Mosley and *Edwards*

The cases that followed *Miranda* make the judicial bias toward the legal profession even clearer. The *Miranda* warnings inform a suspect of two broad rights: the right to remain silent and the right to an attorney. In the *Miranda* opinion itself neither right is favored over the other, and both are treated as critical to safeguarding a suspect's rights. In particular, if a suspect exercises either right, the interrogation must stop: "Once warnings have been given, the subsequent procedure is clear. If the individual

[14] Id. at 480–81.
[15] Id. at 471.

indicates in any manner, at any time prior to questioning, that he wishes to remain silent, the interrogation must cease."[16] Similarly, "[i]f the individual states that he wants an attorney, the interrogation must cease until an attorney is present."[17]

The Court's treatment of these two rights, however, has diverged radically over time, with *Michigan v. Mosely*[18] and *Edwards v. Arizona*[19] serving as the two prime examples. The period between *Miranda* and *Edwards* marked a long and slow erosion of *Miranda* and its protections. Statements taken in violation of *Miranda* were held to be admissible in court under certain circumstances[20] and *Mosely* greatly curtailed the protection for a defendant who asked to remain silent.

In *Mosely,* the Court faced the question of how to handle a second round of questioning after a suspect had already invoked his right to remain silent. The Court cited *Miranda* for the proposition that the "right to cut off questioning" must be "scrupulously honored."[21] Nevertheless, the Court held that an interval of "more than two hours," questioning by another officer about a different crime and a new set of *Miranda* warnings were sufficiently scrupulous.[22]

From the outset, *Mosely* was seen as a significant weakening of *Miranda*.[23] Later cases made it even clearer. *Mosely* listed a series of reasons why the later questioning following a request to remain silent (two or more hours later, a new set of warnings, and different officers/different crimes) is legal. In this circumstance, later courts must decide which of the listed factors are critical and which are not. In *Mosely* it turned out

[16] Id. at 473–74.

[17] Id. at 474.

[18] *Michigan v. Mosely*, 423 U.S. 96 (1975).

[19] *Edwards v. Arizona*, 451 U.S. 477 (1981).

[20] *Harris v. New York*, 401 U.S. 222 (1971), held that a statement taken in violation of *Miranda* (i.e., without the warnings) could be admitted in court to impeach a defendant who took the stand to testify in his own defense.

[21] *Mosely*, 423 U.S. at 104.

[22] Id.

[23] In dissent, Justice William Brennan called *Mosely* another step in *Miranda*'s "erosion and ... ultimate overruling." *Mosely*, 423 U.S. at 112.

that the only factor that really mattered was the relatively short period of time between interrogations. Later cases have made clear that there is no different-crime or different-officer requirement and that the police can scrupulously honor a suspect's right to remain silent by pausing the interrogation for a period as short as an hour or two and then repeating the warnings.[24]

Mosely is thus notable both for its part in the long-term project of eroding *Miranda*'s protections and as the first case to really differentiate between the right to remain silent and the right to counsel. As *Mosely* made clear, its holding on the malleability of a declared desire to exercise the right to remain silent had no effect on the requirements following a request to speak to a lawyer.[25] Although the results of an exercise of either right were treated quite similarly in *Miranda* itself, *Mosely* establishes for the first time that the right to remain silent is to be treated less favorably.[26]

The other post-*Mosely* Supreme Court cases on the treatment of silence at trial are generally unfriendly. The Court recently held that a request to remain silent must be unambiguous and held that silence itself – the very constitutional right that *Miranda* is meant to protect – is ambiguous, so police officers can continue to question a suspect for any amount of time in the face of silence.[27] The Court has held that prearrest and postarrest silence that precedes a *Miranda* warning may be used as evidence of guilt at trial.[28] Post-*Miranda* warning silence, however,

[24] Some of the cases on this issue are gathered in "Custodial Interrogations," at 177 n. 568 (2006).

[25] *Mosely*, 423 U.S. at 101 n. 7.

[26] Anthony X. McDermott and H. Mitchell Caldwell, "Did He or Didn't He? The Effect of *Dickerson* on the Post-Waiver Invocation Equation," 69 *U. Cin. L. Rev.* 863, 896–97 (2001) ("For the first time, a salient distinction was made between the right to counsel and the right to silence. Those suspects requesting the latter thus warranted less protection from the 'menacing police interrogation procedures' than those who requested the former.").

[27] See *Berghuis v. Thompkins*, 2010 WL 2160784, *8–9.

[28] See *Jenkins v. Anderson*, 447 U.S. 231, 238 (1980) (prearrest silence); *Fletcher v. Weir*, 455 U.S. 603 (1982) (per curiam) (allowing the use of postarrest silence if a defendant later takes the stand during her criminal trial).

cannot be used at trial.[29] It is worth noting that a prosecutor could not use a prearrest, postarrest, or post-*Miranda* warning request for a lawyer as evidence of guilt,[30] despite the fact that some jurors might consider a request for a lawyer to be at least as incriminating as a request to remain silent.

Edwards v. Arizona made the distinction between silence and counsel even clearer. *Edwards* was decided in 1981, during a period of erosion for *Miranda* protections.[31] *Edwards* dealt with a situation analogous to that considered in *Mosely*: a suspect had asked for counsel and before counsel had arrived the police resumed their interrogation and the defendant eventually confessed.[32] The Arizona Supreme Court relied on *Mosely* and held that if the confession was gained voluntarily during the second interrogation, *Miranda* was satisfied.[33]

The Supreme Court reversed; *Edwards* is one of the very few later decisions to unequivocally embrace *Miranda*'s language and holding.[34] The Court noted that it had "strongly indicated that additional safeguards are necessary when the accused asks for counsel" and held that once an accused asks for counsel the accused cannot be questioned until she meets with counsel or "initiates further communication."[35] *Edwards* also discussed *Mosley* and made explicit the differential treatment between a request to remain silent and a request for counsel.[36]

Given that *Edwards* is surrounded by *Miranda* cases that refer to the warnings as a nonconstitutionally required, prophylactic

[29] *Doyle v. Ohio*, 426 U.S. 610 (1976).

[30] See, e.g., *State v. Juarez*, 572 N.W. 2d 286, 290 (Minn. 1997).

[31] Leslie A. Lunney, "The Erosion of Miranda: *Stare Decisis* Consequences," 48 *Cath. U. L. Rev.* 727, 745–86 (1999).

[32] *Edwards*, 451 U.S. at 479–80.

[33] *State v. Edwards*, 594 P.2d 72, 77–78 (1979).

[34] *Edwards*, 451 U.S. at 481–82.

[35] Id. at 484–85.

[36] Id. at 485 ("In *Michigan v. Mosley*, 423 U.S. 96 (1975), the Court noted that *Miranda* had distinguished between the procedural safeguards triggered by a request to remain silent and a request for an attorney and had required that interrogation cease until an attorney was present only if the individual stated that he wanted counsel.").

measure,[37] the stridency of the opinion is striking. The Court states that "[t]he Fifth Amendment right identified in *Miranda* is the right to have counsel present at any custodial interrogation"[38] and creates a bright-line requirement that all questioning stop following a request for counsel.

The cases that followed *Edwards* generally built on this bright-line rule.[39] The fact that the Court has followed up on *Edwards* at all is noteworthy. The Court kept the right to counsel question salient through multiple cases, strengthening its protections. In contrast, the Court's last real statement on the effect of an unequivocal request to remain silent was *Mosley*, and this has resulted in a long, slow drift in courts in which even the protections offered by *Mosley* have been diluted.[40]

In *Smith v. Illinois*, one of the first post-*Edwards* cases, the Court reiterated that after an unequivocal request for counsel is made, all questioning must stop and later equivocal statements about wanting a lawyer are of no consequence.[41] In *Arizona v. Roberson,* the Court held that when an accused has requested counsel she may not be questioned later by a new set of detectives about a totally separate crime, even if the second detectives did not know of the earlier request for counsel.[42] The Court recognized the factual similarities to *Mosley* (the second set of detectives investigating a second crime), but again clarified that a request for counsel carried more weight than requesting to remain silent.[43]

In *Minnick v. Mississippi*, the accused requested counsel, met with counsel, and then was questioned by the police without his lawyer present.[44] *Minnick* has a lengthy passage discussing the efficacy of the

[37] See Susan R. Klein, "No Time for Silence," 81 *Tex. L. Rev*. 1337, 1337–38 and n. 6 (2003).

[38] Id. at 485–86.

[39] The main exception is the series of cases that have required a clear request for counsel to trigger *Edwards*, rejecting more equivocal or unclear requests. See, e.g., *Davis v. United States*, 512 U.S. 452 (1994).

[40] See "Custodial Interrogations," 177 n. 568.

[41] *Smith v. Illinois*, 469 U.S. 91, 94–100 (1984).

[42] See *Arizona v. Roberson*, 486 U.S. 675, 680–88 (1988).

[43] *Roberson*, 486 U.S. at 683.

[44] *Minnick v. Mississippi*, 498 U.S. 146, 155–58 (1990).

bright-line *Edwards* rule and well encapsulates a theme that runs throughout all these cases: What is the point of having *Miranda* rights at all if the police can question you regardless of your request for an attorney?[45] In this regard, the Justices' experience as lawyers is extremely relevant. All lawyers know and fear the possibility that their clients will be talking to opposing parties outside the lawyers' presence and say things that can never be retracted or fixed.[46]

In *Montejo v. Louisiana,* the Court did circumscribe the prohibition against police questioning after a lawyer is appointed at an arraignment, but this case expressly upheld "the *Miranda–Edwards–Minnick* line of cases."[47] In fact, these cases will be even more important after *Montejo*, as any new police questioning will require a new waiver of the *Miranda–Edwards–Minnick* right to have counsel present.[48]

In sum, there is now little doubt that the right to counsel is better protected by *Miranda* and its progeny than is the right to remain silent.[49] Aside from the Court's familiarity and natural understanding of the importance of counsel, however, there is not much to support placing the right to counsel above the right to remain silent. To the contrary, the right to remain silent is the more central right protected by *Miranda.*

Insofar as *Miranda* is constitutionally based, it is based squarely on the Fifth Amendment's right to prevent self-incrimination and not the Sixth Amendment's right to counsel. *Miranda* itself referred to self-incrimination.[50] In *United States v. Dickerson,* the Court noted the many

[45] *Minnick*, 498 U.S. at 152–56.

[46] Consider Justice Jackson's concurrence in *Watts v. Indiana*, 338 U.S. 49, 59 (1949): "Any lawyer who has ever been called into a case after his client has 'told all' and turned any evidence he has over to the Government, knows how helpless he is to protect his client against the facts thus disclosed."

[47] *Montejo v. Louisiana*, 129 S.Ct. 2079, 2090 (2009).

[48] *Montejo*, 556 U.S. at 13–16.

[49] See Alexandra Natapoff, "Speechless: The Silencing of Criminal Defendants," 80 *N.Y.U. L. Rev.* 1449, 1481 (2005).

[50] See, e.g., *Miranda*, 384 U.S. at 439 (arguing that coercive nature of custodial interrogations threatens the "privilege under the Fifth Amendment ... not to be compelled to

references in *Miranda* and its progeny to the Fifth Amendment in deciding that the Fifth Amendment required *Miranda*'s holding.[51] The Sixth Amendment's right to counsel, in contrast, does not attach until "prosecution is commenced," not during the police investigation of a crime.[52]

Given that *Miranda* is a Fifth Amendment case, it is somewhat strange that the right to have counsel present during questioning would be elevated above a straightforward and direct invocation of the suspect's right to remain silent. This is especially so because a request for counsel is treated as an invocation of Fifth Amendment rights: "[A]n accused's request for an attorney is *per se* an invocation of his Fifth Amendment rights, requiring that all interrogation cease."[53]

It is dubious to suggest that protecting the right to counsel will do more to counteract coercive police questioning than a robustly enforced right to remain silent. As the Court has repeatedly noted, "any lawyer worth his salt will tell the suspect in no uncertain terms to make no statement to police under any circumstances."[54] In fact, the very first thing any lawyer summoned to a police station by a *Miranda* request will do is find out what the client has already said and strongly advise the client to say nothing further.[55] Given that the main protection presented by the lawyer is silence, should a direct request to exercise the Fifth Amendment right to silence not be treated at least as favorably as a request for the ancillary right to a lawyer during questioning? Instead, a direct request to remain silent requires only a short break in the questioning,

incriminate [oneself]"); id. at 457 (requiring "adequate safeguards to protect precious Fifth Amendment rights").

51 See *Dickerson v. United States*, 530 U.S. 428, 440 and n. 5 (2000) (listing cases that have described *Miranda* as a Fifth Amendment case).

52 See, e.g., *Texas v. Cobb*, 532 U.S. 162, 167–68 (2001).

53 *Fare v. Michael C.*, 442 U.S. 707, 719 (1979).

54 See, e.g., *Escobedo v. Illinois*, 378 U.S. 478, 488 (1964) (quoting *Watts v. Indiana*, 338 U.S. 49, 59 (1949)) (Jackson, J., concurring in result); *Moran v. Burbine*, 475 U.S. 412, 436 n. 5 (1986) (quoting same).

55 See Louis Michael Seidman, "Brown and Miranda," 80 *Cal. L. Rev.* 673, 734–35 (1992).

whereas a request for a lawyer requires a full stop until a lawyer is consulted and, most likely, a full stop of all interrogation.

One obvious difference between a request for a lawyer and a request to remain silent is that the request for a lawyer has a natural ending point (the arrival of the lawyer). Nevertheless, given that *Miranda* is focused on the Fifth Amendment, a request to remain silent should be treated at least as well as a request for a lawyer – that is, a request for silence should be honored until the suspect invites further communication or is provided with a lawyer.

Thus, *Edwards* and its progeny stand out as another sui generis pro-lawyer decision. While the Court was busily eroding the *Miranda* protections on multiple fronts, it chose to retain quite robust protections for an accused that clearly expressed a desire for a lawyer. The advantages to the legal profession are clear: whatever else an accused should know, she should know to request a lawyer first and foremost.

The Right to a Jury versus the Right to Appointed Counsel

Similarly, the right to appointed counsel is now better protected than is the right to a jury. This is surprising because the right to a jury is perhaps the oldest and most important right in American criminal procedure. The framers of the Constitution and the Bill of Rights saw it as absolutely central to the protection of individual rights from the government.

Whereas there has been a long-standing American right to be represented by a lawyer in criminal trials, the right to appointment of counsel is of much more recent vintage.[56] It is indefensible to privilege the right to appointed counsel over the right to a jury as a matter of policy, constitutional theory, or history. The reason that the Supreme Court

[56] I am not arguing that *Johnson v. Zerbst* or *Gideon v. Wainright* are wrong or that because the framers did not contemplate a constitutional guarantee of appointed counsel for the indigent, these cases should be overturned. As I noted earlier, I personally regularly appear as appointed defense counsel for the indigent and recognize how critical it is to allow access to justice.

has favored the right to appointed lawyers over juries is that the Justices personally think that right is more important – a position that is directly related to the fact that they are all lawyers.

The Sixth Amendment states:

> In all criminal prosecutions, the accused shall enjoy the right to a speedy and public trial, by an impartial jury of the State and district where in the crime shall have been committed, which district shall have been previously ascertained by law, and to be informed of the nature and cause of the accusation; to be confronted with the witnesses against him; to have compulsory process for obtaining witnesses in his favor, and to have the Assistance of Counsel for his defense.

Article III, Section 2 of the Constitution likewise states a right to a criminal jury trial for federal crimes: "The Trial of all Crimes, except in Cases of Impeachment, shall be by Jury; and such trial shall be held in the State where the said Crimes shall have been committed."

At the time of the framing there was little question which of these rights was paramount: the right to an impartial jury was seen as one of the Constitution's main bulwarks against government overreaching. The right to criminal jury trials was among the few guarantees of individual rights enumerated in the Constitution of 1789, and it was the only such right to appear in both the original Constitution and the Bill of Rights.

For the framers, the right to a jury was as critical as the right to vote; this was one of the few areas of agreement between the federalists and the antifederalists.[57] "Were I called upon," Thomas Jefferson wrote, "to decide whether the people had best be omitted in the Legislative or Judiciary department, I would say it is better to leave them out of the

[57] "The friends and adversaries of the plan of the convention, if they agree in nothing else, concur at least in the value they set upon the trial by jury." Alexander Hamilton, *The Federalist Papers No. 83*, ed. Clinton Rossiter (New York: NAL Penguin, 1961), 499.

Legislative. The execution of the laws is more important than the making of them."[58]

The right to counsel, though certainly not unimportant, was the subject of little debate[59] and gave federal constitutional standing to a rule that was already in effect in the colonies and at American common law. The Sixth Amendment right to assistance of counsel was a clear rejection of English common law, which allowed defense lawyers in misdemeanor prosecutions, but not in the more serious cases of treason or a felony. Because most felonies at common law were punishable by death, this meant that British defendants were allowed counsel in less serious cases but not in potential death penalty cases. This was justified because judges were seen as neutral and able to protect the rights of the accused and also as an expedience in prosecuting particularly serious crimes.[60]

Although this rule was adhered to in England until 1836, it was rejected by the American colonies. Twelve of the thirteen colonies lawfully recognized the right to appearance of counsel in all criminal prosecutions, with the exception of one or two instances in which it was limited to more serious crimes.[61] Thus, there was naturally little controversy or discussion over the right to counsel. When the framers drafted the Sixth Amendment, the inclusion of the right to counsel formalized a right that was already well established in the states.

[58] Letter from Thomas Jefferson to Abbe Arnoux (July 19, 1789), in 5 *The Founders' Constitution*, eds. Philip B. Kurland and Ralph Lerner (Chicago: University of Chicago Press, 1987), 364. Similarly, John Adams wrote that juries should have "as compleat a Controul, as decisive a Negative, in every Judgment of a Court of Judicature" as the legislature has to veto executive action. John Adams, Diary Notes on the Right of Juries (Feb. 12, 1771), in 1 *Legal Papers of John Adams*, ed. L. Kinvin Wroth and Hiller B. Zobel (Cambridge, MA: Harvard University Press, 1965), 229.

[59] Akhil Reed Amar, *The Bill of Rights: Creation and Reconstruction* (New Haven, CT: Yale University Press, 1998), 278–79.

[60] See David J. Bodenhamer, *Fair Trial* (New York: Oxford University Press, 1992), 39–40.

[61] *Powell v. Alabama*, 287 U.S. 45, 60–66 (1932) offers an excellent overview of the various colonial treatments of the right to counsel.

There are two more important caveats about these rights. First, the rights to a jury trial and counsel were only federal rights, and enforceable only against the federal government. Second, the right to counsel clearly did not encompass the right to appointed counsel, only the right to be represented if one could afford an attorney. The right to appointed counsel was not constitutionally guaranteed in the federal system until 1938 in *Johnson v. Zerbst*[62] and was not guaranteed under the U.S. Constitution in the states until 1963, when *Gideon v. Wainright* guaranteed counsel in felony cases.[63] Along the way Pennsylvania, New Jersey, Connecticut, and a few other states provided for the appointment of counsel by statute, but the practice was not common until the twentieth century.[64]

A defendant's right to have a lawyer if he or she could afford one was thus well established at the time of the passage of the Bill of Rights in both federal and state trials.[65] There certainly was not a right to appointed counsel at the time of the passage of the Bill of Rights, however. If the framers had known that the Sixth Amendment might guarantee a government supplied lawyer to criminal defendants, ratification debates would have likely mentioned it and the right to counsel would have been much more controversial.

In contrast, the right to a jury in criminal trials has been well established in both federal and state jurisdictions from revolutionary times to the present. The state constitutions of all of the original colonies guaranteed a criminal jury trial[66] and by the mid-nineteenth century, every state but California contained such a guarantee.[67]

[62] 304 U.S. 458 (1938).

[63] 372 U.S. 335 (1963).

[64] See Kenneth Katkin, "Incorporation of the Criminal Procedure Amendments: The View from the States," 84 *Neb. L. Rev*. 397, 460–63 (2005).

[65] Note that the original Virginia Constitution did not contain a right to counsel guarantee, nor does the current version.

[66] Albert W. Alschuler and Andrew G. Deiss, "A Brief History of the Criminal Jury in the United States," 61 *U. Chi. L. Rev*. 867, 870 (1994).

[67] Steven G. Calebresi and Sarah E. Agudo, "Individual Rights Under State Constitutions When the Fourteenth Amendment Was Ratified in 1868: What Rights Are Deeply Rooted in American History And Tradition?," 87 *Tex. L. Rev*. 7, 76–77 (2008).

Development of a Right to Appointed Counsel

The development of the modern law establishes that it is the right to counsel that is better protected and offered to more defendants. Strangely, the first of these cases is not even a Sixth Amendment case. In *Powell v. Alabama*, one of the earliest U.S. Supreme Court cases to overturn a state criminal conviction, the Court held that the due process clause of the Fourteenth Amendment required free, effective counsel in a death penalty case.[68]

Powell dealt with the trial of nine black defendants accused of raping two white women on a train passing through Alabama. The trial was an obvious sham. It was held only days after the alleged crime before an all-white jury. The defendants were not allowed to choose their counsel; the trial court appointed two attorneys on the eve of trial, with no time or incentive to investigate or prepare a defense.[69] Among the many patent offenses to justice, the Supreme Court overturned the conviction based on the failure to appoint effective, free counsel.

Powell v. Alabama is an iconic civil rights case and a precursor to *Brown vs. Board of Education* and the criminal procedure revolution of the 1960s. Similar to *Brown*, regardless of the reasoning, there is a visceral correctness to the result in the case. The Justices were certainly right that the trial was an affront to due process of the law.

Nevertheless, the choice to pursue the case as one of an appointment of counsel was curious, and the Court faced a number of logical hurdles. First, why would the due process clause guarantee appointed counsel to defendants in the states when the Sixth Amendment already existed and clearly did not apply to the states? If the authors of the Fourteenth Amendment wanted to include the right to counsel, they could have included it explicitly. The Court had held that a grand jury

[68] *Powell v. Alabama*, 287 U.S. 45 (1932).

[69] Dan T. Carter, *Scottsboro: A Tragedy of the American South* (Baton Rouge: LSU Press, 1979), 11–20.

indictment was not necessary to Fourteenth Amendment due process on essentially those same grounds in 1884 in *Hurtado v. California*.[70] The Court avoided this problem by holding that assistance of counsel is one of the "fundamental principles of liberty and justice which lie at the base of all our civil and political institutions," – that is, the right to the assistance of counsel is so long-standing and fundamental that it must be included in any definition of due process.[71]

Second, because the defendants were indigent and could not afford counsel of their own, the Court had to establish a right to appointed counsel, which was not well recognized in 1932. The Court canvassed the well-established American history of the right to assistance of counsel since before the revolution, along with a series of cases explaining and expanding that right. Nevertheless, to establish a right to appointed counsel the Court needed to rely on a handful of state supreme court cases and the state statutes that granted appointed counsel in certain criminal cases.[72] This elevated the appointment of defense counsel from a legislative decision to a constitutional requirement.

The Court greatly overstated the contemporary practice of court appointment in the following bald and unsupported statement: "The United States by statute and every state in the Union by express provision of law, or by the determination of its courts, make it the duty of the trial judge, where the accused is unable to employ counsel, to appoint counsel for him. In most states the rule applies broadly to all criminal prosecutions, in others it is limited to the more serious crimes, and in a very limited number, to capital cases."[73] As a general rule, such unsupported statements should be viewed with skepticism. At the time of *Powell*, counsel was guaranteed in the federal system by statute and

[70] *Hurtado v. California*, 110 U.S. 516 (1884).

[71] *Powell*, 287 U.S. at 67–69.

[72] Id. at 71–73. For example, Alabama had a statute that guaranteed appointed counsel in capital cases. Id. at 59.

[73] Id. at 73.

only for accusations of treason or other capital crimes.[74] Likewise, the guarantees in the states were hardly as sweeping as *Powell* suggests.[75]

Finally, the defendants in *Powell* actually had been given free counsel. Thus, the Court also had to imply a right to effective assistance of appointed counsel, a right that was not very clearly stated in the opinion and a right that was not fully fleshed out until the 1980s.

Nevertheless, *Powell* established the template for all future appointed lawyer cases: there was much discussion of the critical nature of legal representation and little guidance on the question of what effective legal representation is. In language that would be quoted and cited in later cases expanding the right to appointed counsel, the Court waxed eloquent about the need for lawyers:

> The right to be heard would be, in many cases, of little avail if it did not comprehend the right to be heard by counsel. Even the intelligent and educated layman has small and sometimes no skill in the science of law. If charged with crime, he is incapable, generally, of determining for himself whether the indictment is good or bad. He is unfamiliar with the rules of evidence. Left without the aid of counsel he may be put on trial without a proper charge, and convicted upon incompetent evidence, or evidence irrelevant to the issue or otherwise inadmissible. He lacks both the skill and knowledge adequately to prepare his defense, even though he have a perfect one. He requires the guiding hand of counsel at every step in the proceedings against him. Without it, though he be not guilty, he faces the danger of conviction because he does not know how to establish his innocence. If that be true of men of intelligence, how much more true is it of the ignorant and illiterate, or those of feeble intellect.[76]

The interesting point about *Powell* is that when the Justices read the description of the Scottsboro trial, the part that truly stood out to them was the late appointment of the lawyers and the lawyers' poor

[74] *Bute v. Illinois*, 333 U.S. 640, 660 (1948).

[75] Id. at 663–68.

[76] Id. at 68–69.

performance. Among all the other procedural irregularities and patent unfairness of the trial, the Justices attached themselves to the lawyers. The opinion contains a four-page quote from the colloquy between the Court and counsel before their appointment.[77] Notably, this is the only extensive quoting from the trial record. Moreover, the Court expresses great dismay over representation that was more "pro forma than zealous and active."[78]

In sum, *Powell* is a case in which the Justices were powerfully moved by the actions (and inactions) of the lawyers in the case. Rather than ruling that the trial as a whole failed due process or focusing on the all-white jury, the speed of the trial, or the handling of the witnesses, the Court focused on the lawyers.[79] This led to a decision that created a new constitutional guarantee for appointed, prepared, and competent counsel. The Court limited these rules to capital cases with indigent, illiterate defendants,[80] but the cornerstone for the constitutional requirement for appointed counsel had been laid.

In 1938, the Court used the Sixth Amendment to guarantee appointed counsel in the federal system in *Johnson v. Zerbst*.[81] *Zerbst* is quite similar to *Powell* in several regards. The portion of the opinion that held that the Sixth Amendment requires appointment of a lawyer is quite thin on precedent. That portion of the opinion runs only a page and a half and cites only five cases, none of which held that the Sixth Amendment guarantees a free lawyer for the indigent.[82] There is a very simple reason that the Court's legal analysis was not more thorough: no

[77] Id. at 53–56.

[78] Id. at 58.

[79] In a later case considering the same defendants, the Court did overturn on the basis of racial discrimination in jury selection. See *Norris v. Alabama*, 294 U.S. 587 (1935).

[80] Id. at 71.

[81] *Johnson v. Zerbst*, 304 U.S. 458 (1938).

[82] *Zerbst*, 304 U.S. at 462–63. Three of the cites are reference cites to non-right-to-counsel cases. One of the cites is to *Patton v. United States*, 281 U.S. 276, 308 (1930), a case about waiver of a jury trial, that in turn quotes a Wisconsin Supreme Court case on the same topic that mentions in passing that among other procedural guarantees Wisconsin provided a defense lawyer. Thus, the only nearly relevant support is a quote of double

court had ever held that the Sixth Amendment required a lawyer for every criminal defendant, and it is extremely unlikely that the drafters of the Sixth Amendment would have considered a right to indigent defense within its purview.

As in *Powell*, the Court spends a great deal of time contemplating how essential it is to have a lawyer at a criminal trial, including a lengthy excerpt from *Powell*. *Zerbst* reserved its most powerful and evocative language for the critical role of the lawyer in the criminal process:

> [The Sixth Amendment] embodies a realistic recognition of the obvious truth that the average defendant does not have the professional legal skill to protect himself when brought before a tribunal with power to take his life or liberty, wherein the prosecution is presented by experienced and learned counsel. That which is simple, orderly, and necessary to the lawyer – to the untrained layman – may appear intricate, complex, and mysterious. Consistently with the wise policy of the Sixth Amendment and other parts of our fundamental charter, this Court has pointed to "...the humane policy of the modern criminal law..." which now provides that a defendant "...if he be poor,...may have counsel furnished him by the state,...not infrequently...more able than the attorney for the state."[83]

If the Justices are convinced of anything, they are convinced of the absolute need for defense counsel in criminal cases.

The march toward appointed counsel in all criminal cases stalled temporarily in 1942 with *Betts v. Brady*, which held that the Sixth Amendment applies only in federal courts and that the due process right to counsel from *Powell* did not apply to all criminal prosecutions.[84] *Betts* canvassed the state constitutions and statutes in force at the time of the framing and concluded that (1) the constitutions in force protected

dicta from Wisconsin in 1910. The other cite is to *Powell v. Alabama*, which is a right-to-counsel case, but not a Sixth Amendment case.

[83] *Zerbst*, 304 U.S. at 462–63.

[84] *Betts v. Brady*, 316 U.S. 455, 464–72 (1942).

the right to be represented if one could afford a lawyer, not a right to have an appointed lawyer; (2) the few states that did appoint lawyers did so pursuant to a statute, not as a constitutional requirement; and (3) a review of the state laws and constitutions in effect in 1942 established that very few states considered appointment of counsel a constitutional necessity, although many did appoint counsel by statute in some or all situations.[85]

Essentially, *Betts* contradicts almost every basis for *Powell* and *Zerbst*. It makes clear that the Sixth Amendment and parallel state constitutional provisions were not originally envisioned as requiring appointment of counsel. It establishes that appointment of counsel has been handled as a legislative matter, not a constitutional one. Whereas *Powell* had explicitly relied on the same state legislation as proof of "unanimous accord" on the granting of counsel (notably without any citation to the statutes in force in the individual states),[86] *Betts* used the same information (fully cited this time) to prove the exact opposite.[87]

Betts does quote from *Powell* and expresses some sympathy for the critical nature of defense counsel in criminal trials,[88] but it is clear the *Betts* Court's heart is not in it. *Betts*, like many of the criminal procedure cases of the 1970s and 1980s that similarly followed a time of expanding procedural rights, seems to be a case of criminal procedure fatigue. The Court gratuitously includes information suggesting that the defendant was guilty and a number of other details that support the Court's finding of fundamental fairness.[89]

Twenty-one years later, in *Gideon v. Wainright,* the Court came full circle.[90] The Court flatly overruled *Betts*, quoted *Powell*'s language about

[85] *Betts*, 316 U.S. at 464–72.

[86] *Powell*, 287 U.S. at 73.

[87] *Betts*, 316 U.S. at 468–72. For a roughly contemporary overview of the statutory protections for appointed counsel, see Katkin, "Incorporation of the Criminal Procedure Amendments," 461–63.

[88] Id. at 462–64.

[89] Id. at 472–73.

[90] *Gideon v. Wainwright*, 372 U.S. 335, 344–45 (1963).

the importance of counsel at length, and waxed eloquent over the irreplaceable role of counsel in protecting indigent criminal defendants.[91] *Gideon* thus swept aside the limitations in *Powell* and the arguments in *Betts* and made appointment the rule in all felony cases in both federal and state courts.[92]

Right to Appointed Counsel Outstrips Right to a Jury

In 1968, in *Duncan v. Louisiana*, the Court held that the Sixth Amendment jury right applied to the states.[93] In doing so, the court listed the long history of the fundamental importance of jury trials and the critical importance the framers of the Constitution placed on the jury trial.[94]

In comparison with *Gideon*, *Powell,* or *Zerbst*, however, the Court was much more circumspect in *Duncan*. It lists some critiques of juries and the debate over "the wisdom of allowing untrained laymen to determine the facts in civil and criminal proceedings."[95] Compared with the Court's unbridled enthusiasm for the role of attorneys in the criminal process, the reference to this debate (especially calling jurors "untrained laymen") is striking.

The Court also offered an explicit limitation on its holding: there is no federal constitutional right to a jury for "petty crimes."[96] Louisiana argued that because the defendant was sentenced to only sixty days, the crime at issue was a "petty crime" and thus a jury trial was not required.

[91] Id. at 344–45.

[92] One thing that is likable about *Gideon* is that it does not really bother to go point by point with *Betts* or to prove its case by appealing to a skewed version of what the drafters thought about appointment when they passed the Sixth or Fourteenth Amendments. Instead, the Court simply states the reasons that it is patently unjust for the indigent to face prosecution without a defense lawyer and leaves it at that. This is hard for originalists to swallow, but is much more intellectually honest than trying to paint *Gideon* as an inevitable result of the Sixth or Fourteenth Amendments.

[93] *Duncan v. Louisiana*, 391 U.S. 145, 148–56 (1968).

[94] Id.

[95] Id. at 156–57.

[96] Id. at 157–62.

In *Duncan*, the Court held that there was no right to a jury trial in prosecutions of petty crimes. The Court noted that at English common law at the time of the framing of the Constitution, there was no right to a jury trial for "petty offenses."[97] Further, in 1966 in *Cheff v. Schnackenberg*, the Court had just held that federal petty offenses did not require a jury trial under either the Sixth Amendment or Article III.[98]

The Court then held that the definition of "petty" was based on the potential length of the sentence, not the sentence imposed. This meant that Duncan's case was not petty, because it carried a possible sentence of two years' imprisonment. The Court declined to set a hard and fast rule defining petty crimes, but it did reiterate *Cheff*'s holding that crimes with punishments up to six months qualified as petty.[99]

The Court painted the history of the petty crime exception as clear-cut, but the actual treatment in the federal and state courts was more complicated. For instance, the very first mention of a petty crime exception by the Supreme Court was in 1888 in dicta,[100] and in 1904, the Court was still explaining that the exception even existed.[101] Moreover, Bruce Smith's excellent study of state constitutional history shows that nineteenth-century courts were much more protective of the jury right than *Duncan* and its progeny recognize.[102] Nevertheless, in contrast with *Powell* and *Zerbst*, in which the Court elided or simply rewrote the

[97] Id. at 160–61. For a lengthier treatment of this history, see Felix Frankfurter and Thomas G. Corcoran, "Petty Federal Offenses and the Constitutional Guaranty of Trial by Jury," 39 *Harv. L. Rev.* 917 (1926).

[98] *Cheff v. Schnackenberg*, 384 U.S. 373 (1966).

[99] *Duncan*, 391 U.S. at 159–62.

[100] *Callan v. Wilson*, 127 U.S. 540, 555 (1888).

[101] *Schick v. United States,* 195 U.S. 65 (1904). In *Schick*, the defendant waived a jury trial in a case over a fifty-dollar fine. At first the Court held that the contempt proceedings were petty and thus no jury trial was necessary. Nevertheless, the Court went on to discuss waiver issues and whether the right to a jury could be waived, which seems unusual if it was crystal clear that no jury was necessary in petty cases. Id. at 69–73.

[102] See Bruce P. Smith, "A New Verdict on Criminal Jury Trial in Antebellum America," 59–63. Draft on file with author.

constitutional history, here the Court painted the opposite picture of a clear history of a denial of rights.

The petty crime exception still remains one of the very few areas of the 1960s era incorporation/criminal rights revolution in which individual rights went backward. Both in federal and state law, the petty crime exception was not firmly established at six months of potential imprisonment before *Cheff* and *Duncan*. Afterward, the exception became much more regularized and national.[103] The fact that the petty offense exception remains so well entrenched (and has even been expanded)[104] is a mystery in light of the jury trial's central place in the Constitution and the Bill of Rights.

The right to appointed counsel, however, has found much sunnier shores. In *Argersinger v. Hamlin*, the Court addressed whether the right to appointed counsel extended to misdemeanor prosecutions.[105] In *Argersinger*, the defendant was unrepresented and convicted of carrying a concealed weapon, an offense punishable by up to six months in jail (i.e., a petty offense). The defendant was actually sentenced to ninety days in jail; he challenged his conviction under *Gideon*, arguing that even in misdemeanors counsel must be appointed.

The Supreme Court of Florida followed *Duncan v. Louisiana* and held that if a person accused of a petty offense was not entitled to a jury, she was also not entitled to a free lawyer.[106] The Supreme Court reversed, and held that any time a defendant receives a sentence with any jail time whatsoever, she is entitled to an appointed lawyer. If no appointed lawyer was offered, the verdict must be reversed.[107]

[103] Amar, *The Bill of Rights*, 289–90.

[104] For example, *Lewis v. United States*, 518 U.S. 322 (1996), held that multiple "petty offenses" could be tried without a jury, even though the aggregate potential sentence is more than six months. For an overview of the continued tightening see Colleen P. Murphy, "The Narrowing of the Entitlement to Criminal Jury Trial," 1997 *Wisc. L. Rev.* 133 (1997).

[105] *Argersinger v. Hamlin*, 407 U.S. 25, 37 (1972).

[106] *Argersinger v. Hamlin*, 236 So.2d 442 (Fla. 1970).

[107] *Argersinger*, 407 U.S. at 37.

Some of the language in *Argersinger* is quite familiar. The Court again quotes at length from *Zerbst*, *Powell*, and now *Gideon* on the critical role of the defense lawyer.[108] The Court adds a new concern that appointed counsel can remediate: the rush to push an ever-burgeoning criminal caseload through the courts, with the inevitable result that "casually arranged out-of-court compromise too often is substituted for adjudication."[109] The Court also argues that not all petty offenses are simple and notes the various constitutional issues in vagrancy cases.[110]

In this regard, the case is bizarrely incongruent with the realities of actual criminal defense practice, especially among appointed counsel and public defenders. Suffice it to say that the problems with rushed, out-of-court settlements have not been much helped by appointed counsel in misdemeanor cases. Further, the idea that appointed counsel will be spending days preparing constitutional issues in vagrancy cases is charming in its naiveté. As of 1972, the criminal system was already beginning to resemble an assembly line for pleas, and the appointment of counsel in misdemeanor cases has done nothing to help.[111] To the contrary, if the worry was assembly-line justice, a jury trial right is a much more powerful remedy. Nothing slows down a criminal proceeding like a request for a jury or an actual jury trial.

The Court also draws a sharp distinction between the treatment of the right to a jury and the right to counsel. The Court argues that although "there is historical support for limiting the deep commitment to trial by jury to serious criminal cases, there is no such support for a similar limitation on the right to assistance of counsel."[112] Given the much greater importance of the jury-trial right at the time of the framing, this claim is suspect.

[108] Id. at 31–33.
[109] Id.
[110] Id. at 33–36.
[111] See Jack B. Weinstein, "The Role of Judges in a Government of, by, and for the People: Notes for the Fifty-Eighth Cardozo Lecture," 30 *Cardozo L. Rev.* 1, 49–50 (2008).
[112] *Argersinger*, 407 U.S. at 30.

As support, the Court points to the English common law history that felony defendants could not have a lawyer but misdemeanor defendants could. The Court notes that the Sixth Amendment extended the right to counsel to felony defendants but did not shrink the protection of misdemeanor defendants.[113] Although this is true on its face, the original Sixth Amendment protection was only for the appearance of paid counsel, not for the appointment of free counsel. *Zerbst* in 1938 is the very first Sixth Amendment appointment-of-counsel case. Saying that there is an uninterrupted history of appointment of free counsel to misdemeanor defendants, or even any history of the Sixth Amendment guaranteeing a right to appointed counsel before the mid-twentieth century, is flatly untrue. In fact, given the very mixed history of the petty crime exception, the truth is more likely the exact opposite of the Court's statement.

Regardless of the history, however, there is an underlying question of priorities. In *Gideon*, the Court did not even really argue that its decision was mandated by the history of the Sixth Amendment. It stated a number of reasons that a lawyer was critical and then applied the Sixth Amendment's right to counsel to the states. When it came time to extend the right to a jury, however, the Court found reasons not to – a rare defeat for individual rights in the 1960s.

Why does the Court come to give short shrift to the right to a jury while privileging a right to an attorney? From reading the cases, there are three reasons. The first is clear throughout the cases from *Powell* to *Zerbst* to *Gideon* to *Argersinger*: the Court has a strong belief in the importance of criminal defense lawyers, and the Court will not allow any defendant to serve any jail sentence without the appointment of a free defense lawyer.

Second, the Justices simply think that the right to a lawyer is more important than the right to a jury. The *Argersinger* dissent states, "If there is no accompanying right to counsel, the right to trial by jury

[113] Id. at 30.

becomes meaningless."[114] A review of these cases establishes that this attitude is shared by all the Justices. The right to a jury trial is important, but not as fundamental as the right to an appointed attorney.

Last, jury trials are a hassle for judges. The inclusion of a complaint about "untrained laymen" on juries in *Duncan* makes this bias clear. This simple fact of life makes the Court's worry about assembly-line justice so ironic. Typically, misdemeanor counsel spends much more time talking defendants into taking pleas than they do preparing for hearings or trials in those cases. The current statistics on the minuscule number of criminal trials is evidence of this division of time. Judges are willing to put up with juries in serious cases, but would just as soon handle everything from the bench in smaller cases.

There is one other remarkable feature of *Argersinger*. The Court discusses the ABA's support for its result and quotes from its work extensively.[115] Consider the likelihood that the Court would quote the work of any other trade association as persuasive authority in favor of a required mass purchase of that association's services.

The Court is also not blind to the effect of *Argersinger* on the legal profession. The Court has a lengthy colloquy about how many lawyers would be required to meet the new demand for criminal defense and how many law students were then in law school.[116] In fact, the majority spends more time contemplating the availability of lawyers for the work than the availability of funds to pay for this massive new requirement for criminal defense counsel. This is not to suggest that the ABA's goal in either *Argersinger* or *Gideon* was to increase lawyer salaries, as criminal defense lawyers for the indigent (public defenders or appointed counsel) are notoriously underpaid and overworked.[117] Nevertheless, there is no doubt that *Gideon* and *Argersinger* resulted in increased lawyer employment.

[114] Id. at 46 (Powell, J., dissenting).

[115] Id. at 39; id. at 43 (Burger, C.J., concurring).

[116] Id. at 37 n. 7.

[117] David Cole, *No Equal Justice* (New York: The New Press, 1999), at 89.

The right to a lawyer is now better protected and better funded than the right to a jury trial. This is despite the framers' respect for the jury and the jury's unique role in including ordinary citizens in the judicial process. Reading the cases establishes why: lawyer-judges naturally place more importance on the role of lawyers than that of juries.

Ineffective Assistance of Counsel

With the Court's focus on the centrality of the lawyer to any fair trial, one might expect the Court to be particularly vigilant about the quality of the services it guarantees to the indigent. Unfortunately for criminal defendants, that has hardly been the case. The language and holding of *Strickland v. Washington* make ineffective assistance one of the most obvious areas of lawyer–judge bias.[118] Moreover, in contrast to the strong words of *Gideon*, *Powell,* and *Zerbst*, the law of ineffective assistance of counsel casts great doubt on whether the Court actually cares about the caliber of the representation defendants receive.

The first thing to note is that the Court took its time getting around to expressing an opinion on ineffective assistance of counsel. In comparison with the right to appointed counsel (or, really, almost any other Sixth Amendment right), the Court did not reach ineffective assistance in any comprehensive manner until 1984 in *Strickland v. Washington.* As noted earlier, *Powell* included an implied right to effective counsel,[119] but although the portion of the opinion on the right to appointed counsel became the bedrock of a massive expansion of rights, the portion on ineffective assistance languished for five decades with no expansion or clarification by the Court.[120]

[118] *Strickland v. Washington*, 466 U.S. 668 (1984).

[119] This is because the defendants were actually appointed lawyers, albeit on the eve of trial.

[120] The Court did apply *Powell* in very similar factual circumstances in two later cases: *Reece v. Georgia*, 350 U.S. 85, 89–90 (1955) (lawyer appointed on the eve of trial, and thus ineffective), and *Glasser v. United States*, 315 U.S. 60, 68–70 (1942) (lawyer appointed on the eve of trial to represent codefendant in clear conflict-of-interest case

States and lower federal courts filled this void with a variety of approaches. Courts disagreed on whether a showing of ineffective assistance of counsel required automatic reversal, whether ineffective assistance was subject to harmless error review, or whether the defendant could have a new trial only on a showing of prejudice. Courts also disagreed about the proper standard for weighing effectiveness. Some courts required "reasonable competence" or "customary skill," whereas others required a showing that the lawyer was so awful that it rendered the proceedings a "farce and mockery of justice."[121]

The fact that the right to effective assistance of counsel was so lightly regarded that in some courts it could be enforced only if it rose to the level of a "farce and mockery of justice" speaks volumes about the judiciary's considerable disinterest in these claims. Courts want to presume the lawyering effective and move on. This is partly because many trial lawyer decisions are judgment calls and are hard to second-guess after the fact. It is also partly because many of the defendants claiming ineffective assistance were likely guilty (although that did not control in cases alleging failure to appoint counsel or failure to follow *Miranda*). Another factor, naturally, is every court's hesitance to call a fellow lawyer ineffective. *Diggs v. Welch*, the case that announced the "farce and mockery" standard, is instructive. The court includes a lengthy diatribe against habeas corpus actions and assumes that most prisoner complaints against their lawyers are an "exercise of . . . imagination."[122]

Strickland v. Washington shows the same dynamic. *Strickland* dealt with David Leroy Washington, a Florida death row inmate who had confessed to three "brutal" groups of crimes and received the death penalty. Washington alleged that his counsel had done virtually no investigation

and thus ineffective). The Court also restated the requirement of effective assistance of counsel, without stating any definitive standards, in *McMann v. Richardson*, 397 U.S. 759 (1970) and *United States v. Cronic*, 466 U.S. 648 (1984).

121 For an overview of various state approaches, see Note, "Identifying and Remedying Ineffective Assistance of Criminal Defense Counsel: A New Look After *United States v. Decoster*," 93 *Harv. L. Rev.* 752, 756–58 (1980).

122 *Diggs v. Welch*, 148 F.2d 667 (D.C. 1945).

or advocacy in the sentencing phase. The Court noted counsel's "sense of hopelessness" in two different parts of the opinion and also that counsel had "cut his efforts short" when he learned that Washington had confessed to two of three murders against counsel's advice.[123]

The Court announced a two-pronged test for ineffective assistance of counsel: a defendant must show that his lawyer's representation was deficient (the performance prong) and that the deficient performance affected the outcome (the prejudice prong). The performance prong requires "a showing that counsel's representation fell below an objective standard of reasonableness."[124] The prejudice prong requires a showing that "there is a reasonable probability that, but for counsel's unprofessional errors, the result of the proceeding would have been different."[125] The Court makes clear that if either prong fails, an ineffective-assistance claim fails and that courts can consider either prong first.[126] The combination of these two prongs and the Court's invitation to skip the performance prong to jump right to the prejudice prong means that although the farce and mockery standard[127] is technically dead, its spirit lives on.

Performance

The Court leaves little doubt that it does not want to see attorney performance second-guessed or held ineffective with any great regularity. Consider the great amount of wriggle room that the "reasonably competent attorney" standard offers lawyers and courts. The Court flatly refuses to classify any lawyer activity (other than a lawyer with an actual conflict of

[123] *Strickland*, 466 U.S. at 671–77. My favorite of the six alleged examples of ineffective assistance was counsel's decision not to get an independent psychiatric evaluation before the sentencing phase. Washington had allegedly gone on a ten-day killing spree and had repeatedly ignored the advice of his counsel, including waiving a jury trial, confessing to the crimes, and pleading guilty to all charges, yet counsel did not "request a psychiatric examination, since his conversations with his client gave no indication that respondent had psychological problems." Id. at 673.

[124] Id. at 687–88.

[125] Id. at 694.

[126] Id. at 697.

[127] Discussed earlier at notes 120–21 and accompanying text.

interest) as per se ineffective or unreasonable. Instead, the Court notes that lawyering is an "art," that lawyer behavior cannot be classified, and that there are not "mechanical rules" in the area; as a result, it cannot offer any specific guidance to lower courts about what particular behavior might be ineffective.[128] Although the standard for these cases is flexible, the Court does state that "prevailing norms of practice as reflected in American Bar Association standards and the like" are useful as a guide. Given the long history of judicial discomfort with directly sanctioning, disbarring, or censuring the lawyers who appear before them, this loose standard has, in practice, resulted in findings of ineffective assistance only in the most blatant cases.

The Court virtually guarantees that result by repeatedly emphasizing how deferential reviewing courts should be to lawyers. At points it appears that the Court is struggling to find different ways of expressing its deference. Consider the following:

> Judicial scrutiny of counsel's performance must be highly deferential. It is all too tempting for a defendant to second-guess counsel's assistance after conviction or adverse sentence, and it is all too easy for a court, examining counsel's defense after it has proved unsuccessful, to conclude that a particular act or omission of counsel was unreasonable.... Because of the difficulties inherent in making the evaluation, a court must indulge a strong presumption that counsel's conduct falls within the wide range of reasonable professional assistance; that is, the defendant must overcome the presumption that, under the circumstances, the challenged action might be considered sound trial strategy. There are countless ways to provide effective assistance in any given case. Even the best criminal defense attorneys would not defend a particular client in the same way.[129]

The use of the word "indulge" is particularly evocative. The Oxford English Dictionary defines "indulge" as "Treat (a person) with excessive kindness."

[128] Id. at 693.
[129] Id. at 689.

One might think the language above would be sufficient to protect against reviewing courts looking very carefully at these claims, but the Court keeps coming back to presumptions of effectiveness and deference. On page 690, the Court reiterates "that counsel is strongly presumed to have rendered adequate assistance." On page 691, the Court adds that reviewing courts should apply "a heavy measure of deference to counsel's judgments." Finally, on page 696, the Court reminds us of the "strong presumption of reliability."

The Court mounts a spirited defense for the flexibility of its standard and its exceptional deference to the defense lawyer:

> Any set of rules would interfere with the constitutionally protected independence of counsel and restrict the wide latitude counsel must have in making tactical decisions. Indeed, the existence of detailed guidelines for representation could distract counsel from the overriding mission of vigorous advocacy of the defendant's cause.... Counsel's performance and even willingness to serve could be adversely affected. Intensive scrutiny of counsel and rigid requirements for acceptable assistance could dampen the ardor and impair the independence of defense counsel, discourage the acceptance of assigned cases, and undermine the trust between attorney and client.[130]

We will see this reasoning again, but it is important to parse it here. Remember that the Court is balancing a defendant's right to effective counsel against the factors it lists above. This is the same right to counsel about which the Court waxed eloquent in a string of cases from 1932 to the present. Nevertheless, when those interests bump up against "the constitutionally protected independence of counsel," guess which side wins. Moreover, instead of noting (as it did in *Argersinger*) that there would be plenty of lawyers to serve indigent clients, now the Court finds it critical that the lawyers' performance be judged as deferentially as possible, so they will continue to take these assigned cases. The Court

[130] Id. at 689–90.

also explicitly warns, "Courts should strive to ensure that ineffectiveness claims not become so burdensome to defense counsel that the entire criminal justice system suffers as a result."[131]

The Court assumes that what is good for the lawyers eventually redounds to the benefit of the clients, through better "trust" and more "vigorous advocacy." From the point of view of the defendant, which would be more important – that the lawyer feel as comfortable as possible in making any and all strategic decisions (even decisions that later look to be incompetent) or that the defendant be able to challenge convictions that are the fault of a lazy or ineffective lawyer?

Further, despite the Court's concern for the fragile relationship between the defendant and the lawyer and the overriding concern expressed elsewhere for the sanctity of the lawyer–client privilege, the Court makes it explicit that "inquiry into counsel's conversations with the defendant may be critical to a proper assessment."[132] Thus, we must defer to the lawyers in these cases to preserve the counselor–client trust; however, if there is a challenge to the lawyer's effectiveness, the lawyer's obligation to retain client confidences is gone.

The most notable aspect of these quotes, however, is how much the Court identifies with lawyers and not with criminal defendants. Everything is about respecting, protecting, and deferring to the strategic choices of the lawyers. The test itself requires that any reviewing court avoid the "distorting effects of hindsight" and "evaluate the conduct from counsel's perspective at the time." Note the psychological import of this aspect of an otherwise "objective" inquiry. The reviewing court is explicitly required to put itself in the lawyer's shoes and think about everything the lawyer did from her own point of view. Even more than the repeated calls for deference, the process of asking a judge, who had a long career as a lawyer, to step inside the accused lawyer's head guarantees deference, sympathy, and empathy.

[131] Id. at 697.
[132] Id. at 691.

It is also instructive to compare the Court's overall treatment of the police and other government officials with lawyers. One of the biggest changes of the 1960s was the mass application of the "exclusionary rule," which holds that illegally gained evidence (such as a confession taken without *Miranda* warnings) generally must be suppressed. One of the justifications of the rule is that it punishes the police for bad behavior and, hopefully, encourages them to do better the next time. In comparison, *Strickland* baldly states that "the purpose of the Sixth Amendment is not to improve the quality of legal representation."[133] Far from punishing lawyers who may have done a poor job, the Court goes out of its way to protect them.

Prejudice

Nevertheless, the Court virtually guarantees that even the extremely deferential review it outlines above will rarely occur. This is because the Court requires a defendant to prove prejudice, "a reasonable probability that, but for counsel's unprofessional errors, the results of the proceeding would have been different. A reasonable probability is a probability sufficient to undermine confidence in the outcome."[134] In practice, this has meant that a defendant must prove either innocence or the loss of an important substantive or procedural right. This is quite a stringent standard; many ineffective-assistance claims fail on the prejudice prong.

This works out nicely for courts that want to avoid labeling an attorney's representation ineffective. The Court goes out of its way to make this point:

> In particular, a court need not determine whether counsel's performance was deficient before examining the prejudice suffered by the defendant as a result of the alleged deficiencies. The object of an ineffectiveness claim is not to grade counsel's performance. If it is easier

[133] Id. at 689.
[134] Id. at 694.

> to dispose of an ineffectiveness claim on the ground of lack of sufficient prejudice, which we will expect will often be so, that course should be followed.[135]

Thus, even the prejudice prong is stacked to ensure that courts will not have to address the attorney behavior at issue.

The Upshot

There is also a procedural protection barring many ineffective assistance claims: those claims are generally brought in what is called "collateral proceedings," instead of on direct appeal. This means that the first time ineffective assistance is generally raised is in a federal habeas corpus or state collateral attack on a criminal conviction.[136] These sorts of actions arise only after a criminal defendant has exhausted her direct appeals, which means that they occur years after the original trial. Thus, for anyone serving a sentence of fewer than three to five years, an ineffective-assistance claim is unlikely. This practice insulates all that defense work from review.[137]

Not surprisingly, ineffective-assistance claims are extremely hard to win and courts have proven quite deferential indeed. One example is the series of sleeping-lawyer cases in which the defendants have lost. As one judge famously opined, "The Constitution says that everyone is entitled to an attorney of their choice. But the Constitution does not say that the lawyer has to be awake."[138] Likewise, a Texas appellate court held that a sleeping lawyer's naps might have been a "strategic move" because "the jury might have sympathy for appellant because of" the naps.[139] In

[135] Id. at 697.

[136] See *Massaro v. United States*, 538 U.S. 500, 504–05 (2003).

[137] See Eve Brensike Primus, "Structural Reform in Criminal Defense: Relocating Ineffective Assistance of Counsel Claims," 92 *Cornell L. Rev.* 679 (2007).

[138] Bruce Shapiro, "Sleeping Lawyer Syndrome," *The Nation*, Apr. 7, 1997, at 27–29 (quoting Judge Doug Shaver).

[139] *McFarland v. State*, 928 S.W. 2d 482, 506 n. 20 (Tex. Crim. App. 1996).

analyzing these cases, some courts have used a three-part analysis: Did counsel sleep often? Was counsel unconscious or just resting? Did counsel miss a key part of the trial while asleep?[140] Similarly, reviewing courts have deferentially reviewed allegations of lawyers who were drunk or high at the time of trial and denied some for a lack of prejudice.[141] Disbarment or suspension before, during, or after trials has also been held nonprejudicial by reviewing courts.[142]

The egregious cases are only the tip of the iceberg. The simple fact is that under *Strickland* and its progeny, it is extremely hard for criminal defendants to win an ineffective-assistance claim.[143]

The combination of an extremely robust right to a lawyer, with almost no review of those lawyers' performances, makes constitutional criminal procedure a remarkably designed pro-lawyer environment. Every criminal defendant who faces a likelihood of any incarceration must be assigned a lawyer, and the same lawyer cannot be appointed for several codefendants. The Court makes clear that an actual conflict of interest requires automatic reversal.[144] If the government substantially interferes with counsel's assistance, there is also automatic reversal of a conviction.[145] Thus, in the circumstances in which lawyers benefit (whether they get appointed, whether each defendant gets her own lawyer, and whether the state interferes with the representation), the

[140] See *Burdine v. Johnson*, 262 F.3d 336, 341 (5th Cir. 2001); *Tippins v. Walker*, 77 F.3d 682, 687–90 (2nd Cir. 1996).

[141] Ira Mickenberg, "Drunk, Sleeping, and Incompetent Lawyers: Is It Possible to Keep Innocent People Off Death Row?," 29 *U. Dayton L. Rev.* 319, 323 (2004) and Jeffrey L. Kirchmeier, "Drink, Drugs, and Drowsiness: The Constitutional Right to Effective Assistance of Counsel and the Strickland Prejudice Requirement," 75 *Neb. L. Rev.* 425, 426, 455–63 (1996) have good overviews of these cases.

[142] See Vanessa Merton, "What Do You Do When You Meet a Walking Violation of the Sixth Amendment if You're Trying to Put That Lawyer's Client in Jail?," 69 *Fordham L. Rev.* 997, 1023 and n. 69 (2000).

[143] Stephanos Bibas, "The Psychology of Hindsight and After-the-Fact Review of Ineffective Assistance of Counsel," 2004 *Utah L. Rev.* 1 (2004).

[144] *Strickland*, 466 U.S. at 692.

[145] Id. at 692.

Supreme Court is absolutely unbending in guaranteeing the Constitution's protections.

On the other hand, when lawyers are at risk, as when they have been accused of poor representation, the Supreme Court is suddenly much more circumspect. The Court offers multiple ways to avoid the unpleasant topic of lawyer incompetence. When incompetence is considered, it is under the shadow of deference and presumptions in favor of the accused lawyer. When one adds in the discussion of criminal defense malpractice standards (which are more stringent even than the *Strickland* standard) in Chapter 7, it becomes apparent that criminal defense is an area in which the Court has guaranteed lawyers employment with no meaningful standards for assessing their performance. Ironically, the Court does this in the name of avoiding factory justice, whereas it creates a system that survives only with almost every defendant accepting some sort of plea. I appear regularly in criminal matters and I do not think the majority of criminal defense lawyers or public defenders are incompetent. Nevertheless, I think this is so despite the incentives set up by the Court and certainly not because of them.

4 Civil Constitutional Law

Because direct-mail solicitations in the wake of accidents are perceived by the public as intrusive, the Bar argues, the reputation of the legal profession in the eyes of Floridians has suffered commensurately.... We have little trouble crediting the Bar's interest as substantial.

– *Florida Bar v. Went For It*[1]

But we have never held that the government itself can shut off the flow of mailings to protect those recipients who might potentially be offended. The First Amendment does not permit the government to prohibit speech as intrusive unless the "captive" audience cannot avoid objectionable speech. Recipients of objectionable mailings, however, may effectively avoid further bombardment of their sensibilities simply by averting their eyes. Consequently, the "short, though regular, journey from mail box to trash can... is an acceptable burden, at least so far as the Constitution is concerned."

– *Bolger v. Youngs Drug Products*[2]

THE SUPREME COURT IS A UNIQUELY DESIGNED ENTITY within the structure of the American government. Because of lifetime appointment, the power to interpret the law and the Constitution as stated in *Marbury v. Madison*, and the

[1] *Florida Bar v. Went For It, Inc.*, 515 U.S. 618, 624–25 (1995) (citations omitted).

[2] *Bolger v. Youngs Drug Products Corp.*, 463 U.S. 60, 72 (1983) (citations and quotation marks omitted).

natural independence of the judiciary, the Court's design has been rightfully hailed as an effort to prevent bias in the judicial function. Nevertheless, even Justices of the Supreme Court have a hard time forgetting their past as lawyers. That bias is not limited to criminal procedure. This chapter addresses three other areas of constitutional law: the First Amendment's commercial speech doctrine, the First Amendment's government speech doctrine, and the law of takings.

Bar associations and lawyers have played a bit part in the development of the law in each of these areas. The cases follow a similar pattern. The Supreme Court signals an aggressive new approach. It then follows with a series of cases that generally drift in the direction of either increased constitutional protections for commercial speech or against protection for government-sponsored speech and government takings. In each of these areas small, but important, exceptions were drawn up specifically for lawyers. Although the Supreme Court offers justifications for these exceptions, taken in light of the state of the law as a whole they are classic examples of the lawyer–judge bias.

Lawyers versus Accountants in *Ohralik*, *Edenfield*, and Others

Bar associations have historically spent a great deal of time devising ways to suppress competition within the legal profession.[3] One of the oldest strategies is bans on lawyer advertising. As far back as the medieval English guilds there have been rules against advertising and client solicitation.[4] In America, the ABA and state bar associations began to systematically ban advertising and client solicitation around the turn of the twentieth century.[5] These bans were a key part of the bar's professionalization project and mirrored anticompetitive regulations in other professions. The bans were justified as a protection for the

[3] This topic is covered at length in Chapters 5 and 6.

[4] See Henry Drinker, *Legal Ethics* (New York: Columbia Univ. Press, 1953), 23–24.

[5] See ABA Canons of Professional Ethics, Canons 27 and 28 (1908).

unsuspecting public against "ambulance chasers" and other unscrupulous lawyers.[6] Regardless of the justifications, the results were clearly anticompetitive. Existing practitioners (who were the drafters of these rules) were able to charge inflated prices without worrying about being undercut by competing lawyers advertising or soliciting their clients.

Beginning in the 1970s, the Supreme Court began to overturn the most blatant of these anticompetitive practices. For example, *Goldfarb v. Virginia State Bar* held that mandatory fee schedules violated federal antitrust law.[7]

The lawyer regulation cases that followed generally addressed advertising bans and were decided under the nascent First Amendment commercial speech doctrine. Before 1976, commercial speech had not been protected under the First Amendment.[8] *Virginia Board of Pharmacy v. Virginia Citizens Consumer Council* began a series of Supreme Court cases applying the First Amendment to commercial speech and advertising. *Virginia Board of Pharmacy* held that commercial speech was protected by the First Amendment and struck down a ban on prescription drug price advertising.[9]

The Court's second major commercial speech case, *Bates v. State Bar of Arizona*, held that the State Bar of Arizona could not ban truthful advertising of prices for routine legal services.[10] *Bates* followed *Virginia Board of Pharmacy* by one year and was decided by the same Court. On first reading, *Bates* appears compelled by the reasoning of *Virginia Board*, an 8–1 decision that truthful advertising of drug prices could not

[6] See *Karlin v. Culkin*, 162 N.E. 487, 488–89 (N.Y. 1928) (Cardozo, C.J.) (castigating the "unscrupulous minority" of the bar for "[a]mbulance chasing" and other "evil practices").

[7] *Goldfarb v. Virginia State Bar*, 421 U.S. 773 (1975). *Goldfarb* will be discussed more fully in Chapter 6.

[8] See, e.g., *Valentine v. Chrestensen*, 316 U.S. 52 (1942).

[9] *Virginia Board of Pharmacy v. Virginia Citizens Consumer Council, Inc.*, 425 U.S. 748, 765 (1976).

[10] *Bates v. State Bar of Arizona*, 433 U.S. 350, 363–85 (1977).

be banned. *Bates* similarly involved truthful advertising of prices for legal services.

Nevertheless, the opinions in *Bates* make clear how hard it was for the Court to apply the commercial speech doctrine to the legal profession. The Court split 5–4 on the First Amendment issue; each of the four dissenters noted the special nature of legal services and the unwelcome and "profound changes" the decision would bring to the practice of law.[11]

A year later, the Court decided *Ohralik v. Ohio State Bar Association*.[12] In *Ohralik* the Court held that a ban on in-person client solicitation by lawyers was constitutional.[13] The Court distinguished *Bates* because of the potential for client abuse from in-person solicitation. In retrospect, *Ohralik* is a very unusual commercial speech case. It gives great deference to the interest of the states in regulating lawyers as officers of the court and even notes how a ban on solicitation serves the goal of "true professionalism."[14] This deference to bar association regulation has been a moving target for the Court. In the cases in which the Court strikes down bar regulation, it tends to reject arguments based on "professionalism" or the public image of lawyers.[15] In cases such as *Ohralik*, in which these regulations are upheld, the Court expressly credits them.

Further, *Ohralik* is one of the very few cases in which the Court upheld a blanket prohibition on commercial speech because it might sometimes tend toward "fraud, undue influence, intimidation . . . and other forms of vexatious conduct."[16] As a general rule, the Court has been

[11] Id. at 386 (Burger, C.J., dissenting).

[12] *Ohralik v. Ohio State Bar Association*, 436 U.S. 447 (1978).

[13] *Ohralik* is a case in which the Court favors the wishes of the established bar against the entrepreneurial bar, not a case in which lawyers are favored over clients.

[14] *Ohralik*, 436 U.S. at 460–61.

[15] See *Bates*, 433 U.S. at 368–72; *Zauderer v. Office of Disciplinary Counsel*, 471 U.S. 626, 648 (1985) (holding that "the State's desire that attorneys maintain their dignity in their communications with the public" is not "an interest substantial enough to justify the abridgment of their First Amendment rights").

[16] *Ohralik*, 436 U.S. at 462.

clear that the government can always bar the dissemination of commercial speech that is false, deceptive, or misleading, or that proposes an illegal transaction.[17] *Ohralik* does not, however, ban only false speech. The in-person solicitation rule in *Ohralik* is precisely the type of "blanket prohibition against truthful, non-misleading speech about a lawful product" that, in later cases, the Court reviews with "special care" and that "rarely survive constitutional review."[18]

Four years later, in a case of a ban on advertising attorney specialization, the Court contradicted *Ohralik*'s reasoning exactly by stating that "the States may not place an absolute prohibition on certain types of potentially misleading information . . . if the information also may be presented in a way that is not deceptive."[19] In fact, outside of *Ohralik* and a few cases from the 1980s that are now widely considered overruled, the Court has not sustained any other general ban on advertising or solicitation under the commercial speech doctrine.[20] What is strange about *Ohralik* is not the reasoning of the case itself – it may well be true that in-person solicitation by lawyers carries a likelihood of "vexatious conduct" – it is how inconsistent *Ohralik* is with earlier and later commercial speech cases.

The reasoning of *Ohralik* has been applied only to the legal profession. In *Edenfield v. Fane*, the Court expressly refused to apply *Ohralik* to a rule that barred in-person solicitation by certified public

[17] See *Friedman v. Rogers*, 440 U.S. 1 (1979) (false and misleading); *Pittsburgh Press Co. v. Human Relations Commission*, 413 U.S. 376 (1973) (illegal activity).

[18] *44 Liquormart, Inc. v. Rhode Island*, 517 U.S. 484, 504 (1996).

[19] *In re R.M.J.*, 455 U.S. 455 U.S. 191, 203 (1982).

[20] See, e.g., *Posadas de Puerto Rico Association v. Tourism Company of Puerto Rico*, 478 U.S. 328 (1986), which upheld a ban on advertising for casinos because of the potential harm that gambling might cause to consumers, and *United States v. Edge Broadcasting Co.*, 509 U.S. 418 (1993), which allowed a nonlottery state to bar a foreign state's lottery advertisements. Both these cases are widely considered overruled by *44 Liquormart, Inc. v. Rhode Island*, 517 U.S. 484, 516 (1996), which held a ban on liquor advertising unconstitutional. See Eugene Volokh, "Freedom of Speech and Intellectual Property: Some Thoughts after *Eldred, 44 Liquormart*, and *Bartnicki*," 40 *Hous. L. Rev.* 697, 732–40 (2003).

accountants.[21] The comparison between *Edenfeld* and *Ohralik* is stark and particularly telling. *Ohralik* was an 8–0 decision in which the Court seemed to find it obvious that "the state interests implicated [were] particularly strong" and that in-person solicitation is dangerous and harmful to clients and the profession as a whole. *Ohralik* also accepted the ABA's "three broad grounds" of justification for the in-person ban with little comment.[22] The Court in *Ohralik* shows a particular sensitivity to the concerns of bar associations. The Court's palpable distaste for in-person solicitation by lawyers pervades the entire opinion.

In contrast, the 8–1 *Edenfield* decision was deeply skeptical of a ban on in-person solicitation for accountants. Although *Edenfield* recognized the importance of protecting consumer privacy and discouraging fraudulent solicitation, the Court seemed utterly flummoxed by the assertion that a ban on in-person solicitation could possibly fit those goals. The Court specifically took the Florida Board of Accountancy to task for its lack of underlying evidence supporting a claim of danger to the public, despite accepting similarly "broad" assertions of public danger in *Ohralik*.[23]

Edenfield does attempt to distinguish *Ohralik*, but in so doing it basically limits *Ohralik* to lawyers. *Ohralik* is a "narrow" holding that depends "upon certain unique features of in-person solicitation by lawyers."[24] The main difference appears to be that a lawyer is a "professional trained in the art of persuasion" and thus is much more likely to succeed in taking advantage of a potential client.[25]

[21] *Edenfield v. Fane*, 507 U.S. 761 (1993).

[22] *Ohralik*, 436 U.S. at 460–63.

[23] Compare *Edenfield*, 507 U.S. at 768–73, with *Ohralik*, 436 U.S. at 460–63.

[24] *Edenfield*, 507 U.S. at 774.

[25] Id. at 775. *Edenfield* also notes that the clients in *Ohralik* were unsophisticated and had just suffered a personal loss, making them particularly vulnerable to fraudulent, in-person solicitation. Nevertheless, because *Ohralik* allows a blanket ban on in-person solicitation and there was no evidence in *Ohralik* that most (or even many) potential clients are vulnerable, it is inconsistent to rely too heavily on the characteristics of the individual clients in either *Ohralik* or *Edenfield*.

How ironic it is that the Court upheld a bar association ethical rule on the assumption that lawyers are uniquely dangerous and unprofessional. Moreover, the distinction between the persuasive powers (and relative ethics) of lawyers and accountants is a puzzling example of the Justices using their own impressions of the two professions to come to two contrary holdings on a very similar issue.

The vote tallies on the two cases are notable: *Ohralik* was 8–0 and *Edenfield* was 8–1. The Court considered each case relatively straightforward, regardless of how incompatible they seem. Likewise, *Virginia Board* was an 8–1 decision striking down an advertising ban by pharmacists. A year later, the Court split 5–4 on a similar ban for lawyers in *Bates*. The main difference between the cases was the Court's impression that lawyer advertising was quite distinct from pharmacist advertising.

The Court split contentiously 5–4 (with no majority opinion) in *Peel v. Disciplinary Commission of Illinois* over an attorney advertisement claiming National Board of Trial Advocacy (NBTA) certification as a "civil trial specialist."[26] The plurality spent a good portion of the opinion rosily describing the NBTA certification process and then held that the Illinois Supreme Court's blanket ban on this sort of advertising is exactly the kind of regulation of speech that must fail under the First Amendment.[27]

Justice Sandra Day O'Connor wrote a spirited dissent that begins, "This case provides yet another example of the difficulties raised by rote application of the commercial speech doctrine in the context of state regulation of professional standards for attorneys."[28] She notes that the Court overrules the judgment of the Supreme Court of Illinois, acting under its inherent authority to regulate lawyers, and that the Court should be more "deferential" because "the Supreme Court of Illinois is in a far better position than is this Court to determine which statements are misleading or likely to mislead." Justice O'Connor also notes that

[26] *Peel v. Disciplinary Comm. of Illinois*, 496 U.S. 91 (1990).

[27] Id. at 94–96.

[28] Id. at 119 (O'Connor, J., dissenting).

multiple other state bars have similar rules.[29] In short, Justice O'Connor and her fellow dissenters (Justices Scalia and Rehnquist) greatly credit bar associations and state supreme courts and dissent over the majority's "rote application" of their precedents to the special and unique legal profession.

Four years later, the Court struck down a board of accountancy rule barring an advertising using the terms "CPA and CFP" 7–2 in *Ibanez v. Board of Accountancy*.[30] This case was much easier for the Court than *Peel* (a seven-Justice majority instead of a four-Justice plurality) and the dissent was comparatively quiescent. Again, the main difference between the cases is the Court's greater sensitivity to state bars and state supreme courts.

One odd coincidence is that the accountants keep coming up just after the lawyers and get much worse treatment.[31] The loss in *Edenfield* must have been particularly galling coming on the heels of *Ohralik*. *Ohralik* was decided in 1978, and the accountants added their ban on in-person solicitation in 1979.[32] It is not clear whether the ban was added explicitly in reaction to *Ohralik*, but it certainly seems likely. Regardless, the Supreme Court saw *Edenfield* as a clear case of self-serving professional regulation that was obviously unconstitutional, despite its striking similarity to a regulation the Supreme Court upheld easily in *Ohralik*.

Florida Bar v. Went For It

Ohralik can possibly be explained as an early commercial speech case decided before the Court settled on the more muscular approach of the late 1980s and 1990s. A 1995 case, *Florida Bar v. Went For It, Inc.*, is

[29] Id. at 119–27.

[30] *Ibanez v. Board of Accountancy*, 512 U.S. 136 (1994). One strange quirk of *Ibanez* is that the plaintiff Ibanez was both a lawyer and an accountant. Nevertheless, the rule at issue was from the board of accountancy, not a bar association.

[31] In this scenario, the accountants are Charlie Brown trying to kick a football and the Supreme Court is Lucy.

[32] See 21 Florida Administrative Code Annotated §21A-24.002, history.

harder to explain, especially in light of the earlier cases *In re R.M.J.* and *Shapero v. Kentucky Bar Association.*

In re R.M.J. dealt with, among other things, a Missouri lawyer sending out professional announcement cards that listed certain qualifications (such as membership in bar of the United States Supreme Court) to a broad list of recipients. This mailing was sent to persons outside the Missouri Bar's list of allowed recipients and also included impermissible language on qualifications. The Court rejected the Missouri Bar's rules and specifically held that a ban on mailings cannot be sustained.[33] In a humorous side note, one of the issues was a lawyer advertising his membership in the Supreme Court's bar. The Court held that a lawyer could announce that information, but because membership in the Court's bar requires only a simple application, the Court warned such advertising was "uninformative" and in "bad taste."[34]

In *Shapero v. Kentucky Bar Association*, the Court more explicitly held that a state bar association could not ban truthful and nondeceptive direct mail solicitations to potential clients. The Court distinguished *Ohralik*, holding that a mailed solicitation implicated few of the dangers of in-person solicitation.[35]

Based on these precedents and *Bates v. Arizona*, a federal district court and the Eleventh Circuit struck down a Florida ban on direct mailings to accident victims within thirty days of the accident.[36] *Went For It*, however, upheld the ban.[37]

By the time *Went for It* was decided, the Court's treatment of commercial speech had become much more regimented. Following *Central Hudson Gas & Electric Corp. v. Public Service Commission of New York*, the Court applied an "intermediate scrutiny" test for laws that impinge on commercial speech. The *Central Hudson* test has three prongs: "First,

[33] *In re R.M.J.*, 455 U.S. 191, 193–98, 205–206 (1982).

[34] Id. at 205. It was a case in which the Court wished to avoid guilt by association.

[35] *Shapero v. Kentucky Bar Association*, 486 U.S. 466, 473–78 (1988).

[36] See *McHenry v. Florida Bar*, 21 F.3d 1038 (1994).

[37] See *Florida Bar v. Went For It*, 515 U.S. 618 (1995).

the government must assert a substantial interest in support of its regulation; second, the government must demonstrate that the restriction on commercial speech directly and materially advances that interest; and third, the regulation must be narrowly drawn."[38]

The Court had "little trouble crediting the Bar's interest as substantial" under the first prong of *Central Hudson*.[39] The interests stated were protecting the privacy of accident victims, "preserv[ing] the integrity of the legal profession," defending "the reputation of the legal profession," and "an effort to protect the flagging reputations of Florida lawyers."[40]

There are a few interesting notes about these justifications. It is odd that the court credits the privacy interests of accident victims, especially in a direct-mail case. In *Bolger v. Youngs Drug Products Corp.*, the Court rejected a government ban on "intrusive" and potentially "offensive" advertisements for contraceptives.[41] The Court held that a state interest in protecting mail recipients from offensive materials was of "little weight" because the Court has "consistently held that the fact that protected speech may be offensive to some does not justify its suppression." This is especially so in direct mail cases in which the recipient can exercise the "short, though regular, journey from mail box to trash can."[42]

The Court's use of the privacy interest in *Went for It* seems to resuscitate a part of the *Ohralik* opinion that had been left for dead over the years. *Ohralik* relied on two separate justifications – protecting privacy and potential to mislead – in upholding the ban on in-person solicitation.[43] Later cases had generally treated *Ohralik* as a high-potential-for-deception case and not a privacy case.[44] *Went for It* includes

[38] *Went for It*, 515 U.S. at 624 (citing *Central Hudson Gas & Electric Corp. v. Public Service Commission of New York*, 447 U.S. 557, 564–65 (1980)).

[39] *Went For It*, 515 U.S. at 625.

[40] Id. at 624–25.

[41] *Bolger v. Youngs Drug Products Corp.*, 463 U.S. 60, 71–72 (1983).

[42] Id. at 71–72.

[43] *Ohralik*, 436 U.S. at 460–61.

[44] See, e.g., *In re R.M.J.*, 455 U.S. at 202 (using *Ohralik* as an example supporting the proposition that regulation "is permissible where the particular advertising is

no allegation that the advertising at issue was actually or even potentially false or misleading, however. Instead, the biggest problem seems to be the effect on the public perception of lawyers.

The harm-to-reputation justification is also in direct conflict with the Court's resistance to the suppression of commercial speech on "paternalistic" grounds.[45] The Court had earlier held that lawyer advertising could not be banned on "the mere possibility that some members of the population might find [the advertising] offensive" or that "some members of the bar might find [it] beneath their dignity."[46]

The Court thus had a relatively weak factual and legal case on either privacy or consumer protection grounds. Nevertheless, a close reading of *Went for It* shows the great credit that the Court gave to bar association worries about the low public opinion of lawyers.[47] More than any of the other lawyer advertising cases, *Went For It* evinces a patent sympathy for the plight of lawyer public image and a clear deference to bar associations on these issues. It is hard to imagine that accountants or pharmacists would possibly have received the same treatment. Just as the ban on in-person solicitation allowed by *Ohralik* has been limited to lawyers, the Court has never upheld an advertising ban such as Florida's for any other profession.

Ohralik and *Went For It* thus present a puzzle to students of the commercial speech doctrine. They are now both well-known and venerable precedents, yet in an area of increasing scrutiny of governmental regulation of advertising, they have basically been limited to their facts. Kathleen Sullivan has noted that *Ohralik* and *Went For It* are "difficult to square with the Court's other advertising decisions."[48] The likeliest

inherently likely to deceive or where the record indicates that a particular form or method of advertising has in fact been deceptive.").

[45] *44 Liquormart*, 517 U.S. at 497.

[46] *Zauderer*, 515 U.S. at 648.

[47] *Went For It*, 515 U.S. at 625–34.

[48] Kathleen M. Sullivan, "The Intersection of Free Speech and the Legal Profession: Constraints on Lawyers' First Amendment Rights," 67 *Fordham L. Rev.* 569, 578–79 (1998).

explanation is the natural propensity of the Justices to credit bar associations and look out for the perceived interests of the legal profession.

Physician Speech versus Lawyer Speech – *Rust* and *Velasquez*

In a pair of government-supported speech cases, the Court reached very different results when the speakers were doctors rather than lawyers. Even as the Court attempted to distinguish the two cases, the reasoning and flavor of the opinions make clear the Court's special sympathy and empathy for lawyers.

Rust v. Sullivan dealt with restrictions on speech attached to government funding for family planning services.[49] Title X of the Public Health Service Act authorized grants to public or nonprofit entities for family planning services, but the grants were conditioned on the grantees agreeing not to discuss the option of abortion.[50] The grantees and doctors sued, alleging that the limitation on speech about abortion violated their First Amendment rights.

The Court disagreed by a 5–4 vote. On the First Amendment issue, the Court held that the abortion restriction did not limit speech. Instead, the restriction simply allowed the government to fund one set of activities without funding a different set of activities: "The Government can, without violating the Constitution, selectively fund a program to encourage certain activities it believes to be in the public interest, without at the same time funding an alternate program which seeks to deal with the problem in another way."[51] The Court noted that "a doctor employed by the project may be prohibited in the course of his project duties from counseling abortion" and that the prohibition was not a suppression of speech, but "a prohibition on a project grantee or its employees from engaging in activities outside of the project's scope."[52]

[49] *Rust v. Sullivan*, 500 U.S. 173 (1991).

[50] Id. at 178–81.

[51] Id. at 193.

[52] Id. at 193–94.

The most remarkable aspect of the case is the Court's rather brusque reaction to the speech rights of doctors and the abortion speech ban's possible impingement on the doctor–patient relationship. Even though the majority spends little time arguing it, the doctor–patient relationship was a key argument for the petitioners and was treated at length in their brief, as well as in amicus briefs by the American College of Physicians, the American Medical Association (AMA), and the American College of Obstetricians and Gynecologists.[53] Each of these briefs argued the special nature of the doctor–patient relationship and stressed how critical it was that doctors be free to discuss all medical options with their patients.

The majority curtly disregards these concerns. First, the Court notes that the project doctors "remain free" to pursue "abortion-related activities" outside work.[54] Although this is certainly true, it hardly solves the problem of a restriction on doctor–patient speech.

Second, the Court grudgingly admits that "traditional relationships such as that between doctor and patient should enjoy protection under the First Amendment from Government regulation, even when subsidized by the government." However, the Court simply pooh-poohs this argument:

> We need not resolve that question here, however, because the Title X program regulations do not significantly impinge upon the doctor-patient relationship. Nothing in them requires a doctor to represent as his own any opinion that he does not in fact hold. Nor is the doctor-patient relationship established by the Title X program sufficiently all encompassing so as to justify an expectation on the part of the patient of comprehensive medical advice. The program does not provide post conception medical care, and therefore a doctor's silence with regard to abortion cannot reasonably be thought to mislead a client into thinking that the doctor does not consider abortion an appropriate option for her. The doctor is always free to make clear

[53] Copies of briefs on file with author.
[54] Id. at 198–99.

> that advice regarding abortion is simply beyond the scope of the program. In these circumstances, the general rule that the Government may choose not to subsidize speech applies with full force.[55]

This paragraph well encapsulates the Court's basic lack of respect for the doctor–patient relationship. The fact that the doctor is not compelled to say anything or that the patient does not expect comprehensive advice does not begin to address what doctors considered a major impingement on the critical relationship in their profession. As the dissent put it, "the legitimate expectations of the patient and the ethical responsibilities of the medical profession" demand the provision of all possible medical options.[56] The dissent cited to AMA and American College of Obstetricians and Gynecologists' authority for exactly this proposition.[57]

Rust v. Sullivan has become "infamous" among health law and constitutional scholars for its treatment of the doctor–patient relationship.[58] Reading the case, it is worth wondering whether the Court would possibly have trampled the attorney–client relationship so breezily. Ten years later, the remarkably similar case of *Legal Services Corp. v. Velazquez* answered that question with a resounding "no."[59]

Velazquez dealt with a funding restriction on legal services corporations (LSCs), which are local, government-sponsored providers of free legal services to the poor. Under applicable laws and regulations, LSCs that accepted federal funding were not allowed to challenge the validity or constitutionality of any welfare laws, although they were allowed to represent individual clients on their individual denial-of-benefits cases.[60] In other words, lawyers could dispute the application of individual laws to their clients but were banned from raising facial constitutional objections to federal statutes.

[55] Id. at 200.
[56] Id. at 213–14 (Blackmun, J., dissenting).
[57] Id.
[58] Theodore W. Ruger, "Health Law's Coherence Anxiety," 96 *Geo. L.J.* 625, 643 (2008).
[59] *Legal Services Corp. v. Velazquez*, 531 U.S. 533 (2001).
[60] Id. at 537–40.

The case was almost identical to *Rust*. It dealt with a funding restriction against an activity that annoyed Congress (abortion advice in *Rust*, attacking the legality of welfare laws in *Velasquez*). The restriction fell largely on a professional group (doctors in *Rust*, lawyers in *Velasquez*). Neither restriction limited speech outside work. Neither restriction required any specific speech of the doctors or lawyers. Both restrictions were alleged to impinge on the professional relationship and to force professionals to forgo their typical ethical duties.

The very first sentence of the majority's analysis notes that the government relied on *Rust* to uphold the program restrictions, so the Court immediately attempts to distinguish *Rust*.[61] The Court holds that *Rust* is different because the physician speech in Rust was "governmental speech," and the LSC speech here is private speech funded by the government. The Court relies on the fact that when the LSC attorneys appear in court they advocate on behalf of the client, not the government, so the speech is private, not public.[62] As the dissent notes, however, this distinction is "so unpersuasive it hardly needs response. If the private doctors' confidential advice to their patients at issue in *Rust* constituted 'government speech,' it is hard to imagine what subsidized speech would not be government speech."[63] As commentators have noted, this "incoherent" distinction has "left many scratching their heads."[64]

The real meat of the Court's opinion comes after the discussion of *Rust*, however. The Court is quite disturbed by how the funding limitation affects the ability of attorneys to fully advocate in court and the possibility that courts will not hear every argument they can on behalf

[61] Id. at 540–42.

[62] Id. at 541–43.

[63] Id. at 554 (Scalia, J., dissenting).

[64] The first quote is from Randall P. Bezanson and William G. Buss, "The Many Faces of Government Speech," 86 *Iowa L. Rev.* 1377, 1383 (2001) and the second is from Joseph Blocher, "School Naming Rights and the First Amendment's Perfect Storm," 96 *Georgetown L.J.* 1, 23 (2007).

of welfare recipients. This strikes the Court as wrong on a separation-of-powers basis, and the Court viscerally recoils from this interference in the relationship among lawyers, clients, and courts. The language is quite evocative:

> By providing subsidies to LSC, the Government seeks to facilitate suits for benefits by using the state and federal courts and the independent bar on which those courts depend for the proper performance of their duties and responsibilities. Restricting LSC attorneys in advising their clients and in presenting arguments and analyses to the courts distorts the legal system by altering the traditional role of the attorneys.... [The Government] may not design a subsidy to effect this serious and fundamental restriction on advocacy of attorneys and the functioning of the judiciary.[65]

At the outset, the Court expresses a clear concern over "the independent bar" that courts depend on "for the proper performance of their duties and responsibilities," as well as the concern that the restriction "distorts the legal system" and the "traditional role" of attorneys. It is striking how well the Court understands the way this restriction impinges on courts, lawyers, and clients – and how little it cared that the *Rust* restriction impinged on doctors and patients.

Similarly, in *Rust* the petitioners raised the possibility that the funding restriction would bar medical advice about abortions even in medical emergencies. The Court elided this concern by reinterpreting the regulations.[66] In contrast, in *Velazquez*, the Court discussed the "disturbing example of the restriction [that] if, during litigation, a judge were to ask an LSC attorney whether there was a constitutional concern, the LSC attorney simply could not answer."[67]

The Court's pique at this possibility is so pronounced that the very next sentence cites to *Marbury v. Madison* and the Court's "primary

[65] *Velazquez*, 531 U.S. at 544.
[66] See *Rust*, 500 U.S. at 195.
[67] See *Velazquez*, 531 U.S. at 545.

mission" of interpreting the law and the Constitution. The Court concludes that Congress cannot "wrest the law from the Constitution which is its source."[68] The Court goes on to claim that the restriction "threatens severe impairment of the judicial function" and is "so inconsistent with accepted separation-of-powers principles" that it must be struck down.[69]

Reading the opinion against *Rust*, or even just a plain understanding of the LSC restrictions, the Court's overreaction and umbrage are remarkable. Congress had hardly sought to overturn *Marbury v. Madison* or "wrest the law" away from the judiciary. It simply sought to keep government-paid lawyers from attacking the constitutionality of government programs. As the Court was certainly aware, there are multiple nonprofits and other sources for lawsuits challenging the validity of welfare laws, and the LSC restriction certainly did not insulate all welfare laws and regulations from judicial review.

Moreover, the Court repeatedly uses its understanding of the unique role of lawyers as assistants to judges as support for its decision. The Court twice refers to the importance of an "independent" bar. The Court calls the restriction "serious and fundamental" because it impinges on "the advocacy of attorneys and the functioning of the judiciary." The restriction is "inconsistent with the proposition that attorneys should present all the reasonable and well-grounded arguments necessary for proper resolution of a case" and "the ordinary course of litigation involves the expression of theories and postulates on both, or multiple, sides of an issue." All these problems for the legal profession are repeatedly connected to the effect on the judiciary: "An informed, independent judiciary presumes an informed, independent bar."[70]

[68] Id.

[69] Another exceptional aspect of this portion of the opinion is that outside of *Marbury v. Madison*, the Court does not cite to a single case for two and a half pages of the opinion, relying instead on its basic understanding of the legal profession and the courts. See id. at 545–48.

[70] Each of the above quotes come from id. at 544–48.

Thus, when doctors are limited in the advice they can give their patients by a government restriction, that is just the government choosing not to fund the advice it does not like. When the government tries to limit lawyers from addressing all "the reasonable and well-grounded arguments necessary for proper resolution of a case," it is an impermissible challenge to the American system of justice.

Finally, the Court shows a great deal of concern for the LSC clients displaced by the restriction:

> The restriction on speech is even more problematic because in cases where the attorney withdraws from a representation, the client is unlikely to find other counsel. The explicit premise for providing LSC attorneys is the necessity to make available representation "to persons financially unable to afford legal assistance." There often will be no alternative source for the client to receive vital information respecting constitutional and statutory rights bearing upon claimed benefits. Thus, with respect to the litigation services Congress has funded, there is no alternative channel for expression of the advocacy Congress seeks to restrict. This is in stark contrast to *Rust*. There, a patient could receive the approved Title X family planning counseling funded by the Government and later could consult an affiliate or independent organization to receive abortion counseling. Unlike indigent clients who seek LSC representation, the patient in *Rust* was not required to forfeit the Government-funded advice when she also received abortion counseling through alternative channels. Because LSC attorneys must withdraw whenever a question of a welfare statute's validity arises, an individual could not obtain joint representation so that the constitutional challenge would be presented by a non-LSC attorney, and other, permitted, arguments advanced by LSC counsel.[71]

This statement is questionable as an empirical matter, as there are non-LSC nonprofits that take constitutional challenges to welfare laws. Regardless, the Court's casual note that the patients in *Rust* can simply

[71] Id. at 546–47.

find another doctor if they want more advice shows the difference in concern between the rights of patients versus those of clients. Moreover, the claim that the *Velazquez* clients could not find other lawyers ignores an important caveat: the LSC lawyers could always just limit their representation to individual eligibility and go forward on that basis.[72]

In sum, the greatest difference between *Rust* and *Velazquez* is the difference between the Court's understanding of, and respect for, doctors and lawyers. When Congress impinges on a doctor's professional obligation to give full and unfettered medical advice to patients, it is simply a matter of funding some activities and not others. When Congress encroaches on the "independent bar," however, it is an affront to the separation of powers and a fundamental restriction on the American way of law.

Two years later, in *United States v. American Library Association, Inc.*, the Court made clear that *Rust*, not *Velazquez*, will be the unconstitutional-conditions case that controls and that *Velazquez* will be another lawyers-only case.[73] *American Library* dealt with the constitutionality of the Children's Internet Protection Act, which required libraries receiving federal funds to install Internet filtering software on their computers.[74] Among other arguments, the Court addressed the unconstitutional-conditions argument. The Court quoted at length from *Rust* for the proposition that "when the Government appropriates public funds to establish a program it is entitled to define the limits of that program." Further, in *Rust*, "the Government [was] not denying a benefit to anyone, but [was] instead simply insisting that public funds be spent for the purposes for which they were authorized."[75]

[72] A client who allowed an LSC lawyer to pursue only her individual claims might waive an underlying constitutional argument, even in a later suit brought by a different lawyer.

[73] *United States v. American Library Association, Inc.*, 539 U.S. 194, 198–200 (2003).

[74] Id. at 198–200. All cites are to the four-Justice plurality opinion. There was no majority opinion.

[75] Id. at 211 (quoting *Rust*, 500 U.S. at 178 and 296).

In contrast, the Court distinguished *Velazquez*, leaving it essentially a lawyers-only decision:

> The [*Velazquez*] Court concluded that the restriction on advocacy in such welfare disputes would distort the usual functioning of the legal profession and the federal and state courts before which the lawyers appeared. Public libraries, by contrast, have no comparable role that pits them against the Government, and there is no comparable assumption that they must be free of any conditions that their benefactors might attach to the use of donated funds or other assistance.[76]

Velazquez is thus limited to situations in which the government is funding its own opposition, a situation that is hard to imagine beyond the narrow area of LSC funding. Time will tell, but *Velazquez* seems well suited to fade away as a special case that applies only to lawyers, whereas *Rust* continues as the major unconstitutional conditions case.

Takings – *Brown v. Legal Foundation of Washington*

The Court's pro-lawyer bias is not limited to the First Amendment. A recent Fifth Amendment takings case, *Brown v. Legal Foundation of Washington*, is another case that tangentially involves LSCs and shows the Supreme Court writing around existing precedent to find a way to support LSCs (and lawyers in general).[77]

The Fifth Amendment takings clause has recently been a central concern of the Court. The Fifth Amendment states "nor shall private property be taken for public use, without just compensation." This simple injunction contains (at least) three distinct issues: "whether the interest asserted by the plaintiff is property, whether the government has taken that property, and whether the plaintiff has been denied just compensation for the taking."[78]

[76] Id. at 213.

[77] *Brown v. Legal Foundation of Washington*, 538 U.S. 216 (2003).

[78] *Phillips v. Washington Legal Foundation*, 524 U.S. 156, 172 (1998) (Souter, J., dissenting).

The Court has recently decided two takings cases concerning state Interest on Lawyers Trust Accounts (IOLTA) programs. Every state in the union has an IOLTA program.[79] IOLTA programs take advantage of the fact that lawyers are frequently called on to handle client funds for a short period of time or in amounts small enough that establishing a separate account would be administratively burdensome. In these situations, lawyers are generally required to place the client funds in an IOLTA account. State bar or state supreme court authorities use the interest generated from these accounts to pay for legal services for the poor.[80]

The origin of these programs provides a great example of the unique powers of lawyer self-regulation.[81] IOLTA programs were created in forty-five states under the inherent authority of state supreme courts and by statute in the other five. In Indiana and Pennsylvania IOLTA was originally statutory, but these states' supreme courts invalidated the statutes and created the IOLTA programs by court order.[82] These invalidations are another example of state supreme court jealousy over lawyer regulation: these courts even invalidate statutes with which they agree and then immediately reinstate them under their own inherent authority.

The IOLTA "takings" case is fairly straightforward. Client interest is transferred from the lawyer trust accounts to the government. The plaintiffs argued that the loss of the interest was a loss of their property without just compensation. The first group of IOLTA takings cases held that the interest on client funds was not "property" under the Fifth Amendment, so there was no taking involved and the IOLTA plans owed no recompense to the plaintiffs.[83]

In *Washington Legal Foundation v. Texas Equal Access to Justice Foundation*, the U.S. Court of Appeals for the Fifth Circuit held for the

[79] *Brown*, 538 U.S. at 220.

[80] See id. at 220–26.

[81] Lawyer self-regulation will be discussed more fully in Chapters 5 and 6.

[82] See id. at 221 n. 2.

[83] See *Washington Legal Foundation v. Massachusetts Bar Foundation*, 993 F.2d 962, 975–76 (1st Cir. 1993), for a list of these cases.

first time that IOLTA interest was property subject to the Fifth Amendment takings clause.[84] In *Phillips v. Washington Legal Foundation*, a 6–3 majority of the Supreme Court agreed.[85] The Court held that because "interest follows principal," the interest on client IOLTA funds was the clients' property.[86] Interestingly, the Court did not reach the issue of whether IOLTA funds were actually "'taken' by the State, or what amount of 'just compensation,' if any, [was] due respondents."[87]

Phillips is thus a weird, incomplete case. On one hand, it explicitly left open the question of whether IOLTA programs cause a Fifth Amendment taking. On the other hand, it was hard to imagine after *Phillips* that IOLTA programs did not constitute a compensable taking. In fact, after *Phillips* happily "surprised" IOLTA opponents, they were "tasting victory."[88] Once the Court has found a taking of property, the plaintiffs invariably win, even if the damages are minuscule or nonexistent. For example, in *Loretto v. Teleprompter Manhattan CATV*, the Court held that even if a taking increased the value of a property, it might still be compensable.[89]

Further, the Court's decision in *Webb's Fabulous Pharmacies, Inc. v. Beckwith* seemingly foreclosed IOLTA's most promising argument: that the government was not "taking" anything because the interest itself was government-created value that otherwise would not have existed.[90] In *Webb's*, a Florida statute allowed a county clerk to collect interest on a court interpleader fund. Without the statute and the clerk's actions, the fund would not have earned interest. The Court cited the familiar maxim

[84] *Washington Legal Foundation v. Texas Equal Access to Justice Foundation*, 94 F.3d 996 (1996).

[85] *Phillips v. Washington Legal Foundation*, 524 U.S. 156 (1998).

[86] Id. at 164–72.

[87] Id. at 172.

[88] See Tarra L. Morris, "The Dog in the Manger, The First Twenty-Five Years of War on IOLTA," 49 *St. Louis U. L.J.* 605, 612–15 (2005).

[89] *Loretto v. Teleprompter Manhattan CATV*, 458 U.S. 419, 437 n. 15 (1982); cf. *Phillips*, 524 U.S. at 169–70 (discussing and citing *Loretto* for the same proposition).

[90] *Webb's Fabulous Pharmacies, Inc. v. Beckwith*, 449 U.S. 155 (1980).

that interest follows principal and explicitly rejected the argument that the Florida court "takes only what it creates."[91] The Court found a taking and required the state to disgorge the interest earned to the recipient of the underlying interpleader funds.[92]

Nevertheless, the first few cases after *Phillips* were a mess, as courts struggled to answer the unsettled question of whether IOLTA constituted a taking and what, if any, just compensation was due. The main battleground seemed to be whether to apply the per se test for physical takings or the ad hoc *Penn Central*[93] test for regulatory takings. The choice between the two tests was much more than academic. In takings cases, the choice of the test usually presages the case's outcome. In cases in which the per se test is met, the Court always finds a taking and the only remaining question is just compensation: "When the government physically takes possession of an interest in property for some public purpose, it has a categorical duty to compensate the former owner . . . no matter how small [the compensation due]."[94]

In contrast, "regulatory" takings are analyzed under the ad hoc *Penn Central* standard and frequently result in a finding of no taking at all. A per se taking is more akin to a condemnation proceeding: the government physically takes all or some of the property. A regulatory taking is fuzzier. The Court tries to determine whether the government regulation or action somehow reduces the value of the property and then what, if anything should be paid out:

> Our jurisprudence involving condemnations and physical takings is as old as the Republic and, for the most part, involves the straightforward application of *per se* rules. Our regulatory takings jurisprudence, in contrast, is of more recent vintage and is characterized by

[91] Id. at 163–64.

[92] Id. at 163–65.

[93] *Penn Central Transportation Company v. City of New York*, 438 U.S. 104, 124 (1978).

[94] *Tahoe-Sierra Preservation Council, Inc. v. Tahoe Regional Planning Agency*, 535 U.S. 302, 322–23 (2002).

> essentially *ad hoc*, factual inquiries, designed to allow careful examination and weighing of all the relevant circumstances.[95]

The post-*Phillips* cases followed this logic exactly. The courts that applied the *Penn Central* test found no taking, whereas the per se courts found an unconstitutional taking and required either full repayment or suitable equitable relief. When *Phillips* was considered on remand to the Western District of Texas, the court applied the ad hoc approach and found no taking.[96] On appeal, the U.S. Court of Appeals for the Fifth Circuit applied the per se test, found a taking, and reversed.[97]

The U.S. Court of Appeals for the Ninth Circuit followed a different path. At first, a three-judge panel applied the per se test and found an unconstitutional taking.[98] The Ninth Circuit reversed en banc, applying the ad hoc approach and finding no taking.[99]

The Supreme Court granted certiorari to iron it all out in *Brown v. Legal Foundation of Washington*.[100] Strangely, the Supreme Court broke the mold and found a per se taking of private property for public use, but refused to require any compensation.

One of the issues in a takings case is whether the property is being taken for a public use. This discussion is often pro forma or skipped because it is often quite obvious that a challenged taking is for public use. In *Brown*, however, the Court begins its analysis with a glowing review of the "public use" requirement, calling IOLTA a "dramatic success" serving the "compelling interest" of providing legal services to the

[95] Id. at 321–22.

[96] *Washington Legal Foundation v. Texas Equal Access to Justice Foundation*, 86 F.Supp.2d 624, 643–47 (W.D. Tex. 2000).

[97] *Washington Legal Foundation v. Texas Equal Access to Justice Foundation*, 270 F.3d 180, 186–89 (5th Cir. 2001).

[98] *Washington Legal Foundation v. Legal Foundation of Washington*, 236 F.3d 1097, 1100–01 (9th Cir. 2001).

[99] *Washington Legal Foundation v. Legal Foundation of Washington*, 271 F.3d 835, 854–57 (9th Cir. 2001)(en banc).

[100] *Brown v. Legal Foundation of Washington*, 538 U.S. 216 (2003).

poor.[101] The Court quotes praise from other judges for IOLTA: "IOLTA extracted the earnings from the banks and gave it to charities, largely to fund legal services for the poor. That is a very worthy purpose," and "As a citizen and former member of the bar, I applaud the state's effort to provide legal services for the poor and disadvantaged."[102] It is worth noting how closely this section hews to the bar associations' praise of these programs, even including the statistic that IOLTA funds provide "legal services to literally millions of needy Americans."[103] This section parallels the section in *Went For It* in which the Court uncritically credits each of the bar association factual defenses for the advertising restrictions at issue.[104]

Next, the Court reiterates its holding in *Phillips* that IOLTA interest was the private property of the plaintiffs and held that "a *per se* approach is more consistent with the reasoning in our *Phillips* opinion than *Penn Central*'s ad hoc analysis." Thus, the "interest was taken for a public use when it was ultimately turned over to the foundation," leaving only the question of "just compensation."[105]

At this point, the opinion takes a left turn. The Court turns to valuing the plaintiffs' loss and holds that "just compensation" is measured "by the property owner's loss rather than the government's gain."[106] Because the IOLTA interest is supposed to be generated only when the transaction costs of creating a separate bank account would be more than the interest earned, the Court concludes that the loss was always zero and required no compensation at all.[107]

[101] Id. at 232.

[102] Id. at 232 and n. 7.

[103] That quote is from id. at 232. A comparison of this section of *Brown* with the ABA's amicus brief (on file with author), shows that the Court simply adopted much of the ABA's praise for the IOLTA programs.

[104] See *Florida Bar*, 515 U.S. at 624–25.

[105] *Brown*, 538 U.S. at 235.

[106] Id. at 235–36.

[107] See id. at 239–41.

As noted above, this is a highly unusual result for a per se takings case, especially one in which the calculation of interest is relatively easy and the loss to the various clients at issue was hardly negligible.[108] As the Court itself has repeatedly noted, once a per se or "categorical" taking has been found, it applies a "clear rule" and the government must pay damages, "no matter how small."[109] If there is any clear theme from the Court's per se taking cases, it is that once a per se taking is found, the government will have to pay *something*.[110] Once the Court finds a per se taking, the case is generally all over but the crying. Nevertheless, in *Brown*, the Court found room within its previously relatively uncontroversial calculation of "just compensation" doctrines to deny relief.[111]

Brown is also difficult to square with *Webb's*, especially the *Webb's* Court's explicit rejection of the government-created-value argument. *Brown* distinguished *Webb's* by noting that in *Webb's*, the state of Florida collected both a statutory interpleader fee and the interest generated, as well as noting that the IOLTA interest exists only because of the pooling of funds that would otherwise generate no interest.[112] Nevertheless, in *Webb's*, Florida's entire argument was that the state statute itself created the interest at issue and that in the absence of the statute there would be no interest to collect. The *Webb's* Court rejected that argument, noting that regardless of whether a state statute created the interest, the interest still belonged to the owner of the underlying

[108] For example, in 1999 IOLTA programs generated an estimated $139 million nationwide from client interest. *Washington Legal Foundation v. Legal Foundation of Washington*, 271 F.3d 835, 843 (9th Cir. 2001)(en banc).

[109] *Brown*, 538 U.S. at 234.

[110] See *Loretto*, 458 U.S. at 437 and n. 15 (finding a taking in a situation in which the government action might have actually increased the value of the property overall, and assuming that there will be some finding of compensation); *Phillips*, 524 U.S. at 170 ("The government may not seize rents received by the owner of a building simply because it can prove that the costs incurred in collecting the rents exceed the amount collected.").

[111] It would be an error to call any part of takings jurisprudence wholly uncontroversial. Nevertheless, prior to *Brown*, few of the Court's cases had hinged on the valuation question. The bulk of the work was done on the ins and outs of the taking itself.

[112] See *Brown*, 538 U.S. at 238 n. 10.

principal.[113] As a conceptual matter, this argument looks quite similar to an argument the Court accepted in *Brown*: that without the government-created system pooling IOLTA funds, there would be no net interest. However, in *Brown*, the Court allowed the government to keep the government-created value.[114]

It is still too early to know whether *Brown* will turn out to be a sui generis case that stands outside the mainstream of takings jurisprudence the way that *Ohralik* and *Went for It* stand in the commercial speech area. It seems likely, however, as it is difficult to imagine another type of per se taking in which the government will take something of obvious value to the government and the world at large but of absolutely no value to the individual plaintiff. In fact, the Court's holding that just compensation is measured by the loss to the plaintiffs will likely prove a relative side note as the battle over regulatory and per se takings rages on. As Christopher Serkin has argued, *Brown* will not prove "one of the most important valuation cases in recent years" but will instead be treated as a "prosaic" and fact-specific treatment of fair market value.[115]

Comparing the criminal procedure cases in Chapter 3 with these civil constitutional cases allows several parallels to become clear. The Court often uncritically accepts the arguments or evidence of bar associations, whereas parallel evidence from different professional groups is disregarded. In many of these cases the Court writes around existing precedent to carve out a place for lawyers. As these cases age they stand out from the general course of the law as sui generis exceptions, created just for lawyers, by lawyer-judges.

[113] *Webb's*, 449 U.S. at 161–62.

[114] See *Brown*, 538 U.S. at 235–37.

[115] Christopher Serkin, "Valuing Interest: Net Harm and Fair Market Value in *Brown v. Legal Foundation of Washington*," 37 *Ind. L. Rev.* 417, 421 (2004); Ronald D. Rotunda, "Found Money: IOLTA, *Brown v. Legal Foundation of Washington*, and the Taking of Property Without the Payment of Compensation," 2003 *Cato Sup. Ct. Rev.* 245, 268 (2003) ("When one looks closely at [*Brown*], there is much less to it than meets the eye.").

5 A Short History of Lawyer Regulation

With the influx of increasing numbers, who seek admission to the profession mainly for its emoluments, have come new and changed conditions. Once possible ostracism by professional brethren was sufficient to keep from serious error the practitioner with no fixed ideals of ethical conduct; but now the shyster, the barratrously inclined, the ambulance chaser, the member of the Bar with a system of runners, pursue their nefarious methods with no check save the rope of sand of moral suasion. . . . These men believe themselves immune, the good or bad esteem of their co-labourers is nothing to them so long as their itching fingers are not thereby stayed in their eager quest for lucre.

– ABA Committee on a Code of Professional Ethics, 1906[1]

THE REGULATION OF LAWYERS IN AMERICA IS HANDLED differently from the regulation of any other American profession. Doctors, architects, engineers, teachers, and other professionals are all regulated in the first instance by state and federal legislatures. The legal profession, in contrast, is governed in all fifty states by state supreme courts. As we shall see, these courts delegate the actual nuts and bolts of governing lawyers to bar associations or other administrative bodies. Predictably, this regulatory structure favors the interests of the legal profession over those of the public.

[1] 29 ABA Rep. 601 (1906).

It was not always thus. During most of the nineteenth century, lawyers were largely unregulated; what regulation existed came from legislatures, not courts. There was almost no formal regulation of lawyer behavior, and barriers to entry, such as a bar exam or the law school requirement, were unheard of. Bar associations were weak or nonexistent.

In the late nineteenth century, bar associations began to reform. Priority number one was lobbying courts to step up the regulation of the profession. Over time, state supreme courts have taken control of lawyer regulation and have created the complex web of regulations that now govern the legal profession.

This chapter explains this history in more detail, and Chapter 6 argues that the current regulation of lawyers is much more helpful to the profession than to the public. These chapters discuss two broad types of lawyer regulation: entry and conduct. Entry regulation governs who may join the profession. Current entry regulations include a bar exam, three years of law school (or an equivalent amount of credit hours), a college education, character and fitness examinations, and so forth. Current conduct regulation consists of some version of the American Bar Association's Rules of Professional Conduct, continuing legal education requirements, and the like.

There are a few key historical themes. First, the original selection of lawyer-judges in fourteenth-century England was a result of happenstance, not a studied thought process about who would make the best judges. Almost immediately upon the arrival of lawyer-judges, lawyers began to control their own entry and conduct regulations. Second, the recent American history of lawyer self-regulation begins with the formation of the modern bar associations in the late nineteenth century. Third, these bar associations continually lobbied courts to take up the regulation of lawyers. Fourth, courts obliged, and have since struck down most legislative encroachments into this "inherent power" of the judiciary. Last, the judges' reign has resulted in vastly higher entry barriers and the continual narrowing and clarifying of conduct regulation.

As you read, consider the unusual event of lawyer deregulation during the middle of the nineteenth century. Lawyers have always been more or less unpopular in the United States, but there has never been a stretch in which that unpopularity has resulted in such potent, populist anti-lawyer legislation. For anyone who wonders whether some form of lawyer deregulation could work or who is interested in reining in the legal profession, the mid-nineteenth century is a great starting point.

The First Lawyer-Judges in England

The royal appointment of the first English lawyer-judges was the result of a confluence of multiple overlapping factors, rather than a conscious or systematic design. In fact, the historians who have studied the birth of the twin fundamental institutions of the English common law – the judiciary and the legal profession – are often at odds as to when to pinpoint their respective beginnings. The historians have even more difficulty ascribing reasons for these developments.

Nevertheless, several points are clear. There were "courts" in England even before the Norman Conquest, but they did not resemble our current conception of a court. The early courts were highly localized, staffed by local landowners or lords, and had very informal procedures. There was no legal profession, and litigants pled their own cases.[2]

From the Norman Conquest forward the king and his ministers began to centralize court processes. The reign of Edward I (1272–1307) marked the triumph of a centralized court system and the creation of a nascent legal profession. During this period England saw a professionalization of the judiciary, marked by the prosecution of corrupt judges, the appointment of full-time judges who were paid a salary and made a living as judges, and the rise of an organized legal profession and the first lawyer-judges.[3]

[2] S.F.C. Milsom, *Historical Foundations of the Common Law*, 2nd ed. (London: Butterworths, 1981), 11–25.

[3] Paul Brand, *The Making of the Common Law* (London: Hambledon Press, 1990), 135–68.

Historian Paul Brand has spent much of his career discussing the birth of the legal profession; he often uses the contemporaneous effort to "professionalize" the legal profession by controlling entry and conduct as the surest sign of the development of a recognizable group of lawyers.[4] Thus, for Brand, the mark of the arrival of the British legal profession is the creation of the monopoly over practice in the king's courts.

The highest ranks of the early lawyers were called "serjeants"; by around 1330 the serjeants held a monopoly over practice in the king's courts, and the serjeants likewise gained a monopoly over judicial appointments to the two most prestigious courts, the Common Bench and the King's Bench.[5] Theodore Plucknett called the serjeants of this period a "close guild in complete control of the legal profession."[6] The serjeants controlled legal education and entry into the profession and became the primary source for new judges.

The effect of placing legal education in the hands of the court was enormous. It isolated English lawyers from continental, Roman, and ecclesiastical influence. The structure was independent of university law faculties, in which only Roman civil law and canon law were taught.[7] Lawyers taught each other and learned from court procedures, drawing on their own resources. Thus, English law became a unique, insular system with few foreign ideas, which explains "how the reasoning of a small group of men in Westminster Hall grew into one of the world's two greatest systems of law."[8]

The description of the pomp that came along with the office of serjeant is notable: every new serjeant was required to provide a seven-day feast and give gifts of liveries and gold rings. The benefits were

[4] Id. at 11–15.

[5] Id. at 165.

[6] Theodore Plucknett, *A Concise History of the Common Law*, 5th ed. (Boston: Little, Brown, 1956), 223.

[7] J. H. Baker, *An Introduction to English Legal History*, 4th ed. (Oxford: Oxford University Press, 2005), 155–56.

[8] Id. at 155.

considerable. Every serjeant ranked as a knight and had his own pillar in St. Paul's Cathedral.[9] Below the serjeants was a broader legal profession marked by the Inns of Court and practice in the courts of chancery.[10]

There is a chicken–egg-style conundrum in the creation of the English legal profession and lawyer-judges. Obviously the first lawyer-judge served as a lawyer before becoming a judge. Early historians explained the trend as a natural result of the creation of a nascent legal profession, whose lawyers could be chosen as judges.[11] The creation of the tightly knit serjeant system was a result of multiple synergies: the interest of the king and his counselors in centralized and professionalized courts, the choice of lawyer-judges for the first time, and the close relationship between the privileged lawyer-serjeants and the serjeants in the judiciary.[12]

There are two important takeaway points here. First, even though the system we inherited from these early days may well be the very best possible, it is not because of careful predesign. Second, the arrival of lawyer-judges (in the form of the serjeants appointed as judges in the Common Bench and the King's Bench) came hand in hand with the serjeants having a monopoly on practicing in those courts and the serjeants taking control over entry into the profession, starting a trend that eventually transplanted to America.

Lawyer Regulation in Early America

At the time of the American Revolution, the legal profession was guild-like and locally run. Admission was typically controlled by local courts

[9] Plucknett, *A Concise History of the Common Law*, 223–24.

[10] Baker, *An Introduction to English Legal History*, 155. For a more detailed description of the Inns of Court, see Margaret McGlynn, *The Royal Prerogative and the Learning of the Inns of Court* (Cambridge: Cambridge University Press, 2003).

[11] W. S. Holdsworth, *History of English Law*, Volume 2 (London: Metlmen & Co., 1922), 318.

[12] Brand, *The Making of the Common Law*, 1–20.

after an individual completed a set period of apprenticeship to a licensed lawyer.[13] There was little or no formal control over attorney behavior. These bars were very local and homogenous, so lawyers relied on small, tightly knit communities of practitioners to control the behavior and ethics of other lawyers.[14]

These early bar associations were quite interested in entry regulation. For example, in Hartford, Connecticut, "where after the Revolution the number of attorneys increased rapidly and perhaps unreasonably," a bar association was founded in 1783 to lay down rules and regulations for the admission of apprentices and minimum requirements for legal training and admission to practice.[15] The "Old Bar Record Book" of the early Maine bar, which dissolved in 1829, states that no member of the bar was allowed to use a non-attorney to work as an attorney in the office or appear before courts.[16] In an eighteenth-century New York Bar Association, the members, "to prevent inroads upon their practice, made an agreement not to receive into their offices, as clerks, any young men who intended to pursue the law as a profession."[17] This period later became

[13] Jay F. Alexander, "Legal Careers in Eighteenth Century America," in *The Legal Profession, Major Historical Interpretations,* ed. Kermit L. Hall (New York: Garland, 1987), 2–9.

[14] Bruce Frohnen, "The Bases of Professional Responsibility: Pluralism and Community in Early America," 63 *Geo. Wash. L. Rev.* 931, 931–38 (1995). Common law courts also retained "summary jurisdiction" over the lawyers who practiced before them and could disbar or sanction an errant attorney; see Edward P. Weeks, *A Treatise on Attorneys and Counsellors at Law* (San Francisco: Bancroft-Whitney Co., 1892), 144–223. In keeping with modern trends, however, this power was infrequently invoked. See Fannie M. Farmer, "Legal Practice and Ethics in North Carolina 1820–1860," in *The Legal Profession, Major Historical Interpretations*, ed. Kermit L. Hall (New York: Garland, 1987), 274, 350, and n. 101 (noting that "prior to 1868, no court, so far as the records show, was called upon to disbar an attorney" in North Carolina).

[15] Anton-Hermann Chroust, *The Rise of the Legal Profession in America,* Volume 2 (Norman: University of Oklahoma Press, 1965), 146.

[16] Roscoe Pound, *The Lawyer from Antiquity to Modern Times* (St. Paul, MN: West Publishing, 1953), 191–92.

[17] Chroust, *The Rise of the Legal Profession*, 201.

known as the "golden age" of American law,[18] and it was marked by a rise in the prestige and social status of lawyers.[19]

Jacksonian Democracy

The middle of the nineteenth century, however, ushered in changes in the selection process for judges and entry standards for the legal profession. These changes have often been chalked up to "Jacksonian democracy." Lawyers and judges were seen as elitist and their special treatment as against the natural rights of man.[20] The admission of frontier states to the union also allowed a shift in the treatment of lawyers and judges, as newer and more rural states created their own legal systems.

This period saw the rise of the elected state judiciary and the virtual end to standards of admission for lawyers. For example, New Hampshire, Maine, Wisconsin, and Indiana expressly abolished any requirements for appearing in those states' courts.[21] Likewise, states that maintained a bar admission requirement significantly slackened their standards. In 1800, a set period of preparation for admission was required in fourteen of the nineteen states or territories. In 1840, it was required in eleven of thirty. By 1860, it was required in only nine of thirty-nine.[22]

[18] Maxwell Bloomfield, "Law vs. Politics: The Self-Image of the American Bar (1830–1860)," 12 *Am. J. Leg. Hist.* 306, 307–08 (1968). The "golden age" meme for this period has been criticized by modern legal historians. See Charles W. Wolfram, "Toward a History of the Legalization of American Legal Ethics – I. Origins," 8 *U. Chi. L. Sch. Roundtable* 469, 471, and n. 14 (2001).

[19] Morton J. Horwitz, *The Transformation of American Law, 1780–1860* (Cambridge, MA: Harvard University Press, 1977), 140–59.

[20] Robert Stevens, *Law School: Legal Education in America from the 1850s to the 1980s* (Chapel Hill: University of North Carolina Press, 1983), 7–10.

[21] See Alfred Z. Reed, *Training for the Public Profession of the Law* (New York: Carnegie Foundation, 1921), 87–88.

[22] Pound, *The Lawyer from Antiquity to Modern Times*, 227–28.

During the same period, states moved rapidly to elected judiciaries. In 1832, Mississippi amended its constitution to become the first state to elect all its judges, including those on courts of appeals. Every state that entered the union before 1845 did so with an appointed judiciary. In contrast, from 1846 to 1959 each new state had some form of judicial elections. By 1865, twenty-four of the thirty-four states elected their judges.[23]

The middle of the nineteenth century also saw a significant law reform effort, as legislatures attempted to codify the common law and to eliminate special pleading forms.[24] Consistent with the general populist flavor of the time, codification was meant to simplify the law and break the lawyers' monopoly on pleading lawsuits.

Tellingly, in each of these three reforms, state legislatures – not courts or bar associations – led the way. This is not to say that courts or lawyers were silent. To the contrary, there are multiple examples of irate lawyers and judges. One particularly choleric former Mississippi Supreme Court justice stated that because of elected judges, "Our constitution is the subject of ridicule in all the States where it is known. It is referred to as a full definition of mobocracy."[25] Consider this from a lawyer in 1847: "The voice of the multitude is against the legal community.... The bar finds no favour at the ballot box.... A cry is going out over the land. Radicalism is infectious as the pestilence. The tide of popular will must soon sweep away our prerogative, unless we stay its waters."[26] Pro-lawyer legal historians have likewise written for years about the "demoralization" of the legal profession during the period. In these histories the start of the nineteenth century is the "golden age," the middle period is the reign of the

[23] Joanna M. Shepherd, "Money, Politics, and Impartial Justice," 58 *Duke L.J.* 623, 631–32 (2009).

[24] Charles Warren, *A History of the American Bar* (New York: Howard Fertig, 1966), 508–39.

[25] Edwin Arthur Miles, *Jacksonian Democracy in Mississippi* (Chapel Hill: University of North Carolina Press, 1960), 42.

[26] Bloomfield, "Law vs. Politics," 307.

barbarians, and the turn of the twentieth century finally sees a return to sanity.[27]

Back in the Saddle

In the last third of the nineteenth century and the first third of the twentieth century, the legal profession regained self-regulation behind several interlocking trends. Bar associations formed and immediately began lobbying for higher entry standards and for centralized state supreme court control over lawyer regulation. State supreme courts began to claim an "inherent authority" over lawyers and began to invalidate any legislative attempts to govern lawyers. Many state supreme courts unified their state bar associations – which meant that every licensed attorney in the state was required to join the bar association – and these unified bar associations were frequently in charge of lawyer regulation.

Not surprisingly, the same period saw a dramatic tightening of rules of entry, as well as a shift from lawyer apprenticeships to law schools. Bar associations and courts also began to adopt the first formal regulation of lawyer conduct through the creation and adoption of the ABA Canons of Legal Ethics.

Beginning in the 1870s, lawyers began to form organized bar associations, starting in local city bar associations and later in state and national associations.[28] Among these new bar associations was the ABA, founded in 1878 in Saratoga, New York, by "seventy-five gentlemen from twenty-one jurisdictions, out of approximately 60,000 lawyers then practicing in the United States."[29] In general, the members of these new bar associations were drawn by invitation from the "elite" of practice. From the

[27] A great example is W. Raymond Blackard, "The Demoralization of the Legal Profession in Nineteenth Century America," 16 *Tenn. L. Rev.* 314 (1940). The works of Warren, Pound, and Chroust cited herein are in the same vein.

[28] Lawrence M. Friedman, *A History of American Law*, 2nd ed. (New York: Simon & Schuster, 1985), 648–52.

[29] Reed, *Training for the Public Profession of the Law*, 220.

outset, the new bar associations focused on the punishment of the "activities of a notorious fringe of unlicensed practitioners" and "shystering and unprofessional conduct,"[30] as well as requiring higher qualifications for admission to practice.[31]

From its inception the ABA pilloried what it considered to be the undesirable element in the bar and proposed a tightening of bar admission standards because low admissions standards had contributed to "extraordinary numbers" of the "ignorant" and "unprincipled" becoming lawyers.[32] This subject "received more attention from the Association during the Saratoga era than any other."[33] In 1891, the ABA Committee on Legal Education produced a sixty-page report on entry to the profession that proved remarkably prophetic. The report recommended a number of changes that would eventually come to fruition, including state supreme court control over entry, written bar exams, a three-year requirement for law schools, and specific law library and facility requirements.[34] The report's very first resolution was to "strongly recommend that the power of admitting members to the Bar, and the supervision of their professional conduct, be in each state lodged in the highest courts of the State."[35]

To understand why, consider the experience of the nascent Virginia State Bar Association, which was formed in 1888 and immediately sought to raise entry standards in the state. Its first try was a bill proposed to the general assembly requiring a new, written bar examination. This act was defeated. In 1896 the bar tried again, but this time suggested that

[30] Friedman, *A History of American Law*, 649–50.

[31] W. Hamilton Bryson and E. Lee Shepard, "The Virginia Bar, 1870–1900," in *The New High Priests: Lawyers in Post-Civil War America,* ed. Gerald W. Gawalt (Westport, CT: Greenwood Press, 1985), 171–72.

[32] 2 ABA Rep. 212 (1878).

[33] Edson R. Sunderland, *History of the American Bar Association and Its Work* (Chicago: American Bar Association, 1953), 72–73.

[34] 14 ABA Rep. 301–360 (1891).

[35] 14 ABA Rep. 349 (1891).

admission be handled by the state supreme court; this time, the act passed. The first written bar examination was given less than a year later, on January 8, 1897.[36]

During this period, state supreme courts around the country began claiming an "inherent authority" to regulate the legal profession as an outgrowth of the constitutional separation of powers between the legislative and judicial branches. The Illinois Supreme Court's decision to raise entry standards at the turn of the twentieth century is an early example. Before 1897, graduates of Illinois law schools received automatic admission to the bar without taking an exam, on a showing of good character.[37] This was known as the law school "diploma privilege." In 1897, the Illinois Supreme Court adopted admission rules that required three years of law school and the taking of a written bar exam for admission.[38] Students from existing two-year law schools (who would have been automatically licensed under the previous regime) petitioned the Illinois legislature for assistance, and the legislature obliged by passing a law exempting these students from the new rules. When these applicants petitioned the Illinois Supreme Court to be licensed, the court invalidated the law and refused their admission in a case called *In re Day*.[39]

The court invalidated the act because the legislature had "assumed the exercise of a power properly belonging to the courts."[40] The court's reasoning is critical because it is emblematic of the inherent power cases generally. *Day* was also favorably featured in a contemporaneous *Harvard Law Review* article and widely cited and imitated afterward.[41]

[36] Bryson and Shepard, "The Virginia Bar, 1870–1900," 171–72.
[37] Thomas M. Alpert, "The Inherent Power of the Courts to Regulate the Practice of Law: An Historical Analysis," 32 *Buff. L. Rev.* 523, 537 (1983).
[38] Id.
[39] *In re Day*, 54 N.E. 646 (1899).
[40] Id. at 648.
[41] Blewett Lee, "The Constitutional Power of the Courts over Admission to the Bar," 13 *Harv. L. Rev.* 31 (1899).

Article 3 of the then Illinois Constitution stated, "The powers of the government of this state are divided into three distinct departments – legislative, executive and judicial; and no person, or collection of persons, being one of these departments, shall exercise any power properly belonging to either of the others, except as hereinafter expressly directed or permitted."[42] Based on this language, the court determined that the question was whether the power to admit attorneys to practice law was properly in the legislative or judicial department – in other words, whether entry to the legal profession was a judicial or legislative type of power.[43]

In deciding this question in favor of the judiciary, the court relied on two basic arguments. First, the court argued that in England and America, the courts "have always controlled the admission of attorneys."[44] Given that legislatures all over the country had slackened admission standards within the same century, that the Illinois legislature had been heavily involved in the admission of lawyers from Illinois' inception as a state,[45] and that the history in England is hardly unequivocal,[46] this claim is at best questionable.

[42] *In re Day*, 54 N.E. at 648.

[43] Id.

[44] Id. at 650.

[45] Id. at 654–57 (Phillips, J., dissenting).

[46] The historical claims as to England before 1776 are also questionable. For example, C.W. Brooks, *Pettyfoggers and Vipers of the Commonwealth* (Cambridge: Cambridge University Press, 2004), 138–39, reports that between 1580 and 1629, Parliament considered at least eight bills to limit the size of the legal profession. Parliament also granted courts the right to admit attorneys and solicitors, required judges to examine applicants, and set the number of years of required study as a clerk to a licensed practitioner. Reed, *Training for the Public Profession of the Law*, 11. See also Alpert, "The Inherent Power of the Courts to Regulate the Practice of Law," 532 ("The English and American experiences before the Revolution provide little basis for the contention that control of the legal profession was or would have been regarded by the framers of the first state constitutions as an inherently judicial task and thus protected from legislative encroachment.").

Second, the court argued that the admission of attorneys was an essential judicial power, as lawyers served as "officers of the court" and were closely involved in the administration of justice:

> It would be strange, indeed, if the court can control its own court room, and even its own janitor, but that it is not within its power to inquire into the ability of the persons who assist in the administration of justice as its officers.... The fact that the legislature may prescribe the qualifications of doctors, plumbers, horseshoers, and persons following other professions or callings, not connected with the judicial system, and may say what shall be evidence of such qualifications, can have no influence on this question. A license to such persons confers no right to put the judicial power in motion or to participate in judicial proceedings. The attorney is a necessary part of the judicial system, and his vocation is not merely to find persons who are willing to have lawsuits. He is the first one to sit in judgment on every case, and whether the court shall be called upon to act depends on his decision.[47]

Two justices dissented. First, they presented a very persuasive description of the Illinois legislature's long history of involvement in the admission of attorneys. Second, they noted that the legislature controls entry into other professions and flatly stated, "The control exercised by the legislature, being the exercise of a police power ... cannot be held to be an impairment of judicial power nor the assumption of such judicial power by the legislature."[48]

There are a few important points to note about the reasoning of this case and the other inherent authority cases that followed.[49] The cases are

[47] *In re Day*, 54 N.E. at 652–53. My favorite part of this quote is that the Illinois legislature apparently licensed "horseshoers" in 1899.

[48] Id. at 657.

[49] There are a long series of inherent authority admission cases that follow similar reasoning. See, e.g. *In re Bailey*, 248 P. 29, 30 (Ariz. 1926) ("[T]here is no more important duty, nor one whose performance is more necessary to the proper performance of the courts, than to see that their officers are of proper mental ability and moral character."); *Ex Parte Steckler*, 154 So. 41, 45 (La. 1934) (holding that the state supreme court

constitutional in nature and they rely solely on the creation in each state of three different branches of government: the legislative, executive, and judicial. Because the courts are analyzing state constitutions, legislatures have no power, short of a constitutional amendment, to overrule these cases.

The thinness of the court's basis in actual constitutional language is significant. It is certainly true in Illinois and every other state that the constitution creates a judicial branch. It is also true that the creation of a judicial branch necessarily assumes that the judiciary will settle legal disputes, however defined. That said, the court's use of the existence of a judicial branch to create whole areas of responsibility outside of the obvious power to decide lawsuits is a massive leap.

The Illinois Supreme Court claimed an *exclusive* power over the admission of lawyers.[50] Even if the court was correct that the history and structure of the Illinois Constitution means that courts must have some baseline of control over the attorneys that appear before them, why is the power not shared between the legislature and the judiciary? It would have been very easy to limit the decision to truly hazardous legislative acts – that is, encroachments that endanger the administration of

has ultimate authority over bar admission because "[a] proper administration of justice depends as largely upon the conscience, competence and conduct of the members of the bar, as upon the work of the men on the bench."); *In re Sparks*, 101 S.W.2d 194, 197 (Ky. Ct. App. 1936) ("The power to regulate the conduct and qualifications of its officers does not depend upon constitutional or statutory grounds. It is a power which is inherent in this court as a court – appropriate, indeed necessary, to the proper administration of justice."); *Ayres v. Hadaway*, 6 N.W.2d 905, 908 (Mich. 1942) ("Attorneys practicing in the district courts of this state are officers of the courts in which they practice. Their position is an honorable one; they are the trusted advisers of the court. There can be no doubt that the court has ample power to protect itself against dishonorable and corrupt practitioners." [quoting *In re Disbarment Proceedings of William L. Newby*, 107 N.W. 850, 852 (Neb. 1906)]). Courts also frequently complained of legislative efforts to "destroy the courts" by admitting "persons without legal learning, and wanting in the proper ethics of the profession." *In re Thatcher*, 22 Ohio Dec. 116 (Lucas Co. Common Pleas Ct. 1912), quoted in Alpert, "The Inherent Power of the Courts to Regulate the Practice of Law," 539–40.

[50] Id. at 648 ("If [the power of admission] is judicial in its nature, the legislature [is] expressly prohibited from exercising it.").

justice. Presumably, the court did not do so because the current legislation clearly did not pose a grave threat. These very applicants would have been admitted under the rules of three years earlier, and the legislature did not try to change the rules going forward, as the statute was limited retroactively to students from 1899 and before.[51]

This is an especially salient point because it shows how aggressive the court was in interpreting its own powers. The inherent judicial power is one of the constitutional areas in which the judiciary's power completely bars other branches from encroachment or involvement. In later cases, we see state supreme courts invalidating legislative actions with which they actually agree. For example, the supreme courts of both Kentucky and Michigan invalidated state statutes unifying their bars as a violation of the inherent powers of the courts and replaced them with court-ordered unified bars.[52]

Consider the personal, turf-battle aspect of these cases. Later cases held that the inherent authority extends to any power that "is essential to the existence, dignity and functions of the judiciary."[53] The inclusion of "dignity" in some of these cases gives a flavor to the courts' feelings on these matters. They are not interested in merely defending their existence or their efficacy at deciding legal disputes. Instead, they seek to defend their "dignity." This connects nicely to the public choice insight that government actors often engage in internecine power battles.

Finally, consider the massive conflict of interest in these decisions. In each of these cases the state supreme court itself is defining the extent and reach of its own power. Moreover, the justices are doing so as former lawyers who are being heavily lobbied by bar associations. The inherent authority cases strongly evince the lawyer–judge bias: when faced with an issue that affects lawyers the courts reach the conclusion that best suits the profession, often by reasoning that seems somewhat questionable.

[51] Lee, "The Constitutional Power of the Courts over Admission to the Bar," 234–35.

[52] Glenn R. Winters, *The Unified Bar in the United States* (Chicago: American Judicature Society, 1973), 5.

[53] *In re Integration of State Bar of Oklahoma*, 95 P.2d 113, 113 (Okla. 1939).

These inherent-authority cases had multiple uses. Many state supreme courts followed Illinois' lead and seized entry regulation from the legislature.[54] Moreover, in reaction to bar complaints, many state supreme courts launched *sua sponte* investigations of the unauthorized practice of law. These actions defined the practice of law broadly to include multiple out-of-court functions, enjoined corporations from the practice of law, and sanctioned attorneys who assisted those corporations.[55] Courts also used their inherent authority to appoint lawyers to represent indigent defendants at the state's expense.[56]

Courts also relied on inherent authority to make many bar associations unified or mandatory. Today, the bar is unified (i.e. integrated) in thirty-six states and the District of Columbia.[57] In states with unified bars, a lawyer must be a member of and pay dues to the state bar association to practice law in that state. In ordering the unification of the bar, state supreme courts regularly noted their interest in increasing the quality of the lawyers appearing before them.[58]

Not all these state bars were unified by court order. In fact, state legislatures unified the bar in the first group of states.[59] This trend changed in 1939 when the Oklahoma state legislature repealed its ten-year-old unified bar statute. In response, the Oklahoma Supreme Court reunified the

[54] See note 49 for some examples.

[55] Henry M. Dowling, "The Inherent Power of the Judiciary," 21 *ABA J.* 635, 636–37 (1935).

[56] See *Hendryx v. State*, 29 N.E. 1131 (Ind. 1892).

[57] See Terry Radtke, "The Last Stage of Professionalizing the Bar: The Wisconsin Bar Integration Movement, 1934–1956," 81 *Marq. L. Rev.* 1001, 1001 (1998).

[58] See, e.g., *Application of the Montana Bar Association*, 368 P.2d 158, 162 (Mont. 1962) (integrating the bar by court order because "[t]here is need for improvement in our court, the district and justice courts, and the bar of which we are members"); *In re Integration of the Nebraska State Bar Association*, 275 N.W. 265, 267–68 (Neb. 1937) (approving integration because "the court has an immediate interest in the character of the bar, for the court's own sake"); *Petition of the Florida State Bar Association*, 40 So. 2d 902, 908–09 (Fla. 1949) (same).

[59] The first fifteen bars were unified by statute, although some of those statutes were later invalidated under the inherent authority approach, with the bar unification then replaced by court order. See Winters, *The Unified Bar in the United States*, 4–5.

bar under the inherent authority doctrine.[60] As historian Dayton McKean has noted, the process of obtaining bar unification by court order proved "so much easier than lobbying a bill through a legislature against the opposition of other professional associations, perhaps only to meet a governor's veto, that the use of statutes has been all but abandoned since the Oklahoma decision" and all the remaining states unified via court action and the use of the inherent authority doctrine.[61]

Obviously, a mandatory bar association has significant benefits for the legal profession in those states. In many of these states, the supreme courts ceded control over the profession to the unified bars,[62] making lawyers in those states the most self-regulated professionals in the world.[63] Further, as in a closed union shop, the mandatory collection of dues and the associated political clout of having *all* lawyers be members of the bar association were significant advantages to the profession.

Between 1870 and 1940, there was a large growth in bar associations, and membership in some of those bar associations became mandatory. State supreme courts became increasingly interested in, and territorial over, the regulation of lawyers. One would expect the regulation of lawyers to move more into line with the wishes of bar associations during this period – and that was certainly the case.

Entry

The work of the ABA and other nascent bar associations paid immediate dividends on entry. By 1890, twenty-three of thirty-nine jurisdictions

[60] Dayton D. McKean, *The Integrated Bar* (Boston: Houghton Mifflin, 1963), 46–49; *In re Integration of State Bar of Oklahoma*, 95 P.2d 113 (Okla. 1939).

[61] McKean, *The Integrated Bar*, 49–50.

[62] Benjamin H. Barton, "An Institutional Analysis of Lawyer Regulation – Who Should Control Lawyer Regulation, Courts, Legislatures or the Market," 37 *Ga. L. Rev.*1167, 1208–09 (2003).

[63] Susan A. Martyn, "Lawyer Competence and Lawyer Discipline: Beyond the Bar?," 69 *Geo. L.J.* 705, 707 (1981); Nancy J. Moore, "The Usefulness of Ethical Codes," 1989 *Ann. Surv. Am. L.* 7, 14–16 (1989).

required a formal period of study or apprenticeship.[64] This period also marked a replacement of informal (and very easy) oral bar exams with written exams in many jurisdictions. By 1917, thirty-seven states had centralized boards of bar examiners to oversee written exams.[65]

Law schools also came into increased prominence. There were twenty-eight American law schools with 1,600 students in 1870. There were fifty-four schools with 6,000 students in 1890, and one hundred schools with 13,000 students by the turn of the twentieth century. In 1870, one-quarter of new bar admittees were law school graduates. By 1910, two-thirds were.[66]

The greatest tightening happened during the depression in the 1930s; by the 1940s, the modern system of bar admissions was basically in place. By the end of the 1930s, most states began to require some years of college in advance of law school, most states required graduation from an ABA-accredited law school (instead of apprenticeship), a set number of years (usually three) of law school, a formal character and fitness test, the elimination of the diploma privilege, and a harder, written bar exam run by a central authority under the unified bar or the state supreme court.[67]

In each of these moves the profession gained greater power over who became a lawyer and developed different ways to keep competitors out of the market. As Chapter 6 argues, barring entry to the profession and the prosecution of the unauthorized practice of law raises lawyer earnings by restricting the supply of legal services and eliminating cheaper replacement services.

Conduct

From the outset, the new bar associations were gravely concerned with what they considered to be the immoral element of the profession. The

[64] Stevens, *Law School*, 25.

[65] Kermit L. Hall, *The Magic Mirror: Law in American History* (New York: Oxford University Press, 1989), 215.

[66] Jerold S. Auerbach, *Unequal Justice* (New York: Oxford University Press, 1976), 94.

[67] Richard L. Abel, *American Lawyers* (New York: Oxford University Press, 1989), 40–73.

push to raise entry standards was often pitched as an effort to keep immoral lawyers out of the bar altogether. The ABA and other bar associations initially turned to the Canons of Legal Ethics to battle a new breed of lawyers who "believe themselves immune, the good or bad esteem of their co-laborers is nothing to them provided their itching fingers are not thereby stayed in their eager quest for lucre."[68] It is also interesting to note how the impetus for the canons changed over time. The original impetus for the creation of the canons was a speech by President Theodore Roosevelt (in full trustbusting mode) excoriating the legal profession as a tool of the very wealthy.[69] By 1906 the canons had morphed into a tool to battle the "increasing influx" of shysters.[70] Ironically, it was exactly these "shysters" who were most likely to come from immigrant or impoverished backgrounds; these same lawyers were also most likely to be plaintiffs' lawyers serving those populations.[71]

The ABA adopted the canons in 1908[72] and by 1914, the canons had been adopted by thirty-one of the forty-five state bar associations.[73] At first, the canons were nonenforceable and hortatory in nature, but they were sporadically cited by courts as persuasive authority.[74] As state bars became mandatory, the canons suddenly became an enforceable code of conduct for the state's licensing agency. The ABA and other bar associations reacted to the increasing enforceability of the canons in two now-familiar ways.

First, the ABA pursued extensive redrafting and retooling of the canons in pursuit of "additional guidance" to lawyers.[75] The controversial issues in this period were all over the suppression of competition: the

[68] 29 ABA Rep. 601–02 (1906).
[69] 28 ABA Rep. 380–89 (1905).
[70] 29 ABA Rep. 681 (1906).
[71] Auerbach, "Unequal Justice," 44–53.
[72] 31 ABA Rep. 55–85 (1908).
[73] 37 ABA Rep. 560–61 (1914).
[74] Barton, "The ABA, the Rules and Professionalism," 430–32.
[75] See 56 ABA Rep. 155–78 (1933) (stating that thirteen additional canons were adopted in 1928 as a "specific guide" to situations unforeseen in the drafting of the original canons); see also 51 ABA Rep. 130–31 (1928); 60 ABA Rep. 350–52, 761–67 (1937).

ABA debated at length about contingency fees, lawyer advertising, and the division of fees.[76]

Following the canons, the ABA took two more stabs at simplifying and clarifying its rules of conduct. In 1969, the ABA adopted the Code of Professional Responsibility.[77] The code formally divided the canons' hortatory material from the mandatory, and made the mandatory much clearer and more "black letter" in nature.[78] Throughout the twentieth century, bar associations sought to clarify and distill the minimum standards of lawyer conduct from the broader pronouncements within the canons. The code very consciously makes this distillation patent: the moral and ethical were physically placed in a separate category from the minimum rules. Thus, the code is the ABA's first explicit division between what would later come to be called "professionalism" and minimum rules: the disciplinary rules govern lawyer conduct, and the canons and ethical considerations are relegated to food for thought.

Next, the ABA decided to jettison the hortatory altogether and focus solely on the minimum rules in the Model Rules of Professional Conduct. The original draft of the rules included new rules limiting client confidentiality, requiring pro bono work, and new regulations of conflicts of interest. These new proposals were extremely controversial; the drafters presented successively milder versions until the approval of the final version in 1983.[79] The rules are now in effect (with some local modifications) in forty-eight states and the District of Columbia.[80] As such,

[76] Barton, "The ABA, the Rules and Professionalism," 430–33; Auerbach, *Unequal Justice*, 46–50.

[77] See ABA, "Association's House of Delegates Meets in Dallas, August 11–13," 55 *ABA J.* 970 (1969).

[78] Samuel J. Levine, "Taking Ethics Codes Seriously," 77 *Tul. L. Rev.* 527, 531 (2003).

[79] See Ted Schneyer, "Professionalism as Bar Politics: the Making of the Model Rules of Professional Conduct," 14 *L. & Soc. Inquiry* 677, 702–24 (1989).

[80] See Center for Professional Responsibility, "Dates of Adoption of the Model Rules of Professional Conduct," available at http://www.abanet.org/cpr/mrpc/alpha_states.html.

the ABA has a high level of control over lawyer conduct regulation and has spent the past one hundred years continuously refining and narrowing the rules.

Second, bar associations began to establish ethics committees to advise lawyers on following the canons.[81] From the outset, the work of these ethics committees was meant to bring clarity and specificity to the ethical duties of lawyers under the canons, and although their opinions were advisory and unofficial, they certainly had a strong influence.[82] These opinions are unusual in two respects: they were offered before the conduct had occurred or at least before the issues had been adjudicated (which means they were "advisory opinions") and were ex parte (nonadversarial). American law has a long-standing bias against advisory opinions and nonadversarial proceedings. Courts almost always want two sides to a dispute (to argue both sides of a problem), and courts also hate to handle problems before they become "ripe."

For comparison, consider a criminal court setting up a question line for potential criminals in which they could call up and get opinions ahead of time about the legality of their future conduct. Usually the burden on determining the legality of an action is on the individual and the courts will sort out the legality later. In lawyer regulation, however, the opposite is true. Lawyers can call ahead and get a written response approving their behavior. These opinions can be used in any subsequent disciplinary proceeding,[83] although neither disciplinary authorities nor courts are bound by those opinions.[84]

[81] The New York County Lawyers' Association (NYCLA) ethics committee started in 1912 and the ABA followed in 1913. See Ted Finman and Theodore Schneyer, "The Role of Bar Association Ethics Opinions in Regulating Lawyer Conduct: A Critique of the Work of the ABA Committee on Ethics and Professional Responsibility," 66 *UCLA L. Rev.* 67, 69 (1981) (same); 36 ABA Rep. 147 (1913).

[82] See Finman and Schneyer, "The Role of Bar Association Ethics Opinions in Regulating Lawyer Conduct," 83–88.

[83] Barton, "The ABA, The Rules, and Professionalism," 433–34.

[84] Peter A. Joy, "Making Ethics Opinions Meaningful: Toward More Effective Regulation of Lawyers' Conduct," 15 *Geo. J. Legal Ethics* 313, 314 (2002).

The bar's continual attention to the ease of compliance is based partly in the somewhat palatable goals of clarity and predictability, but it is also certainly motivated by self-interest. For example, the ABA drafted its most recent spate of changes with an explicit eye toward limiting the possible use of the rules in lawyer malpractice suits.[85]

The irony is that the effort to make compliance easier has done almost nothing to increase enforcement.[86] Lawyer disciplinary authorities are notoriously underfunded, and actual enforcement of anything beyond blatant violations of the rules is rare.[87]

Antitrust

In reading about bar association control over entry and conduct, one might wonder whether this behavior has raised any antitrust concerns. Should we not be concerned when a trade association has such significant control over the terms and conditions of a government-created monopoly such as a law license? Although bar associations have made some changes in response to antitrust law, the existence of a state action defense – in the form of state supreme courts claiming the exclusive right to regulate lawyers – has left the role of the bar in lawyer regulation largely beyond antitrust challenge.

Courts first applied antitrust law to other professions long before addressing the legal profession. In 1943, the Supreme Court applied the Sherman Antitrust Act to a doctor-run price-fixing scheme in *American Medical Association v. United States*.[88] This holding rejected an earlier

[85] Id. at 439 and n. 106.

[86] Deborah L. Rhode, *In the Interests of Justice: Reforming the Legal Profession* (New York: Oxford University Press, 2000), 158–61 (describing infrequency and general leniency of bar sanctions).

[87] The ABA itself has concluded that attorney discipline is, and always has been, a neglected area; its research shows that the public thinks attorney discipline is "too slow, too secret, too soft and too self-regulated." ABA Commission on Evaluation of Disciplinary Enforcement, *Lawyer Regulation for a New Century* (Chicago: American Bar Association, 1992), 12–16.

[88] *American Medical Association v. United States,* 317 U.S. 519 (1943).

understanding that professionals were not engaged in commerce under the Sherman Act.[89]

It was another thirty-two years until the Supreme Court addressed lawyer price-fixing in *Goldfarb v. Virginia State Bar*.[90] In *Goldfarb* the Court addressed a fee schedule promulgated by a state and county bar. The lower court held that the bar associations were organs of the state and therefore the fee schedules were protected by the state action doctrine, which immunizes any direct government action from antitrust review. The Supreme Court noted that the Supreme Court of Virginia had not ordered fee schedules and that the bar was essentially acting on its own in setting and enforcing fee schedules.[91] The Court made sure to note, however, that "in some instances the State may decide that forms of competition usual in the business world may be demoralizing to the ethical standards of a profession" and that the "interest of the States in regulating lawyers is especially great since lawyers are essential to the primary governmental function of administering justice, and have historically been 'officers of the courts.'"[92]

On its face, *Goldfarb* appears to be an opinion that strongly checks bar association authority. *Goldfarb* is one of the very first cases that opponents of the lawyer–judge bias regularly mention as evidence that courts do not favor lawyers. Nevertheless, *Goldfarb* has proven to be a remarkably weak case. Although it does grudgingly hold that the practice of law is subject to antitrust review, that is a point that should have been obvious from *American Medical Association v. United States*, from 1943.

Moreover, the key limiting factor in the *Goldfarb* decision was the lack of state action protection because the bar acted outside the Virginia

[89] See *FTC v. Raladam Co.*, 283 U.S. 643, 653 (1931) (medical practitioners "follow a profession and not a trade"); *Federal Baseball Club v. National League of Professional Baseball Clubs*, 259 U.S. 200, 209 (1922) (lawyers arguing cases are not engaged in commerce).

[90] *Goldfarb v. Virginia State Bar*, 421 U.S. 773 (1975).

[91] Id. at 773, 788–92 (1975).

[92] Id. at 792.

Supreme Court's grant of authority. Later cases alleging antitrust violations have foundered on this exact point. For example, in *Hoover v. Ronwin,* an unsuccessful bar applicant sued the Arizona Supreme Court's Committee on Examinations and Admissions under the Sherman Act.[93] The argument was that the bar exam was an effort by the bar association to limit competition. The Committee on Examinations and Admissions was made up of seven members of the state bar selected by the court from a list supplied by the Arizona State Bar Association's board of governors.[94] Thus, the decision-making structure was somewhat similar to the structure found to be non-state action in *Goldfarb* – the state supreme court delegated substantial authority to an arm of the bar association. In fact, the U.S. Court of Appeals for the Ninth Circuit held exactly this in denying state action protection in the same case.[95] Nevertheless, the Supreme Court found state action and held that the bar admission machinery did not violate the Sherman Act.[96]

Following this case, other attempts to curb ABA or state bar action through antitrust suits have been defeated by the state action defense. For example, in *Lawline v. American Bar Association,* the petitioner sued the ABA over the Model Rules barring lawyers from joining in partnerships with nonlawyers and the prohibition on lawyers assisting in the unauthorized practice of law. The plaintiffs argued that the ABA drafted these rules, the Supreme Court of Illinois adopted them basically verbatim, and the rules violated the Sherman Act. The U.S. Court of Appeals for the Seventh Circuit held that the plaintiff's harm was a result of the actions of the Illinois Supreme Court, not the ABA, found state action, and dismissed the case.[97]

Likewise, in *Massachusetts School of Law v. ABA,* an unaccredited law school sued the ABA over its accreditation standards and the fact that unaccredited schools were at a disadvantage because their graduates

[93] *Hoover v. Ronwin*, 466 U.S. 558 (1984).
[94] Id. at 586 (Stevens, J., dissenting).
[95] *Ronwin v. State Bar of Arizona*, 686 F.2d 692, 696–97 (9th Cir. 1982).
[96] *Hoover*, 466 U.S. at 568–74.
[97] *Lawline v. American Bar Association*, 956 F.2d 1378, 1383–85 (7th Cir. 1992).

could not become lawyers in almost every American state, including Massachusetts. The U.S. Court of Appeals for the Second Circuit cited *Hoover* and *Lawline* and found state action because the Massachusetts Supreme Court itself made the decision to allow only graduates of ABA accredited schools to sit for the bar, not the ABA.[98]

Following the *Massachusetts School of Law* case, the Department of Justice filed a case against the ABA for its law school accreditation practices. This case was later settled pursuant to a consent decree.[99] The consent decree limited the ABA's ability to set floors on the salary of professors, but otherwise left most ABA practices untouched. In the spring of 2006, the Department of Justice argued that the ABA had violated multiple parts of the consent decree. In a stipulation, the ABA acknowledged the violations and agreed to reimburse the United States $185,000 in fees and costs incurred in the department's investigation. Notwithstanding the violations, the department allowed the settlement decree to expire in 2007.[100]

In sum, *Goldfarb* has basically become a price-fixing case, not a case that generally holds the regulation of lawyers up to antitrust scrutiny. In fact, the later cases have consistently applied the state action defense (or settled on favorable terms), leaving the great bulk of bar association activity in the category of protected state action.

Some Conclusions

What conclusions can be drawn from the history of lawyer regulation? Lawyers covet the opportunity to govern themselves. The best way to

[98] *Massachusetts School of Law at Andover, Inc. v. American Bar Association*, 107 F.3d 1026, 1035–37 (3rd Cir. 1997); see also *Staver v. American Bar Association*, 169 F. Supp. 2d 1372, 1380 n. 7 (M.D. Fla. 2001) (denying an injunction against the ABA for failing to accredit Barry Law School and citing to *Massachusetts School of Law*).

[99] *United States v. ABA*, 934 F. Supp. 435 (D.D.C. 1996). The settlement involved Justice Department and ABA lawyers, not the judge. Nevertheless, the settlement terms certainly reflected those lawyers' best guess at how the suit might end.

[100] Thomas O. Barnett, "Interoperability Between Antitrust and Intellectual Property," 14 *Geo. Mason L. Rev.* 859, 869 (2007).

accomplish this goal is to convince judges to take over the regulation. Since the late nineteenth century, lawyers have relentlessly lobbied state supreme courts to take over their regulation, and these courts have been quite receptive. Judges will go to some lengths to claim power over the legal profession, even invalidating legislation with which they otherwise agree. Last, when judges are later tasked with deciding whether lawyer regulation violates antitrust principles, those judges are loath to find any violations.

One would guess that the level of self-regulation reached by lawyers would be unlikely to benefit the public. Chapter 6 demonstrates that this is indeed the case.

6 Current Lawyer Regulation

> People of the same trade seldom meet together, even for merriment or diversion, but the conversation ends in a conspiracy against the public, or in some contrivance to raise prices.
>
> – Adam Smith[1]

AMERICAN LAWYERS HAVE A UNIQUE REGULATORY STRUCTURE. Every other profession – from cosmetology to medicine – is regulated in the first instance by state or federal legislatures.[2] State legislatures generally set up regulatory agencies for each licensed profession, although the efficacy of these agencies is a subject of some debate.[3] Moreover, as predicted by public choice theory, each regulated profession often dominates its state board. This is partly because each board needs "experts" to help with regulation and those experts naturally come from the profession itself, and partly because each profession lobbies the legislature and the board for as much control as possible.

That said, at least every other American profession must push its policies and regulation through a legislature made up of members who

[1] Adam Smith, *The Wealth of Nations* (Amherst, NY: Prometheus Books, 1991), 137.

[2] S. David Young, *The Rule of Experts: Occupational Licensing in America* (Washington, DC: Cato Institute, 1987).

[3] See id. for a rather negative take. See Eliot Friedson, *Professionalism Reborn: Theory, Prophecy, and Policy* (Chicago: University of Chicago Press, 1994) for a more sanguine take on "professionalism" and regulation.

generally practice another profession (ironically, many state legislators are lawyers). As such, state legislatures serve as a check on the other professions. If any profession overreaches or the regulation grows too self-interested, the state legislature can always jump in. The recent history of tightened regulation of the medical profession on the federal and state level is instructive.[4]

Why Judges Are a Poor Choice to Regulate Lawyers

Remember the discussion of public choice theory in Chapter 2 – all industries seek helpful government regulation, and professions are no different. For purposes of our analysis, the key insight is not that regulation will tend to favor the regulated over the public – that is axiomatic. The critical point is that the choice of a governing institution can affect the equilibrium between the narrow professional interest and the public interest. If the public can influence an institution more easily and cheaply, the equilibrium shifts in favor of the public. Likewise, as industry costs of purchasing regulation rise, more public-minded legislation should result. If the government entity makes public input particularly difficult, however, the equilibrium shifts in favor of the narrow interests.

There are institutional, personal, and political reasons that courts are a poor choice for regulatory authority over lawyers. At first blush, one would assume that judges would have the advantage of immunity to lobbying. Our paradigm of judicial integrity naturally assumes that judges and courts are independent of external influences.[5] Nevertheless, when regulating lawyers, state supreme courts act as *legislators*, not

[4] See, e.g., Clark J. Lee, "Federal Regulation of Hospital Resident Work Hours: Enforcement with Real Teeth," 9 *J. Health Care L. & Pol'y* 162 (2006).

[5] See, e.g., Symposium, "Judicial Independence and Accountability Symposium," 72 *S. Cal. L. Rev.* 311 (1999). In fact, even typically skeptical public choice scholars have preferred judicial decision makers to legislative ones, because theoretically the judiciary is less likely to be swayed or lobbied by interest groups. Einer R. Elhauge, "Does Interest Group Theory Justify More Intrusive Review?," 101 *Yale L.J.* 31, 44–48 (1991).

adjudicators,[6] and are hardly independent in that role. In fact, state supreme courts are uniquely vulnerable to lobbying by lawyers.

As noted in Chapter 2, all state supreme court justices are former lawyers, which usually means that they view the legal system and lawyer regulation from a lawyer's point of view. Most state supreme court justices are also elected and count on lawyers for donations and political support.

Finally, even though justices are not open to lobbying in the traditional sense (paid lobbyists or nonprofits entreating them on a particular issue), they are very open to informal lawyer lobbying – at bar association meetings, at conferences in chambers, by their clerks, or simply at social gatherings with their current and former colleagues, partners, or associates. Lawyers and bar associations have a high level of access to and influence over justices. The interests, social status, and thought processes of the judiciary and lawyers substantially dovetail.

Although state supreme courts are quite susceptible to lawyer and bar association lobbying, they are particularly inaccessible to lobbying by the public. As a logistical matter, courts are not set up to be lobbied.[7] The public cannot stop at a justice's chambers to complain about lawyer regulation. Justices do not have large staffs to respond to constituent complaints or lobbying. Courts are organized to minimize the effect of public opinion and lobbying on judges.

Moreover, courts have a "new institutional" aversion to lobbying. Recurrent calls for judicial independence have a powerful effect on the

[6] None of the hallmarks of adjudication is present in state supreme courts' regulation of lawyers. There is no case or controversy, presumably any interested party has standing, and the court is free to adopt any rule, regardless of breadth or precedent. In fact, in ruling on the Wisconsin Supreme Court's decision to create a unified bar by court order, the U.S. Supreme Court held that the act was legislative – not judicial – in character. See *Lathrop v. Donahue*, 367 U.S. 820, 824–25 (1961).

[7] See *United States v. Grace*, 461 U.S. 171, 183 (1983) (remarking that courts "are not subject to lobbying, judges do not entertain visitors in their chambers for the purpose of urging that cases be resolved one way or another, and they do not and should not respond to parades, picketing or pressure groups").

way in which justices view their institutional roles and jobs. For the great bulk of a state supreme court justice's work, immunity from public opinion and lobbying is laudable. When courts regulate lawyers, however, this immunity becomes problematic.

Even if state supreme courts were more open to lobbying, however, there is a substantial difficulty of public ignorance and apathy about state supreme courts and lawyer regulation. Transaction costs and the expense of public education on the issues contribute substantially to the power of interest groups in the political system. Thus, the deeper the ignorance about the nature and role of the government body involved, the steeper the cost of organizing the public. Most voters do not know the names of their state supreme court justices or that justices regulate the legal profession.[8] The programs that evaluate judicial performance before elections (presumably for the benefit of the voters) wholly ignore the judicial role in lawyer regulation.[9] Thus, even in the occasional high-salience judicial election, lawyer regulation is not an issue. In general, most people tend to think that bar associations control lawyer discipline[10] and do not connect lawyer regulation to state supreme courts.

Ironically, even if these barriers could be overcome, it would still prove difficult to vote an offending justice out over lawyer regulation. Judicial elections focus on a justice's abilities as a judge, not as a regulator of lawyers. Because judging is the great bulk of any justice's job, this voting strategy makes perfect sense. The lack of state supreme court accountability for lawyer regulation makes the problems associated with public choice theory particularly acute, because the only real public

[8] Deborah L. Rhode, *In the Interests of Justice: Reforming the Legal Profession* (Oxford: Oxford University Press, 2000), 158–65.

[9] See Arizona Commission on Judicial Performance Review, *Voter Information Guide* (Phoenix: State of Arizona, 2000).

[10] In many cases, of course, they are right. In multiple states, the supreme court has delegated all or most of the regulation of lawyers to bar associations.

check on the power of interest groups is the power to vote an offending legislator out of office.

A short travelogue of the steps a citizen would need to take to alter lawyer regulation helps elucidate the multiple hurdles involved in any lobbying effort. Consider, for example, the necessary steps for a group of citizens seeking to raise the rate of disbarments for unethical lawyer conduct.[11]

In a unified-bar state, the group would have to appeal to the state bar association. The state bar association is unlikely to support any measures that disbar more lawyers; lawyers already view the disciplinary system skeptically. The group could take its complaint to the state supreme court, although it is difficult to imagine how the group would gain access. As noted above, state supreme courts are purposefully designed to avoid the possibility of lobbying by disgruntled citizens.[12]

Even if the group could attract the supreme court's attention, the odds of the supreme court bucking the bar association are slim, as evinced by the current state of lawyer regulation and bar discipline. If the state supreme court did not overrule the bar association's decision, it would be extremely difficult for the citizen group to punish the supreme court justices. If the justices are appointed, their removal would require impeachment proceedings – a nearly impossible task. If they are elected, the group would have to organize an opposition campaign. The campaign would likely flounder because it would require substantial voter education about the role of state supreme courts, as well as education on the state of lawyer discipline. Even with an educated electorate, voters

[11] This topic will be covered in greater detail later, but note that disciplinary authorities routinely dismiss up to 90 percent of complaints with no formal investigation and fewer than 2 percent of complaints result in any public discipline at all, let alone disbarment. Rhode, *In the Interests of Justice*, 159–60.

[12] Alternatively, the citizens could complain to the state legislature. State legislative control over the legal profession is circumscribed by the inherent authority doctrine, but it is more likely that a state supreme court justice would listen to a state legislator than to a group of concerned citizens.

presumably vote for justices first and foremost on the basis of their abilities as judges, not as regulators. In comparison, a complaint to the legislature is a more straightforward process.

Courts are also not natural legislators. It cuts against the grain of their institutional mission and self-image. Courts consider themselves mainly interpreters of the law, not policy makers. Nearly every supreme court shrinks (at least in judicial opinions) from the bugaboo of "judicial legislating."[13] It is difficult for justices to alter their mindset of being simple adjudicators narrowly deciding disputes. Furthermore, whatever policies or interpretations courts do produce tend to occur piecemeal, in small incremental steps, constrained by stare decisis. Judges are thus unused to crafting broad new programs or approaching societal problems from a policy-making perspective.

Membership on supreme courts also turns over much more slowly than in other government bodies, allowing great institutional consistency. Courts are, therefore, a uniquely conservative (in the nonpartisan sense) institution. Although this institutional conservatism has numerous advantages to a judicial body, it hampers adaptability in policy making.

Moreover, there is no reason to believe that judges will make particularly good legislators. State supreme court justices are selected or elected because of their abilities as judges, not as attorney regulators. There is nothing in the selection process for judges that suggests that they will be natural administrators of lawyer regulation.[14]

[13] See, e.g., *Jewish Home and Infirmary of Rochester, New York, Inc. v. Commissioner of New York State Department of Health*, 640 N.E.2d 125, 130 (N.Y. 1994) (eschewing an invitation to "the forbidden realm of judicial legislating"); *Rose v. Council for Better Education*, 790 S.W.2d 186, 211 (Ky. 1989) ("[W]e do not engage in judicial legislating. We do not make policy. We do not substitute our judgment for that of the General Assembly."); *Lanier v. State*, 635 So. 2d 813, 819 (Miss. 1994) (refusing to "engage in judicial legislating in order to circumvent the statutory scheme"); and *Phillips v. Duro-Last Roofing, Inc.*, 806 P.2d 834, 836–37 (Wyo. 1991) (avoiding the opportunity to "engage in comprehensive judicial legislating").

[14] Cynical readers may wonder whether any of our legislators are selected for their legislative abilities.

State supreme courts are also very busy. Much has been made about the "caseload crisis" in the federal and state courts, including state appellate courts.[15] State supreme courts are relatively small and cannot grow because of logistical and constitutional concerns. Given that judges are faced with a scarcity of resources and a desire for a modicum of leisure, something has to give. Justices are naturally reluctant to forgo their responsibilities as judges, so the abdication of their regulatory responsibilities is a convenient solution. This is especially so because state supreme courts approach the task of regulating lawyers with little joy or alacrity.[16] Few, if any, state supreme court justices pursued their position to regulate attorneys. In practice, state supreme courts tend to treat lawyer regulation the way that trial courts treat discovery disputes – as a less palatable aspect of the job.

Therefore, we would expect supreme courts to delegate as much of their authority over lawyer regulation as they can, to preserve leisure and to maximize the time and energy they have to spend on their primary job – deciding cases. The degree of delegation depends on the consequences of overdelegation. The public has limited opportunities to punish justices for overdelegation – but lawyers are well organized, care greatly, and have significant chances to punish judges. Thus, we would expect state supreme courts to delegate as much authority as they can without upsetting lawyers.

In practice, this has been exactly the outcome. State supreme courts have satisfied their own and lawyers' interests by delegating virtually all their regulatory authority under the vaunted system of "lawyer self-regulation." This delegation kills two birds with one stone: state supreme courts maximize delegation and please the only players who care,

[15] See, e.g., Richard A. Posner, *The Federal Courts: Crisis And Reform*, 2nd ed. (Cambridge, MA: Harvard University Press, 1999), 53–124; ABA Committee on Standards of Judicial Administration, *Standards Relating to Appellate Delay Reduction* (Chicago: American Bar Association, 1988), 11.

[16] Charles W. Wolfram, *Legal Ethics* (St. Paul, MN: West Publishing, 1986), 37 ("The relationship between the unified bar and the court that has often created it is sometimes that of unruly offspring and compliant parent.").

lawyers. Lawyers are happy because they maximize their control (or capture to use a more loaded term) over their regulation. The ultimate example of this phenomenon is the unified bar: state supreme courts literally delegate almost all their regulatory authority back to lawyers. A more universal example is state supreme court reliance on the ABA to draft the rules that govern lawyer behavior.

A comparison between two different areas of lawyer regulation, one that lawyers care about and one that they do not, demonstrates this bias in practice. First, consider entry barriers. From the late nineteenth century, bar associations have lobbied relentlessly for higher entry barriers. These efforts have proven enormously successful, and entry is now guarded by well-oiled machines and multiple and growing requirements.

In comparison, attorney discipline is a low priority for bar associations, for obvious reasons. The ABA itself, among others, has determined that attorney discipline is and always has been a neglected area.[17] Attorney discipline is underfunded.[18] There are backlogs for investigations.[19] In most states the process is secret.[20] Up to 90 percent of the complaints are summarily dismissed, partly because many complaints are over fee disputes or "mere negligence" that is not generally covered by the Model Rules of Professional Conduct.[21] The comparison shows how the regulatory preferences of lawyers are well reflected in the actual processes.

State legislatures have few of these difficulties. Although state legislators would certainly bend to lawyer lobbying, there is no reason

[17] Rhode, *In the Interests of Justice*, 158–65.

[18] Susan P. Koniak and George M. Cohen, "Under Cloak of Settlement," 82 *Va. L. Rev.* 1051, 1121 (1996).

[19] See Lisa J. Frisella et al., "State Bar of California," 17 *Cal. Reg. L. Rep.* 203, 205 (2000) ("In his initial February 1999 report, Justice Lui reported that the Bar's discipline system faces an unprecedented backlog of over 7,000 open complaints and reports against attorneys from consumers and courts.").

[20] John P. Sahl, "The Public Hazard of Lawyer Self-Regulation: Learning from Ohio's Struggle to Reform its Disciplinary System," 68 *U. Cin. L. Rev.* 65, 108 (1999).

[21] Rhode, *In the Interests of Justice*, 159–60.

to believe that legislators would favor lawyers over any other group. Nationally, only about 15 percent of state legislators are lawyers.[22] Lawyers are not particularly popular with the public or most legislatures. Law reviews, bar publications, and newspapers are filled with anecdotal and statistical evidence displaying the public's low esteem for the legal profession, and politicians have responded to those sentiments.[23] Insofar as legislators are responsive to their constituents, lawyers would have a more difficult time obtaining preferential legislation.

State legislatures have, in fact, passed or proposed a number of lawyer-unfriendly statutes. These include Texas's passage of a sunset provision for the Texas state bar,[24] Arizona's repeal of its statutes regarding unauthorized practice of law,[25] Kentucky's move to allow nonlawyers to practice before administrative agencies,[26] Virginia's decision to allow nonlawyers to perform real estate closings,[27] Florida's and Michigan's consideration of a move to legislative regulatory control,[28] and the California legislature's continuing tussles with the state bar.[29]

[22] National Conference of State Legislatures, *State Legislators' Occupations* (Washington, DC: National Conference of State Legislators, 1996), 11.

[23] Consider the advice of political consultants that "[i]t's almost impossible to go too far when it comes to demonizing lawyers." See Luntz Research Companies, *Language of the 21st Century* (Alexandria, VA: Luntz Research Co., 1997), 128.

[24] Charles Aycock, "President's Opinion," 63 *Tex. B.J.* 430 (2000).

[25] Jonathan Rose, "Unauthorized Practice of Law in Arizona: A Legal and Political Problem That Won't Go Away," 34 *Ariz. St. L.J.* 585 (2002).

[26] The statute was ruled unconstitutional by the Kentucky Supreme Court in *Turner v. Kentucky Bar Association*, 980 S.W.2d 560 (Ky. 1998).

[27] This statute was also ruled unconstitutional in *Fears v. Virginia State Bar*, 2000 WL 249247 (Va. Cir. Ct. Mar. 1, 2000).

[28] In 1996 members of the Florida state legislature proposed removing regulation of the bar from the Florida Supreme Court. See John A. Devault, "First, Let's Put the Lawyers Under the Legislature," *Fla. B. J.*, January 1996, at 8; F. Raymond Marks and Darlene Cathcart, "Discipline Within the Legal Profession: Is It Self-Regulation?," 1974 *U. Ill. L.F.* 193, 194 (1974) (noting the introduction of a bill in the Michigan legislature for lay control of the bar, and the defeat of this effort by the bar association and the state supreme court).

[29] Tamara Hall, "Senate Bill 1413: The Answer to Senate Bill 60 Plebiscite and Its Constitutionality Under the Inherent Powers Doctrine," 27 *Golden Gate U. L. Rev.* 601

In short, state supreme courts have some major difficulties as lawyer regulators.[30] These weaknesses have resulted in entry and conduct regulation that greatly favors the legal profession.

Entry: High Costs, Few Benefits

Both lawyers and justices have powerful reasons to favor inflated entry standards to the profession. Raising entry barriers has been the sine qua non of the formation of modern bar associations and lawyer lobbying. Lawyers, of course, have an excellent reason to favor higher entry standards: they decrease the supply of lawyers and raise the price for legal services. Barriers to entry, such as the bar requirements, naturally result in fewer practitioners, greater demand for existing lawyers, and higher prices. The amount of extra expense is determined by the availability of substitute goods. If a consumer can substitute a nonregulated product for legal services, regardless of barriers to entry, price inflation will be dampened. Prohibitions on the unauthorized practice of law, however, explicitly ban any substitute goods.

The higher prices are a windfall for the current members of the profession. They enjoy the higher prices without having to meet the new, higher standards because they are "grandfathered" in.[31] This explains why every complaint about *current* practitioners is solved by a burden on *future* practitioners.[32] Consider the growing use of the Multistate

(1997) (describing one legislative effort to eliminate California's unified bar); Frisella, "State Bar of California," 203–05.

[30] A full institutional analysis of the strengths and weaknesses of state supreme courts would need a comparison to every other possible venue, including federal legislative action, U.S. Supreme Court control, deregulation, and so on. I lay out my version of that comparison in Benjamin H. Barton, "An Institutional Analysis of Lawyer Regulation – Who Should Control Lawyer Regulation, Courts, Legislatures, or the Market?," 37 *Ga. L. Rev.* 1167-1250 (2003).

[31] Simon Rottenberg, "Introduction," in *Occupational Licensure and Regulation*, ed. Simon Rottenberg (Washington, DC: American Enterprise Institute, 1980), 5.

[32] This also explains why any occupation will fight deregulation tooth and nail. If the entry barriers were suddenly dropped altogether, the existing practitioners could not recoup their own investment in passing the entry regulations.

Professional Responsibility Examination (MPRE) as a response to claims of unethical lawyers. The original bar associations' drive to establish the bar examination and extensive legal education as a response to perceived lawyer incompetence or the current uptick in bar failure rates are also examples.[33]

In each of these cases, the stated problem is current practitioners who are allegedly unethical or incompetent. The obvious regulatory solution to a problem with current practitioners is regulation aimed at the incompetent or the unethical in the form of conduct regulation, disbarment, or other sanctions. These moves would be unpopular, however, so the burden is shifted to new applicants.

Although rising entry standards have multiple benefits to lawyers, there is little evidence that the benefit to consumers is equivalent to the higher cost of services. Despite the bar exam and legal education requirements, there are continuing questions about the competency of the bar.[34] Consider, for example, the increase in legal malpractice claims since the 1980s.[35]

Perhaps the most damning evidence of the efficacy of the bar exam is a consideration of the skills of the newest members of the bar. What legal tasks, if any, can we guarantee that a newly admitted lawyer can perform? Without further training or experience, most would shudder to imagine this newly minted lawyer immediately trying a case or drafting a complex contract. This failing alone casts serious doubts on the utility of current entry regulations. Even after a minimum of three years of college, three more years of law school, a two-to-three-day bar examination,

[33] As of 2001, "the percentage of test takers passing the bar has dropped sharply since 1994." Deborah J. Merritt et al., "Raising the Bar: A Social Science Critique of Recent Increases to Passing Scores on the Bar Exam," 69 *U. Cinc. L. Rev.* 929, 929 (2001).

[34] See Lorenzo A. Trujillo, "The Relationship Between Law School and the Bar Exam: A Look at Assessment and Student Success," 78 *U. Colo. L. Rev.* 69, 80–81 (2007); Warren E. Burger, "The Special Skills of Advocacy: Are Specialized Training and Certification of Advocates Essential to Our System of Justice?," 42 *Fordham L. Rev.* 227, 234 (1973) ("One-third to one-half of the lawyers who appear in serious cases are not really qualified.").

[35] ABA Standing Committee on Lawyers' Professional Liability, *Profile of Legal Malpractice Claims: 2000–2003* (Chicago: American Bar Association, 2005), 16.

the MPRE, and the character and fitness process, there are few concrete skills that new members of the bar are guaranteed to have, nor is there any guarantee that these same lawyers will gain any or all of those skills on their own with the passage of time or that the lawyers will not lose what little they knew when they passed the bar during their careers as licensed attorneys.

The irony, of course, is that the bar examination is actually quite difficult. Even students who have completed the requisite years of prelegal and legal education frequently fail the bar. The relative difficulty of the bar examination, in comparison with the paucity of actual skills that it guarantees, suggests that the exam is designed more to limit the number of lawyers than to guarantee any set level of competence – in other words, the entry regulations are set to limit competition with existing lawyers rather than to protect the public.

Stifling Innovation

Having strict guidelines for legal education and the bar examination regiments the training for the profession in a way that is sure to cramp technological, philosophical, or pedagogical evolution. With few exceptions, anyone who wants to be a lawyer in America must attend an ABA-accredited law school as a precursor to taking the bar exam and gaining a license. The ABA accreditation standards are complex, are very specific, and require attendance at a particular type of law school.[36]

This means that any large-scale changes to legal education must go through the ABA – and there have been few changes. Most American law schools are remarkably alike.[37] We teach a similar first-year curriculum, we hire similar-looking candidates to become professors, and we

[36] See ABA Section of Legal Education & Admissions to the Bar, *Standards for Approval of Law School*, available at http://www.abanet.org/legaled/standards/standards.html. The AALS, a voluntary association of law schools, has another equally complex set of membership standards. AALS, *AALS Handbook: Membership Requirements*, available at http://www.aals.org/about_handbook_requirements.php.

[37] See Susan Sturm and Lani Guinier, "The Law School Matrix: Reforming Legal Education in a Culture of Competition and Conformity," 60 *Vand. L. Rev.* 515 (2007).

model our classes on the courses we ourselves took in law school. In fact, given the massive changes in the country as a whole since the late nineteenth century, it is striking how comparable current law schools are to the Harvard Law School of the 1870s.[38]

The sameness of legal education makes a lot of sense for most of the players involved. It makes sense for law professors because innovation is hard and, at times, painful. It makes sense for law schools and universities because the traditional case law method is relatively inexpensive. A bare-bones law school is inexpensive to staff and run. As a result, many universities are able to make money on their law schools (which is not true of many other graduate programs).[39] The universities and law faculties work with the ABA and the Association of American Law Schools (AALS) to create detailed standards that limit variation or innovation within law schools.

This benefits existing or current lawyers because law school is long, expensive, and hard. When the students graduate, they are not prepared to practice right away, which means less competition for existing lawyers. It is hard to imagine a system that is harder or more expensive to circumnavigate than lawyer entry, while still so ill-preparing its students for their future careers.

Thus, the system works great for all the players except for the students. A colleague once quipped, "It works out great. No one suffers but the students, and they're used to it!" The students, however, have no choice but to go to law school if they want to be attorneys.

Compare law school to business school. No one *needs* to go to business school. Many businesspeople will even advise students against going to business school if they can avoid it.[40] If a student can get a good job without an MBA, he of she should skip the investment in time and money. Moreover, no business in particular has to hire MBAs. If an

[38] See Robert W. Gordon, "The Geologic Strata of the Law School Curriculum," 60 *Vand. L. Rev.* 339 (2007).

[39] See George Anastaplo, "Legal Education, Economics, and Law School Governance: Explorations," 46 *S.D. L. Rev.* 102 (2001).

[40] Louise Story, "Bye Bye B-School," *New York Times*, September 16, 2007, at F1.

MBA is seen as valueless, businesses can always hire economists, college graduates, or whomever they want.

Accordingly, business schools are very responsive to both sides of their customer base: they work hard to make the education worth it to the students who enroll, and they work hard to ensure that their graduates offer significant value to employers.[41] MBA programs must justify their existence to both students and employers; this fact alone makes them more innovative and focused on necessary business skills.[42] Law schools, though, are protected by the licensing requirement and are comparatively hidebound and nonresponsive.

Negative Effects on the Poor and Middle Class

The combination of a limited number of practitioners and the very high costs associated with becoming licensed means that an entire price

[41] A brief aside: Over the years, my law school has had a variety of budget difficulties. During one of these stretches we went to speak to the business school about its relatively superior budget position. The business school's administrators mentioned the school's very successful and lucrative Center for Executive Administrative Education as a significant revenue source. The center's motto is "proven results faster" and it features various short, but expensive, executive training programs. The business school professors wondered whether there was anything similar we offered at the law school.

In thinking about whether we could create some kind of high-level program for our alumni, I came to the conclusion that law schools have little to sell that is comparable with what business schools sell. In fact, when I thought about it, law schools have a better chance of getting our alumni to pay us *not* to teach them what we teach the law students than the other way around.

[42] The accreditation standards for the Association to Advance Collegiate Schools of Business (AACSB) are much more flexible and focused on each school's individual mission. See AACSB, "Accreditation," available at http://www.aacsb.edu/accreditation/ (noting "mission-linked accreditation standards"); AACSB, "Accreditation standards," available at http://www.aacsb.edu/accreditation/business/std_faq5.asp (stating that AACSB standards encourage innovation and "are quite flexible in the construction of both content and delivery of education programs"). For an overview of the "mission linked" accreditation method, see Robert H. Jansen and James A. Yunker, "AACSB Mission-Linked Standards: Effects on the Accreditation Process: Doing Things the Hard Way – Problems with Mission-Linked AACSB Accreditation Standards and Suggestions for Improvement," 75 *J. Ed. Bus.* 343 (2000).

category of the market – the less expensive category – is eliminated. This means that consumers who would prefer cheaper services, but can afford to pay more, must either spend more than they would like on legal representation or go without it. There is evidence of a great unmet demand for legal services for the middle class.[43]

Those who cannot afford to pay the cost for the higher-quality product must either go without or receive subsidized services. Both pro bono legal services and LSCs aim to meet this demand, but they are drops in the bucket.[44] Ironically, high entry standards have historically had a substantial negative impact on the number of poor, female, or minority lawyers.[45] Thus, the poor face two barriers to legal representation: they face substantial barriers to becoming lawyers and too often cannot afford services in the open market.

In presenting this argument, I have sometimes heard gasps from audiences accompanied by the following question: "Are you suggesting that there are *too few lawyers*?" What I am suggesting is that there are both too many and too few lawyers. There are too many lawyers chasing the most remunerative work, as defense counsel for corporations or wealthy individuals and as plaintiffs' attorneys for injured consumers or stockholders. There are too few lawyers willing to do everything else.

Of course, an easy solution would be to deregulate big chunks of the legal system, such as divorce, custody disputes, landlord–tenant litigation, and small claims and make those systems so easy that a lawyer would be superfluous. The United Kingdom has recently launched a major deregulation of its legal profession along these exact lines.[46]

[43] See George C. Harris and Derek F. Foran, "The Ethics of Middle-Class Access to Legal Services and What We Can Learn from the Medical Profession's Shift to a Corporate Paradigm," 70 *Fordham L. Rev.* 775 (2001).

[44] See Deborah L. Rhode, "Access to Justice: Again, Still," 73 *Fordham L. Rev.* 1013 (2004). LSCs were discussed more fully in Chapter 4.

[45] See Daria Roithmayer, "Barriers to Entry: A Market Lock-In Model of Discrimination," 86 *Va. L. Rev.* 759 (2000).

[46] Robert Denney, "What's Hot and What's Not in the Legal Profession," *Law Practice*, January/February 2005, 13.

American lawyers have always battled these sorts of reforms for obvious reasons;[47] these systems remain designed primarily for the benefit of the lawyers and judges, regardless of the effect on the public. In particular, the situation for poor people seeking divorces is scandalous.[48]

Brutal Costs for Entrants

Although some prospective lawyers might choose to pursue four years of college and three years of law school even if it were not required, it is very unlikely that all would. These educational requirements cost students in both tuition and lost income while in school. The amount of post-law school student debt is at an all-time high.[49] The bar exam itself imposes substantial costs. Most students take an additional bar examination preparatory course. Given the lengthy educational requirements, the students who fail are unlikely to give up; because the exam is generally offered only every six months, however, another period of underemployment or unemployment ensues pending the next bar exam. The unfortunate students who never pass have paid a small fortune for a nonexistent credential.

Regardless of the damage to the consumers, though, these market distortions have a significant cost to the profession itself. On the front end, potential students' impression that all lawyers work at corporate law firms or are millionaire plaintiffs' lawyers draws in individuals who would otherwise choose other pursuits, just for the hope of the high earnings. On the back end, once these students graduate from law school, the costs they have incurred along the way guarantee that many are forced to consider salary first and career and personal satisfaction second.[50]

[47] See Deborah L. Rhode, *Access to Justice* (New York: Oxford University Press, 2004).

[48] See Carolyn D. Schwartz, "Pro Se Divorce Litigants," 42 *Family Court Rev.* 655 (2004).

[49] See John A. Sebert, "The Cost and Financing of Legal Education," 52 *J. Legal Educ.* 516 (2002).

[50] See Edward Rubin, "Should Law Schools Support Faculty Research?," 17 *J. L. & Contemp. Legal Issues* 139, 146–47 and n. 18 (2008). Some have argued that the artificially inflated price and salaries associated with entry barriers have drawn individuals who

The grave unhappiness of lawyers and law students provides anecdotal evidence that both these effects may be occurring.[51]

But What about Consumer Protection?

The ABA and the courts have defended entry regulation as a protection for the public from incompetent or unethical lawyers.[52] This rationale is not particularly persuasive. There are actually two underlying parts to the "protection from incompetent lawyers" defense. The first part is what economists call *information asymmetry*. In this area, it means that consumers lack sufficient information to gauge a good lawyer from a bad lawyer or even a dangerous lawyer. The second part is that the harm a bad lawyer can cause is so severe that we need to protect clients ex ante from damage, rather than just paying them money ex post after any damages occur. Classic examples of irremediable damages are harms to health or safety, because it is very hard to recompense victims for severe injuries.

Ex ante is a term of art that refers to regulation, such as entry regulation, that tries to address a problem before it happens. Because ex ante regulation naturally looks forward, it is usually more expensive and

would otherwise prefer another line of work into an occupation for which they are less suited. See Young, "The Rule of Experts," 51–52.

[51] See Lisa G. Lerman, "What Needs Fixing? The Slippery Slope From Ambition to Greed to Dishonesty: Lawyers, Money, and Professional Integrity," 30 *Hofstra L. Rev.* 879 (2002).

[52] See, e.g., ABA, *ABA Model Code of Professional Responsibility* (Chicago: ABA, 1983), EC 1–2 ("The public should be protected from those who are not qualified to be lawyers by reason of a deficiency in education or moral standards or of other relevant factors but who nevertheless seek to practice law."); ABA Commission on Professionalism, *In the Spirit of Public Service: A Blueprint for the Rekindling of Lawyer Professionalism* (Chicago: ABA, 1986), 10; *In re Schwartz*, 862 P.2d 215, 218 (Ariz. 1993) (stating that the purpose of attorney discipline is not to punish the offender, but to protect the public and the justice system); *In re Ruffalo*, 390 U.S. 544, 550 (1968) (noting that disbarment is "designed to protect the public"); *In re Agostini*, 632 A.2d 80, 81 (Del. 1993) (stating that sanctions are aimed at protecting the public and fostering confidence in the justice system).

far-reaching than addressing damages ex post, because regulating before requires a guess about what might happen and who might be harmed. Recompensing afterward limits payment to only the injured. As such, ex ante regulation should be used only in areas in which it does not make sense to simply repay injured people after the fact.

If either information asymmetry or irremediable harms is not a problem, the "incompetent practitioner" justification is seriously weakened. If the quality of the product is relatively easy to judge, the need for ex ante regulation is much less. Similarly, if the damages are the kind that money can cover, it will likely work better to simply repay injured parties after the fact. Defenders of lawyer regulation have asserted that both information asymmetry and irremediable harms are serious problems in the legal market.[53]

Neither information asymmetry nor irremediable harms is present in most areas of legal practice. The majority of lawyers hold positions with governments, law firms, corporations, or nonprofit organizations.[54] Law firms have been getting larger and the number of lawyers working as sole practitioners has been shrinking precipitously.[55]

The lawyers within these firms are increasingly specialists. The agglomeration of these specialist lawyers in larger organizations lessens information asymmetry because it is easier to judge the track record of a large organization than that of an individual practitioner. Large, successful firms have also done the legwork of finding quality associates and partners.

[53] Joseph R. Julin, "The Legal Profession: Education and Entry," in *Regulating the Professions, A Public Policy Symposium*, eds. Roger D. Blair and Stephen Rubin (Lexington, MA: Lexington Books, 1980), 204.

[54] Bureau of Labor Statistics, *Occupational Outlook Handbook, 2008–09*, available at http://www.bls.gov/oco/ocos053.htm.

[55] Catherine G. O'Grady, "Preparing Students for the Profession: Clinical Education, Collaborative Pedagogy, and the Realities of Practice for the New Lawyer," 4 *Clinical L. Rev*. 485, 495 (1998).

Customers of legal services, especially corporations, are also becoming increasingly sophisticated and knowledgeable through the use of in-house counsel and information clearinghouses.[56] In short, although multiple commentators and lawyers have decried the death of a "profession" and the birth of a "business," the changes in the structure of the legal market have substantially decreased information asymmetries. Corporations, large law firms, or the government hire lots of lawyers and have sufficient institutional expertise to make any protection unnecessary. Accordingly, for most purchasers of legal services, there is virtually no problem with information asymmetry.

Even for small firms and sole practitioners there are many informal ways to collect information, such as seeking recommendations from family and friends, working with the same lawyers over time, gauging success by the length of time a firm or lawyer has been in the market, or estimating a firm's success by surveying its offices or the cars in the parking lot.[57] Increased attorney advertising and growing competition for clients has led all lawyers, from sole practitioners to large law firms, to focus more on "selling" themselves, granting consumers more information in selecting an attorney, despite the fact that bar associations have often fought against the free flow of information by barring or limiting attorney advertising and keeping their disciplinary proceedings confidential.

Even if information asymmetry is a substantial problem, it is still quite a leap to defending our current system. The answer to information asymmetry is more information, not entry barriers. A system that required more disclosures to potential clients might prove more workable than the current system and would certainly be less expensive. Likewise, making all lawyer complaints public and opening the lawyer disciplinary system would help.

[56] See Association of Corporate Counsel, *ACC Value Challenge*, available at http://www.acc.com/advocacy/valuechallenge/index.cfm.

[57] When I worked in private practice I drove a Toyota Tercel and had one client complain that my car made him feel as though he had a bad lawyer.

Further, most damages that result from legal work are not irremediable. In the bulk of civil cases and legal transactions, the potential damages for error can be stated in terms of money. For example, a court seeking to redress a wronged client after a civil trial, a botched tax return, or a bankruptcy will have the money damages awarded or incurred as a basis for damages. Thus, there is a baseline to make the client whole in a way that does not exist with products or services that may cause bodily harm or death.

Because the potential harm from most legal transactions can be estimated in monetary terms, savvy clients can handicap the potential harms involved and account for them in their behavior. For example, in most civil lawsuits a knowledgeable defendant will have some basis for measuring the risks involved and can purchase the appropriate level of legal services or insurance. If the client chooses incorrectly, it is a result of a poor tactical decision, not a flaw in the market. This is not to say that a client who loses a business or a personal fortune through a botched lawsuit has not suffered a serious harm. The critical point is that the harm should be remediable through a later malpractice action, making the harm quite different from death or dismemberment.

Compare doctors and lawyers on this point. It makes a lot of sense to keep incompetent doctors out of the practice of medicine ex ante, because the harms they impose are often irremediable. No matter how much a later wrongful death or medical malpractice suit would pay out for a botched surgery that kills the patient, the odds are that the patient would rather be alive than have the heirs collect damages. In contrast, lawyers rarely deal in situations of life, death, or physical harm.

Criminal defense lawyers actually do deal in matters of life and liberty, so it may make sense to require some sort of ex ante regulation in criminal law. For example, death penalty jurisdictions generally require some type of extra certification for the lawyers who defend death-eligible defendants. Ironically, though, it is almost impossible to collect against a criminal lawyer in malpractice or to have a case overturned for ineffective assistance of counsel. As such, the area that needs the most protection offers the least ex post.

The "incompetent lawyer" justification for regulation cannot justify regulation of the legal market as a whole because the entire market is not affected by information asymmetry or serious harms. Instead, limited subsections of the market, such as lawyers who represent clients in serious criminal matters or lawyers who tend to represent more vulnerable clients, may need to be regulated.

The need for regulation should thus be understood as a sliding scale. The more serious and irreversible the potential harm, the greater the justification for regulation to counteract information asymmetry. As the harms become more quantifiable and foreseeable, the need for ex ante regulation lessens because the danger of an irremediable harm lessens. Obviously, this has not been the actuality of lawyer regulation, which treats the entire profession monolithically and, if anything, disadvantages the most vulnerable clients.

Judges on Entry

You should now be convinced that entry barriers are too high and that lawyers have a number of reasons for favoring this system. Lawyers are not alone – doctors, accountants, engineers, and even hairdressers have similarly lobbied legislatures for tougher entry. But because judges are former lawyers and are in charge of the system, it is worth separately considering the special interests that judges have in entry.

Lawyers push for stricter entry requirements to suppress competition and increase their wages; judges do so to ease their jobs. Many of the studies of judicial preferences have noted that although judges cannot be paid more regardless of how they decide cases, judges strongly value leisure – that is, a reduction or streamlining in their case load or their administrative responsibilities.[58] In the American court system, judges rely heavily on lawyers to process and prosecute the cases on their dockets. Lawyers are in charge of filing suits, discovery, researching and

[58] See Gregory C. Sisk et al., "Charting the Influences on the Judicial Mind: An Empirical Study of Judicial Reasoning," 73 *N.Y.U. L. Rev.* 1377, 1483–85 (1998).

presenting the law in arguments and briefs, and assembling their cases before the courts. A cursory review of the Federal Rules of Civil and Criminal Procedure establishes that lawyers (or, in some cases, pro se litigants) are primarily responsible for almost all the legal and factual research, as well as the procedural aspects, of every case on a judge's docket. Accordingly, the quality of the lawyering is critical to a judge: the better the lawyers, the easier the job.[59] Justices have had a powerful incentive to support and mandate the ratcheting up of entry standards throughout the twentieth century.

The language of the state supreme court decisions claiming the regulatory authority that allowed higher entry barriers is further evidence. Courts have frequently noted that lawyers, as "officers" of the court, were critically "necessary to the proper performance of the courts."[60]

[59] Compare, for example, judicial frustration with pro se litigation, Deborah L. Rhode, "Access to Justice," 1806 and n. 119 (2001) with the judicial pleasure in a well litigated case. See Charles E. Ramos and Alvin K. Hellerstein, "A View from the Judiciary," 5 *Fordham J. Corp. & Fin. L.* 129, 139 (2000) (offering "an unpaid advertisement" for the commercial courts division in Manhattan based on the "well litigated" cases and the "wonderful attorneys").

[60] *In re Bailey*, 248 P. 29, 30 (Ariz. 1926) ("[T]here is no more important duty, nor one whose performance is more necessary to the proper performance of the courts, than to see that their officers are of proper mental ability and moral character."); *Ex Parte Steckler*, 154 So. 41, 45 (La. 1934) (holding that the state supreme court has ultimate authority over bar admission because "[a] proper administration of justice depends as largely upon the conscience, competence and conduct of the members of the bar, as upon the work of the men on the bench."); *In re Sparks*, 101 S.W.2d 194, 197 (Ky. Ct. App. 1936) ("The power to regulate the conduct and qualifications of its officers does not depend upon constitutional or statutory grounds. It is a power which is inherent in this court as a court – appropriate, indeed necessary, to the proper administration of justice."); *Ayres v. Hadaway*, 6 N.W.2d 905, 908 (Mich. 1942) ("Attorneys practicing in the district courts of this state are officers of the courts in which they practice. Their position is an honorable one; they are the trusted advisers of the court. There can be no doubt that the court has ample power to protect itself against dishonorable and corrupt practitioners" (quoting *In re Disbarment Proceedings of William L. Newby*, 107 N.W. 850, 852 (Neb. 1906)). Courts also frequently complained of legislative efforts to "destroy the courts" by admitting "persons without legal learning, and wanting in the proper ethics of the profession." *In re Thatcher*, 22 Ohio Dec. 116 (Lucas Co. Common Pleas Ct. 1912).

Likewise, in ordering the unification of the bar, state supreme courts have regularly noted their interest in the quality of the lawyers appearing before them.[61]

The judicial urge to assist the "best" of the bar and require higher standards can also be seen in the historical battle between the "upper" (white middle-class male) bar and the "lower," entrepreneurial bar (immigrants and minorities who had to struggle for business). At the turn of the twentieth century, bar association membership was almost exclusively from the "best" of the bar.[62] Complaints against the entrepreneurial bar had a particular resonance with state supreme court justices, who naturally considered themselves part of the "finest men" of the profession.[63]

In each of the efforts to tighten bar admission or punish unethical attorneys, there was an implied (and sometimes blatant) effort to bar immigrants, Jews, and blacks from joining the profession.[64] For example, Pennsylvania devised a system whereby every applicant to the bar needed the support of three current members of the bar, a system that effectively barred African American applicants from bar membership from 1933 to 1943 and strongly discouraged Jews from applying.[65] Bar associations and judges railed against "shysters" and "ambulance

[61] See, e.g., *Application of the Montana Bar Ass'n*, 368 P.2d 158, 162 (Mont. 1962) (integrating the bar by court order because "[t]here is need for improvement in our court, the district and justice courts, and the bar of which we are members"); *In re Integration of the Nebraska State Bar Association*, 275 N.W. 265, 267–68 (Neb. 1937) (approving integration because "the court has an immediate interest in the character of the bar, for the court's own sake").

[62] John A. Matzko, "The Best Men of the Bar: The Founding of the American Bar Association," in *The New High Priests: Lawyers in Post-Civil War America,* ed. Gerald W. Gawalt (Westport, CT: Greenwood Press, 1985), 75–90.

[63] Rodney L. Mott et al., "Judicial Personnel," in *Judicial Behavior: A Reader in Theory and Research*, ed. Glendon Shubert (Chicago: Rand McNally, 1964), 205 (from 1900 to 1929, more than 70 percent of the state supreme court justices studied received "the highest rating of Martindale ability").

[64] Jerold S. Auerbach, *Unequal Justice* (New York: Oxford University Press, 1976), 102–29.

[65] See id. at 125–28.

chasers" as lawyer discipline was formalized and entry standards were tightened, a clear signal of the upper bar's disdain for the entrepreneurial bar. Chief Judge Benjamin Cardozo of the New York Court of Appeals decried an "unscrupulous minority" of the bar for "[a]mbulance chasing" among other "evil practices" and held that the court had authority to investigate and punish "professional misconduct" by an "act of its own motion." These actions were taken in response to complaints from bar associations, which Judge Cardozo termed "the organs of [the profession's] common will."[66] Also consider the vitriol in the ABA quote that precedes Chapter 5, decrying "the shyster" and his "itching fingers" and "eager quest for lucre."[67]

The entry system is thus a joint effort of the regulated and the regulators; it reflects their joint interests in the system much more so than an honest appraisal of what would be best for the public. It is worth asking whether aggressive conduct regulation might be a much better way of addressing the few areas that need consumer protection. Right now the legal profession is hard to get into, but even harder to get thrown out of. A more rational answer is to make it easier to get in *and* easier to get out.

Conduct

Given the variety and difficulty of the entry regulations, one would expect a similar level of attention to the competence of existing practitioners. Any comparison of conduct regulation with entry regulation belies any serious concern about substandard practitioners, especially if it means actually impinging on current lawyers.

There are rules that require competent representation, diligence, communication with clients, safekeeping client property, and consultation with clients concerning the objectives of the representation and

[66] *Karlin v. Culkin*, 162 N.E. 487, 488–89 (N.Y. 1928). Consider the irony of Judge Cardozo, himself Jewish, assisting bar association programs that frequently targeted Jews, immigrants, and African Americans.

[67] 29 ABA Rep. 601 (1906).

"the means by which they are to be pursued."[68] These regulations cover little more than what would already be required by the common law covering contracts, fiduciaries, and agency relationships.[69] Insofar as the regulation duplicates or perhaps subtly alters existing obligations, it is of questionable value.

Moreover, the provisions requiring competence and hard work are stated extremely broadly and are rarely prosecuted. State disciplinary bodies "treat individual instances of incompetence and neglect as not violative of the rules of professional conduct or as a minimal violation not worthy of disciplinary action."[70]

Further, many of the rules restrict open communication or are otherwise anticompetitive. Attorney regulation has a long tradition of restricting advertising, client solicitation, client referrals, statements concerning lawyer credentials, and law firm affiliation.[71] Lawyers are also explicitly barred from unauthorized practice in another jurisdiction or assisting in unauthorized practice.[72] Law firms may not be owned or operated by nonlawyers.[73] The Supreme Court has overturned some of the more aggressively anticompetitive versions of these regulations, including bans on advertising,[74] fee schedules,[75] and strict residency requirements.[76]

[68] See ABA Model Rules of Professional Conduct 1.1, 1.2, 1.3, 1.4, and 1.15 (2008).

[69] Stephen Gillers, "What We Talked About When We Talked About Ethics: A Critical View of the Model Rules," 46 *Ohio State L. J.* 243, 255–56 (1985).

[70] ABA Center for Professional Responsibility, *Lawyer Regulation for a New Century: Report of the Commission on Evaluation of Disciplinary Enforcement* (Chicago: ABA, 1992), 11–14.

[71] The Model Rules that address these issues are ABA Model Rules of Professional Conduct 7.1, 7.2, 7.3, 7.4, and 7.5 (2008). The Code provisions were DR 2–101, DR 2–102, DR 2–103, DR 2–104, and DR 2–105. See ABA, *Model Code Of Professional Responsibility* (1983), available at http://www.law.cornell.edu/ethics/aba/mcpr/MCPR .HTM.

[72] ABA Model Rules of Professional Conduct, Rule 5.5 (2008).

[73] Id. at Rule 5.4.

[74] *Bates v. State Bar of Arizona*, 433 U.S. 350 (1977).

[75] *Goldfarb v. Virginia State Bar*, 421 U.S. 773 (1975).

[76] *Supreme Court of New Hampshire v. Piper*, 470 U.S. 274 (1985).

The bar has sought to suppress and control these activities as a protection against the creeping commercialization, or lack of professionalism, of the bar. Commentators, however, have seen a clear effort to repress competition and maintain or raise prices.[77]

Even bedrock regulatory features such as client confidentiality and conflict of interest rules tend to favor the legal profession over the public.[78] Lawyers face very strict rules on client confidentiality. A lawyer generally cannot reveal a client confidence except to prevent reasonably certain death or substantial bodily harm or to prevent a crime or fraud that is "reasonably certain to result in substantial injury to the financial interests or property of another."[79] Even in those circumstances, the ABA's Model Rules say only that a lawyer "may," not must, break client confidence.[80]

As noted in the discussion of the attorney–client privilege (which basically makes any private communications between lawyer and client inadmissible) in Chapter 8, the combination of that evidentiary privilege with the rules on client confidentiality offers a powerful and unique product to potential clients. If you have a problem that you need to discuss and you want your discussions to remain private in a later legal action, a lawyer is the advisor for you.

Moreover, confidentiality rules carry substantial costs for any justice system's search for truth. Maintaining strict confidentiality raises the

[77] Lester Brickman, "ABA Regulation of Contingency Fees: Money Talks, Ethics Walks," 65 *Ford. L. Rev.* 247, 252–54 (1996).

[78] I have kept the section on conduct regulation purposefully short. This is partly because there is already a great deal of excellent work on the pro-lawyer bias to the Model Rules of Professional Conduct. Some of my favorites include Deborah Rhode, *In the Interests of Justice* (Oxford: Oxford Univ. Press 2000); Stephen Gillers, "What We Talked About When We Talked About Ethics: A Critical View of the Model Rules," 46 *Ohio St. L.J.* 243 (1985); and William H. Simon, *The Practice of Justice* (Cambridge: Harvard Univ. Press, 1998). A full treatment might also swallow the rest of the book whole.

[79] ABA Model Rule of Professional Conduct 1.6 (2008).

[80] Id. There are some variations in this rule, and some states do require that lawyers report certain types of future misconduct. See *Restatement (Third), The Law Governing Lawyers* § 67 and Reporter's Note (2000).

possibility of legal error, including the possibility that an innocent criminal or civil defendant may face unjustified sanctions. Daniel Fischer has also noted that confidentiality rules raise legal costs because each side in a lawsuit has an incentive to dig longer and harder in discovery to try to discover what, if anything, has been hidden by the attorney–client privilege.[81]

These costs are measured against the mythic need for open communication between lawyers and clients. However, there is no empirical evidence that these rules actually encourage frank communication between lawyers and clients and even less evidence of an honest balancing between the benefits of that communication and the overall costs.

Similarly, the conflict-of-interest rules appear to favor zealous advocacy to clients by requiring a lawyer to decline representation under almost any circumstance that could even potentially present a conflict of interest.[82] These strict rules are defended as necessary to fully protect clients. However, there is little doubt that they have another effect: the generation of more business for more lawyers. The classic example is divorce cases. Usually, even in amicable divorces, the lawyers recommend that both spouses get their own lawyers to prevent a potential conflict of interest. If there are children, the court will sometimes appoint a guardian ad litem (often a lawyer) to protect the interests of the child. If other parties, such as grandparents, become involved in a custody dispute, the lawyers can multiply exponentially.

In many cases, this level of care may offer a salutary protection to client interests. Nevertheless, a closer look at the mechanics of the rules themselves shows that lawyers actually have substantial leeway in this area. The lawyer's conflict-of-interest rules are similar to the general rules governing principals and agents and are actually broader in some contexts.[83]

[81] Daniel R. Fischel, "Lawyers and Confidentiality," 65 *U. Chi. L. Rev.* 1 (1998).

[82] ABA Model Rules of Professional Conduct 1.7 and 1.8 (2008).

[83] For example, compare Rules 1.7 and 1.8 with *Restatement (Third) Of Agency* §§ 8.02–06 (2006).

Nevertheless, the Model Rules also allow a looser standard of waiver for those conflicts.[84] Even in cases in which "the representation of one client will be directly adverse to another client" or "there is a significant risk that the representation of one or more clients will be materially limited by the lawyer's responsibilities to another client," a lawyer can represent both parties if the lawyer reasonably believes she can and if each client involved offers written consent.[85] The Model Rules thus offer lawyers a great deal of latitude in these situations. Because clients will rarely want to lose one lawyer just to start paying another lawyer and because most clients have a much looser definition of conflicts of interest than do most lawyers,[86] the waiver rules mean that lawyers can often keep the conflicted cases they want and abandon the conflicted cases they do not want.

Finally, remember that the enforcement of these rules is particularly lax and disbarment is rare, reserved for the very worst offenders who are caught red-handed. Likewise, judges have been quite reticent to impose sanctions of any kind on shoddy lawyering in their courts,[87] nor do they report lawyers to bar disciplinary authorities, despite being in an exceptionally good position to observe violations of the rules.[88]

[84] Compare Rule 1.7 with *Restatement (Third) Of Agency* § 8.06 (2006).

[85] ABA Model Rules of Professional Conduct Rule 1.7 (2008).

[86] For example, parties negotiating a partnership agreement often want to use a single lawyer, seeing no conflict, whereas lawyers see each individual partner as a potential conflict. See, e.g., Kenneth J. Abdo and Jack P. Sahl, "Entertainment Law Ethics," 22 *Ent. & Sports Law*. 2, 3–4 (2004).

[87] Wayne D. Brazil, "The Adversary Character of Civil Discovery: A Critique and Proposals for Change," 31 *Vand. L. Rev*. 1295, 1343 (1978) (pointing out that judicial reticence to sanction discovery abuses is likely a result of "judges' understanding [as] former lawyers").

[88] ABA Standing Committee on Professional Discipline, *The Judicial Response to Lawyer Misconduct* (Chicago: ABA, 1984), iii (citing research showing that "judges represent a minority of the complaints, even against easily detected serious misconduct directly affecting the administration of justice").

This reticence is puzzling given that greater enforcement might actually improve the administration of justice and the ease of any particular judge's job. In this case, judicial sympathy for lawyers apparently trumps any individual interest in sanctions and lends credence to the idea that the lawyer–judge bond is powerful enough to overwhelm judicial self-interest.

7 Torts

A defendant attorney owes no duty to the plaintiff. The attorney's paramount duty is to the trial court, as a licensed attorney and officer of the court, and to his client. No cause of action in negligence can lie because the overriding public policy guarding free access to the courts and the fact that the attorney's legal duty is to his own client demands a finding that the attorney owes no duty to an adverse party that would give rise to a claim in negligence, whether to investigate fully the client's claim prior to filing suit or to avoid filing a suit which he knew or should have known was frivolous.

– *Clark v. Druckman*[1]

THIS CHAPTER ADDRESSES THE LAW OF TORTS. IT BEGINS with legal malpractice, which is the law that covers clients suing lawyers for harmful, substandard performance. Medical malpractice is used as a comparison point, as the medical and legal professions are somewhat similar, but it is much easier to successfully sue a doctor than it is to successfully sue a lawyer in the United States.

The chapter closes with a discussion of the law of wrongful prosecution – the tort that allows persons who have faced either a baseless criminal prosecution or a civil suit to sue for damages. It is easier to sue

[1] I eliminated some ellipses and brackets in this quote for ease of reading. It is from *Clark v. Druckman*, 624 S.E.2d 864, 869 (W.Va. 2005) (quoting *McKenna Long & Aldridge, LLP v. Keller*, 598 S.E.2d 892, 894 (Ga. 2004)).

an accusing criminal witness or tort plaintiff than it is to sue the lawyer or prosecutor who actually brought the case, despite the fact that the lawyer is often the person in the better position to assess the merits of such a suit.

Legal Malpractice

It is much harder to prove legal malpractice than medical malpractice. This is because lawyers have enjoyed several unique advantages as defendants in malpractice actions and because doctrinal changes that have been applied in medical malpractice have been barred or adopted much more slowly in legal malpractice. Courts have justified many of these differences on the now-familiar ground that lawyers are special and need special treatment.

Legal malpractice is generally treated as a tort action based in negligence. The traditional negligence action requires proof of four elements: (1) a duty between the plaintiff and the defendant; (2) a breach of that duty; (3) causation – proof that the breach caused the plaintiff's injury; and (4) damages from the injury. Because these four elements are hundreds of years old, each has its own quite complicated law. Still, the general framework encompasses the ways in which an injured party can sue a negligent injurer for recompense.

When applied to lawyers, the framework is adjusted slightly. Legal malpractice requires a relationship establishing a duty of care; "skill and knowledge in providing legal services to the client; a breach of that duty; and a connection of legally recognized causation between the breach and resulting harm to the client."[2] Expert testimony establishes the existence of a duty and a breach of that duty. The question is usually whether the lawyer exercised typical diligence and skill.[3]

[2] *North Bay Council, Inc. v. Bruckner*, 563 A.2d 428, 430 (1989) (Souter, J.).

[3] See Wilburn Brewer, "Expert Witness Testimony in Legal Malpractice Cases," 45 *S.C. L. Rev.* 727, 757 (1994).

Causation

The single biggest distinction between legal malpractice and medical malpractice is the requirements for causation. In a legal malpractice action that arises from a botched litigation, the aggrieved former client must prove "but for" causation – that is, that the client would have been successful in the underlying lawsuit but for the attorney's malpractice.[4] This is what is known as the "case-within-the-case" requirement: the legal malpractice plaintiff must first prove that she would or should have won the underlying case and then prove that she did not win the case because of the lawyer's malpractice. Here is a typical court description of the process:

> To prove damages and proximate cause, the plaintiff must show that, but for the alleged negligence of the attorney, the result in the underlying action would have been different. In this respect, a plaintiff must prove a case within a case, as he or she must prove the merits of the underlying case as part of the proof of the malpractice case.[5]

The majority of courts add a second caveat: the plaintiff must prove not only that she would have won the underlying judgment but also that she would have collected it.[6] A minority of states hold that the burden should be on the defendant attorney to prove (often as an affirmative defense) that the client's putative judgment was uncollectible.[7]

The case-within-a-case standard has been applied to nonlitigation areas, such as transactional malpractice claims. For example, a plaintiff in a legal malpractice action over a contract negotiation would have to

[4] See, e.g., Meredith J. Duncan, "Legal Malpractice by any Other Name: Why a Breach of Fiduciary Claim Does not Smell as Sweet," 34 *Wake Forest L. Rev.* 1137, 1143–44 (1999).

[5] See, e.g., *Barnes v. Everett*, 95 S.W.3d 740, 744 (Ark. 2003). The case-within-a-case requirement is the rule in the "vast majority" of states. See Stephen E. McConnico et al., "Unresolved Problems in Texas Malpractice Law," 36 *St. Mary's L.J.* 989, 1009 and n. 99 (2005).

[6] See, e.g., *Garretson v. Miller*, 99 Cal. App. 4th 563, 568–69 (Cal. Ct. App. 2002).

[7] See *Hoppe v. Ranzini*, 385 A.2d 913, 920 (N.J. 1978).

prove not only that a lawyer should have bargained over a missing term, but also that the opposing party would have accepted the missing term.[8]

The case-within-a-case standard is difficult to meet, both theoretically and practically. As a theoretical matter, the plaintiff faces two issues of proof: proving the underlying malpractice and then proving that she would have won in a re-creation of the botched original trial. Although causation is always an issue in any tort action, it is the central issue in legal malpractice cases.[9] This is because causation requires the malpractice plaintiff to win two trials: the original litigation and the later malpractice suit.

Proving the underlying case against the original attorney is quite challenging. The original attorney may know the facts, law, and weaknesses of the case backward and forward. The original attorney also has access to client confidences; despite the purported sanctity of client confidences, the Model Rules of Professional Conduct explicitly allow a lawyer to reveal client confidences to defend a malpractice action.[10] Furthermore, if the attorney's lax performance affected the discovery process, the malpractice plaintiff may have an extremely hard time piecing together the underlying evidence years later, especially when the original defendant is not a party to the malpractice action for purposes of discovery. That said, it is true that legal malpractice defendants often have a hard time getting the defendant in the original case (who is often a doctor who hates lawyers, especially the lawyer that sued him in the original case) to cooperate in the legal malpractice defense.

The case-within-a-case structure makes civil litigation legal malpractice claims quite difficult to prove, but criminal defense malpractice is practically impossible to prove for most criminal defendants. In the great

[8] See R. Todd Hogan and Franz Hardy, "Defending the Transactional Legal Malpractice Case: Trends and Considerations for Defense Counsel," 73 *Def. Couns. J.* 332, 333 and n. 3 (2006).

[9] John Leubsdorf, "Legal Malpractice and Professional Responsibility," 48 *Rutgers L. Rev.* 101, 148 (1995).

[10] ABA Model Rule of Professional Conduct 1.6(b)(5) (2008).

majority of states, a legal malpractice plaintiff who was a criminal defendant must prove more than the case-within-a-case – she must prove actual innocence.[11] Because many criminal defendants defeat prosecutions through motions suppressing illegally obtained evidence, such as confessions taken in violation of *Miranda v. Arizona* or other procedural arguments, the actual innocence requirement immunizes a great deal of criminal defense lawyering from scrutiny. It also means that many criminal defendants have no recourse if their lawyer misses an obvious procedural or investigatory irregularity in their cases, even if that argument might have been the defendants' best hope for an acquittal or a plea to a lesser crime.

Furthermore, in most jurisdictions a plaintiff cannot pursue a legal malpractice action unless the plaintiff has first been cleared of the previous charges on appeal (known technically as *postconviction relief*).[12] The postconviction relief requirement has a further downside: in many jurisdictions, the collateral estoppel doctrine is employed to bar malpractice actions against criminal defense attorneys if an ineffective assistance claim has been raised and denied.[13] Recall the discussion in Chapter 3 of the many challenges involved in proving ineffective assistance of counsel;[14] this means that even a defendant who wins on appeal and is set free can be barred from a later malpractice action if the court rejected the ineffective-assistance claim while granting relief on other grounds. Combine this treatment of criminal legal malpractice with the discussion in Chapter 3 of ineffective assistance, and it is clear that criminal defense work is virtually free from review or possible liability. Not all of this is a result of lawyer favoritism, however. Courts have long hesitated to allow

[11] See Joseph H. King, "Outlaws and Outlier Doctrines: The Serious Misconduct Bar in Tort Law," 43 *William and Mary L. Rev.* 1011, 1030 (2002).

[12] Meredith J. Duncan, "The (So-Called) Liability of Criminal Defense Attorneys: A System in Need of Reform," 2002 *B.Y.U. L. Rev.* 1, 30–31 and n. 159 (2002).

[13] Meredith J. Duncan, "Criminal Malpractice: A Lawyer's Holiday," 37 *Ga. L. Rev.* 1251, 1270–71 (2003).

[14] See David Cole, *No Equal Justice: Race and Class in the American Criminal Justice System* (New York: The New Press, 1999), 78.

tort suits by plaintiffs (such as the criminal defendants who might bring a legal malpractice suit) who are guilty of serious misconduct themselves.[15]

The strict treatment of causation in legal malpractice is in sharp contrast to the general loosening of causation requirements in other areas of tort law. Perhaps the best example is the medical malpractice doctrine of "lost chance." Joseph King describes the lost-chance doctrine as follows:

> [W]hen a defendant tortiously destroys or reduces a victim's prospects for achieving a more favorable outcome, the plaintiff should be compensated for that lost prospect. Damages should be based on the extent to which the defendant's tortious conduct reduced the plaintiff's likelihood of receiving a better outcome.... In other words, a plaintiff's right to damages for the loss of a chance should not be restricted to situations in which the plaintiff proves that it was more likely than not that he would have received a better outcome in the absence of the tortious conduct.[16]

Basically, loss of chance is a way around the strict logic of "but for" causation. In a medical malpractice case, lost chance can allow a finding of causation when strict "but for" causation would not. For example, if a patient has cancer and has only a 40 percent chance of survival, under strict rules of causation there is no recovery when a late diagnosis reduces the chance of survival to 10 percent: it was more likely than not that the plaintiff would have died regardless. This scenario also occurs in legal malpractice – assume a plaintiff has a 40 percent chance of winning a lawsuit, but the lawyer forgets to subpoena a critical witness and the chances of winning shrink to 10 percent. In both these cases the plaintiffs lose under strict "but for" causation because the cancer patient would have likely died and the plaintiff would have likely lost regardless of the alleged negligence. Loss of chance, however, elides this stricture and allows a medical malpractice plaintiff to collect damages for the lost chance of survival, even if the original chance was not better than even.

[15] See King, "Outlaws and Outlier Doctrines: The Serious Misconduct Bar in Tort Law."

[16] Joseph H. King, "Reduction of Likelihood: Reformulation and Other Retrofitting of the Loss-of-Chance Doctrine," 28 *U. Memphis L. Rev.* 491, 492 (1998).

Although the logic of loss of chance applies in multiple areas of the law, in America it has been largely confined to medical malpractice cases[17] and it has been adopted in a majority of states.[18] The applicability of loss of chance to legal malpractice is obvious; multiple commentators have suggested that loss of chance would ameliorate much of the unfairness of the case-within-a-case requirement.[19] The few courts to consider the issue have consistently denied efforts to extend loss of chance to legal malpractice.[20]

One route that has enjoyed limited success is arguing that legal malpractice reduced the settlement value of a case.[21] This is not technically an application of loss of chance, but if widely accepted it could serve a similar purpose. Outside very limited areas, lawyers remain protected by the rule of "judgmental immunity" regarding settlement advice.[22] The majority of courts have rejected potential settlement value in favor of the case within a case, in part because holding otherwise renders "professionals liable as guarantors, as almost all cases have some value."[23] This quote begs the question of why negligent lawyers should not recompense the original settlement value of cases in which they have committed malpractice.

[17] See Todd S. Aagard, "Identifying and Valuing the Injury in Lost Chance Cases," 96 *Mich. L. Rev.* 1335, 1335 n. 5 (1998).

[18] See *Roberts v. Ohio Permanente Medical Group, Inc.*, 668 N.E.2d 480, 485 (Ohio 1996).

[19] See Polly A. Lord, "Loss of Chance in Legal Malpractice," 61 *Wash. L. Rev.* 1479 (1986). Loss of chance has actually been suggested by the *Restatement (Third) of the Law Governing Lawyers* §53 comment B, which is odd because the restatement usually attempts to "restate" existing law, not suggest changes in the law. Nevertheless, this comment, which suggests that loss of a "substantial chance of prevailing" in a lawsuit may be recoverable, cites only foreign cases and dicta in one U.S. case as support.

[20] See *Daugert v. Pappas*, 704 P.2d 600 (Wash. 1985); *Beatty v. Wood*, 204 F.3d 713, 718–19 (7th Cir. 2000).

[21] McConnico, "Unresolved Problems in Texas Malpractice Law," 1009–10.

[22] Ronald E. Mallen and Jeffrey M. Smith, *Legal Malpractice*, 5th ed. (St. Paul, MN: West Group, 2000), §30.41; 7 *Am. Jur. 2d, Attorneys at Law* (St. Paul, MN: Thomson West, 2008), §201.

[23] Mallen and Smith, *Legal Malpractice*, §32.8.

As noted earlier, a minority of jurisdictions have rejected loss of chance in medical malpractice. In doing so, some courts have pointed to legal malpractice as a cautionary example of why loss of chance should not be adopted or why it should not be expanded beyond medical malpractice. For example, in *Kramer v. Lewisville Memorial Hospital*, the Texas Supreme Court rejected loss of chance for medical malpractice because of an explicit worry that it might leak over to legal malpractice:

> Furthermore, assuming we adopt the loss of chance doctrine in the context of this medical malpractice action, it is doubtful that there is any principled way we could prevent its application to similar actions involving other professions. If, for example, a disgruntled or unsuccessful litigant loses a case that he or she had a less than 50 percent chance of winning, but is able to adduce expert testimony that his or her lawyer negligently reduced this chance by some degree, the litigant would be able to pursue a cause of action for malpractice under the loss of chance doctrine.[24]

State courts have also dissented to the adoption of loss of chance in medical malpractice by pointing to the possible impact on the legal profession. In *Perez v. Las Vegas Medical Center*, the Nevada Supreme Court adopted loss of chance over Justice Steffen's dissent, which argued that loss of chance "would be equally just and applicable in such actions involving other professions, including the legal profession."[25]

The psychology of these cases is quite striking. Although courts all over the country have adopted loss of chance for medical patients, the mere mention of applying it to lawyers is enough to convince some judges

[24] *Kramer v. Lewisville Memorial Hospital*, 858 S.W.2d 397, 406 (1993). The dissent in *Kramer* countered this argument by citing *Daugert v. Pappas* for the proposition that loss of chance could be and has been limited to medical malpractice. *Kramer*, 858 S.W.2d at 410 (Hightower, J., dissenting); see also *Hardy v. Southwestern Bell Telephone Co.*, 910 P.2d 1024, 1029 (Okla. 1996) (refusing to extend loss of chance outside of the medical malpractice context and noting *Daugert v. Pappas*' rejection of loss of chance for legal malpractice).

[25] *Perez v. Las Vegas Medical Center*, 805 P.2d 589, 599 n. 5 (Nev. 1991) (Steffen, J., dissenting); see also *Dumas v. Cooney*, 1 Cal. Rptr. 2d. 584, 593 (Cal. App. 1991) (noting that "the lost chance theory has troubling implications," such as a possible application to lawyers).

not to adopt the doctrine at all. When a judge hears about a patient who lost a 45 percent chance of surviving because of a doctor's malpractice, courts can see why that loss should be recompensed. When a court hears about a client who lost a 45 percent chance of winning because of a lawyer's malpractice, the suit is dismissed.

Privity

The doctrine of privity was one of the pillars of tort law that eventually disintegrated in reaction to the Industrial Revolution. In the nineteenth and early twentieth centuries, British and American courts held that a plaintiff must prove privity – the equivalent of a contractual relationship – with a defendant to proceed in a product liability lawsuit. Thus, in the 1842 English case of *Winterbottom v. Wright*, a plaintiff who drove a mail coach manufactured by the defendant, but bought by his employer, could not sue the manufacturer for alleged defects because the plaintiff lacked contractual privity with the manufacturer. As the court stated, "There is no privity of contract between these parties; and if the plaintiff can sue, every passenger, or even any person passing along the road, who was injured by the upsetting of the coach, might bring a similar action."[26]

In 1879, the U.S. Supreme Court extended this doctrine to legal malpractice in *National Savings Bank of District of Columbia v. Ward*.[27] *Ward* involved a factual scenario that remains quite familiar today: the improperly performed title search. A property owner hired a lawyer to do a title search. When the title search came back clear, the owner used the title search to procure a mortgage on his property from the National Savings Bank of District of Columbia. The title search turned out to be faulty and the bank eventually sued the lawyer. Because the bank was not the lawyer's client, however, the court dismissed the case for lack of privity.[28]

[26] See *Winterbottom v. Wright*, 152 Eng. Rep. 402 (Ex. 1842).
[27] *National Savings Bank of District of Columbia v. Ward*, 100 U.S. 195 (1879).
[28] Id. at 198–99.

Over the course of the early and mid-twentieth century, the general requirement of privity crumbled and third-party liability for tortious conduct became the rule rather than the exception.[29] The privity doctrine lasted longer in legal malpractice, though, and remains a substantial challenge to third-party plaintiffs.[30]

The area of trusts and estates has been particularly ripe for these types of controversies because the injured party is almost always not the client: the injured party is typically a relative of the decedent who received less or nothing because of the lawyer's negligence. The requirement of contractual privity to bring a legal malpractice claim made will drafting a virtual malpractice-free zone before the privity requirement began to weaken for lawyers in the 1960s.[31]

Even as privity has weakened in legal malpractice, it has done so more slowly, and in a different and more limited way, than elsewhere in torts. As a general rule, the test for third-party liability in other torts is "foreseeability": if the injury to the third party could have been foreseen, third-party liability attaches.[32]

Third-party liability in legal malpractice is often more limited, and state courts use different approaches. California, for example, uses a multifactor balancing test considering "the extent to which the transaction was intended to affect the plaintiff, the foreseeability of harm to him, the degree of certainty that the plaintiff suffered injury, the closeness of

[29] David G. Owen, "The Evolution of Products Liability Law," 26 *Review of Litigation* 955, 965–66 (2007).

[30] See John H. Bauman, "A Sense of Duty: Regulation of Lawyer Responsibility to Third Parties by the Tort System," 37 *S. Tex. L. Rev.* 995, 1004–14 (1996) (noting that "privity limitations persisted in the field of legal malpractice even as the courts lifted them in other areas"); Charles W. Wolfram, "A Cautionary Tale: Fiduciary Breach as Legal Malpractice," 34 *Hofstra L. Rev.* 689, 695 (2006).

[31] See "Developments in the Law, Lawyers' Responsibilities to the Client: Legal Malpractice and Tort Reform," 107 *Harv. L. Rev.* 1557, 1560–61 (1994).

[32] W. Jonathan Cardi, "Reconstructing Foreseeability," 46 *B.C. L. Rev.* 921, 921–22 (2005). One exception is torts that involve only economic loss, such as negligent misrepresentation. In those cases, courts take a more limited view of third-party liability; see *Restatement (Second) of Torts* §552. Some will-drafting cases do resemble negligent misrepresentation cases (when they deal with bad advice instead of bad drafting, for example).

the connection between the defendant's conduct and the injury suffered, the moral blame attached to the defendant's conduct, and the policy of preventing future harm."[33]

Other states basically use the contract law of third-party beneficiaries. If the primary purpose of the attorney–client relationship was to benefit the third party, the third party is a proper legal malpractice plaintiff.[34] This bar is substantially higher than that of foreseeability. The question is the purpose of the relationship, not whether the injury was foreseeable. Finally, a minority of courts allow third-party suits if the reliance on the lawyer's advice or actions was foreseeable.[35]

Most of these doctrines rely on contract or quasi-contract types of reasoning to establish third-party liability.[36] This means that privity is still lurking in the area of legal malpractice. These courts have a hard time opening themselves fully to third-party legal malpractice, so they stick to the tighter restrictions of contract or contractlike theories.

Doctors have fared much worse than lawyers have on third-party liability. Doctors are basically held to the simple foreseeability test and certainly do not enjoy the quasi-contractual protection that lawyers do.[37] Doctors and psychiatrists frequently find themselves on the cutting edge of plaintiff-friendly foreseeability decisions. For example, doctors who fail to warn patients about a drug's side effects have been held liable to third parties injured in a later car accident allegedly caused by the drug.[38]

[33] *Biakanja v. Irving*, 320 P.2d 16, 19 (Cal. 1958).

[34] See, e.g., *Pelham v. Griesheimer*, 440 N.E.2d 96, 100 (Ill. 1982); *Schreiner v. Scoville*, 410 N.W. 2d 679 (Iowa 1987).

[35] See *Williams v. Ely*, 668 N.E.2d 799, 805 (1996). For an overview of this case law, see *Restatement (Third) of the Law Governing Lawyers* §51 comment f and Reporter's Notes.

[36] Some courts have limited accountant third-party liability in a manner consistent with liability of lawyers; see Jay M. Feinman, "Liability of Accountants for Negligent Auditing: Doctrine, Policy, and Ideology," 31 *Fla. State L. Rev.* 17, 20 (2003).

[37] See Dale L. Moore, "Disparate Treatment of the Allocation of Power Between Judge and Jury in Legal and Malpractice Cases," 61 *Temp. L. Rev.* 353, 358–72 (1988).

[38] Gregory G. Sarno, Annotation, "Liability of Physician, for Injury to or Death of Third Party, Due to Failure to Disclose Driving-Related Impediment," 43 *A.L.R. 4th* 153 (1986).

Tarasoff v. Regents of University of California is a particularly striking example.[39] In *Tarasoff*, a mental patient being treated at Cal Berkeley's teaching hospital allegedly told his psychiatrist that he was going to kill a particular female student. When the mental patient later killed her, the student's parents sued the psychiatrist. The district court held no liability, but the Supreme Court of California reversed, holding that the psychiatrist had a duty to warn the student about the threat. This holding was despite the psychiatrist's duty of confidentiality and relied on a "special relationship" between the psychiatrist and the killer/patient and simple foreseeability.[40] The discussion in Chapter 4 of the Supreme Court's different treatment of doctors' and lawyers' advice to clients in *Rust* and *Velazquez* reappears here. The *Tarasoff* court considers the "special relationship" between this doctor and patient to be a reason to find liability, rather than a reason to protect the doctor. Consider whether a court would ever have held that a lawyer had a duty to violate confidentiality to protect a third party. The few cases that have raised *Tarasoff* in the context of lawyers have found no such duty.[41]

Nevertheless, the third-party liability standards in the states described earlier are actually the liberal ones. Nearly a hundred years after the American law of privity was first reversed by Justice Cardozo's opinion in *MacPherson v. Buick Motor*,[42] nine states retain a strict privity rule in legal malpractice actions.[43] Given that the privity requirement has

[39] *Tarasoff v. Regents of University of California*, 551 P.2d 334 (Cal. 1976).

[40] Id. at 339–48.

[41] See *Seibel v. City & County of Honolulu*, 602 P.2d 532 (Haw. 1979) (prosecuting attorney not liable for murder committed by released defendant); *Hawkins v. King County Department of Rehabilitation Services*, 602 P.2d 361 (Wash. App. 1979).

[42] *MacPherson v. Buick Motor*, 111 N.E. 1050 (N.Y. 1916); Murray H. Wright and Edward E. Nicholas, III, "The Collision of Tort and Contract in the Construction Industry," 21 *U. Rich. L. Rev.* 457, 465–67 (1987) (noting rapid acceptance of *MacPherson*).

[43] See Martin L. Fried, "The Disappointed Heir: Going Beyond the Probate Process to Remedy Wrongdoing or Rectify Mistake," 39 *Real Prop. Prob. & Tr. J.* 357, 384 (2004) (listing the nine states – Alabama, Arkansas, Maine, Maryland, Nebraska, New York, Ohio, Texas, and Virginia – and citing supporting statutes [Arkansas] or cases).

disappeared in other areas of tort and has been subject to general derision, the fact that nine states have retained it is quite striking.[44] The justification for this retention is the potential harm to clients if third-party liability was allowed and the fear of unlimited liability for lawyers:

> [T]he rule protects the attorney's duty of loyalty to and effective advocacy for his or her client. While the testator/client is alive, the lawyer owes him or her...a duty of complete and undivided loyalty....[C]ourts [also] fear that absent the strict privity rule there would be no limit as to whom a lawyer would be obligated....In threatening the interests of the attorney, the interests of potential clients may also be compromised; they might not be able to obtain legal services as easily in situations where potential third party liability exists.[45]

> At common law, an attorney owes a duty of care only to his or her client, not to third parties who may have been damaged by the attorney's negligent representation of the client. Without this 'privity barrier,' the rationale goes, clients would lose control over the attorney-client relationship, and attorneys would be subject to almost unlimited liability....This [rule ensures] that attorneys may in all cases zealously represent their clients without the threat of suit from third parties compromising that representation.[46]

This reasoning is remarkable on several levels. First, the reliance on protecting the wishes of the original client is rather disingenuous in the area of wills because the original client is dead and can no longer sue the attorney. Further, it is hardly helpful to say that courts are protecting the original client's interests when the work of the lawyer allegedly flies in the face of that client's stated desires. In some cases the third party may have a specious claim. That is an issue for proof, however. The blanket

[44] See Melvin A. Eisenberg, "Third-Party Beneficiaries," 92 *Colum. L. Rev.* 1358 (1992) for an example of a critique of privity's survival in this area.

[45] *Noble v. Bruce*, 709 A.2d 1264, 1270 (Md. 1998).

[46] *Robinson v. Benton*, 842 So. 2d 631, 636–37 (Ala. 2002) (quoting *Barcelo v. Elliott*, 923 S.W.2d 575, 577–79 (Tex. 1996)).

rule of privity means that even meritorious claims of negligence are barred at the door.

Second, these courts rely on an original argument defending privity – the concern of unlimited liability to third parties – that was rejected repeatedly as courts displaced the privity requirement in virtually every other context. Compare language from *Winterbottom*, one of the original privity cases – "if th[is] plaintiff can sue, every passenger, or even any person passing along the road, who was injured by the upsetting of the coach, might bring a similar action" – with *MacPherson*'s rejection of privity – "Yet the defendant would have us say that [there was only] one person whom it was under a legal duty to protect. The law does not lead us to so inconsequent a conclusion. Precedents drawn from the days of travel by stage coach do not fit the conditions of travel today."[47] Ironically, in some states stagecoach law remains alive and well to protect lawyers. When the subject changes to privity and lawyers, the threat of unlimited liability is suddenly a very real and cognizable danger.

Third, the worry about clients is quite telling, as the same arguments have been utterly disregarded in the doctor–patient scenario. The possibility of third-party liability could certainly affect the doctor–patient relationship or cause the doctor to worry more about third parties than about her own patients. Courts generally consider this effect a *benefit* of third-party liability for doctors and psychiatrists: the whole point of third-party liability is to make doctors consider risks outside the doctor–patient relationship. The relationship between a lawyer and client, however, is so sacrosanct that future lawsuits by injured nonclients are barred out of the mere chance that allowing those suits might disrupt the original relationship. Once again, courts are able to sympathize with lawyers while disregarding similar concerns for doctors.

Last, the worry that clients "might not be able to obtain legal services as easily in situations where potential third party liability exists" is also one that has been explicitly rejected in other tort areas, notably products

[47] *Winterbottom*, 152 Eng. Rep. at 402; *MacPherson*, 111 N.E. at 1058.

liability and medical malpractice. One of the tort reformers' favorite criticisms is that court decisions have greatly reduced or eliminated access to health care and certain products. Tort advocates consider this a benefit – unsafe products or dangerous doctors are priced correctly or eliminated altogether.[48] When lawyers are involved, however, courts worry that certain services will be unavailable to clients owing to the costs of liability.

The Rules of Professional Conduct

As noted in Chapters 5 and 6, one of the keys to the success of lawyer self-regulation is that state supreme courts have adopted the ABA's Model Rules of Professional Conduct in cases and as conduct regulation. Forty-eight state supreme courts have adopted these rules with modifications. Courts have also used the rules to decide cases in areas as diverse as noncompete agreements among lawyers, lawyer advertising, and client confidences.

There is one notable exception: malpractice actions. Remember that legal malpractice, as other negligence-based torts, requires a finding of a duty and a breach of that duty as part of a claim. It would seem that a list of binding professional obligations, such as each state's rules of professional conduct, would be a natural place to define each lawyer's duties. Moreover, one might think that the ABA and the states would encourage this use, as adding legal malpractice actions as enforcement mechanisms for the rules would greatly increase the likelihood that lawyers would follow them.

The Model Rules state quite clearly, however, that "[v]iolation of a Rule should not itself give rise to a cause of action against a lawyer nor should it create any presumption in such a case that a legal duty has been breached."[49] Courts have been mixed in the ways they apply the rules

[48] See Benjamin H. Barton, "Tort Reform, Innovation, and Playground Design," 58 *Fla. L. Rev*. 265, 274–77 (2006).

[49] ABA Model Rules of Professional Conduct Preamble and Scope (2008).

in malpractice actions. The majority of courts have presented a compromise position: the Model Rules cannot stand in as the duty of care and a violation of the rules is not negligence per se, but they can be considered as evidence of duty and breach.[50] A few courts have allowed the rules to inform the duty of care question more directly, by creating a rebuttable presumption of a breach of duty if the rules are violated.[51] A very few courts have held that the Model Rules of Professional Conduct are flatly inadmissible in a legal malpractice action.[52] Ironically, even in these jurisdictions lawyer-defendants retain the right to introduce ethical standards in defense of their actions.[53]

Damages

The damages for legal malpractice are also distinct.[54] Punitive damages are rarely awarded in legal malpractice cases.[55] The decision as to

[50] See Marc R. Greenough, "The Inadmissibility of Professional Ethical Standards in Legal Malpractice Actions after *Hizey v. Carpenter*," 68 *Wash. L. Rev.* 395, 400 (1993).

[51] A rebuttable presumption means that the jury can assume that the Rules are the proper standard of care, but that the lawyer has a chance to rebut that assumption. *Evans v. Dickstein*, 2005 WL 1160621, at *1 (Mich. App., May 17, 2005) ("This Court has previously rejected the argument that violation of the Rules of Professional Conduct is negligence per se. Instead, this Court has favored the proposition that a violation of the Rules of Professional Conduct is rebuttable evidence of malpractice and does not relieve a plaintiff 'of the obligation to present expert testimony.'" (quoting *Beattie v. Firnschild*, 394 N.W. 2d 107, 109 (1986)).

[52] See *Ex parte Toler*, 710 So.2d 415, 416 (Ala. 1998); *Orsini v. Larry Moyer Trucking, Inc.*, 833 S.W.2d 366, 369 (Ark. 1992); and *Hizey v. Carpenter*, 830 P.2d 646, 653–54 (Wash. 1992). A court in Ohio held that evidence that a lawyer was disciplined by the state disciplinary authorities must be excluded in a malpractice action. *Krischbaum v. Dillon*, 567 N.E.2d 1291 (Ohio 1991).

[53] Developments in the Law, "Lawyers' Responsibilities to the Client," 1567.

[54] Legal malpractice damages usually consist of the difference between the result the former client actually received and the result the client should have received, as determined by the case within a case portion of the trial. See Susan S. Fortney and Vincent R. Johnson, *Legal Malpractice Law* (St. Paul, MN: Thomson/West, 2008), 181–83.

[55] Id. at 183–85; 188–91; David J. Meiselman, *Attorney Malpractice: Law and Procedure* (Rochester, NY: The Lawyers Co-Operative Publishing Co., 1980), 55–63. Consider

whether to allow the jury to award punitive damages rests with the discretion of the trial judge.[56]

Emotional-distress damages are also usually not recoverable in a legal malpractice action. Emotional-distress damages have generally been limited to truly egregious cases, sometimes under a foreseeability standard and sometimes as a matter of public policy. Judges rarely find that a lawyer can foresee emotional damages from her malpractice.[57]

Long-Russell v. Hampe is a good example.[58] The plaintiff in *Long-Russell* alleged that she paid a lawyer to help her with a custody dispute and to avoid eviction from her home. The lawyer apparently accepted a fee and did nothing. Predictably, the plaintiff ended up evicted and without custody of her children.[59] The court held that she was not entitled to damages for emotional distress. This was partly because there were no physical damages in the case, partly because in Wyoming a legal malpractice case is based on a hybrid of negligence and contract, and partly because the court thought that allowing damages for emotional distress in legal malpractice actions would allow "fraudulent claims" and be a "burden on the judicial system and defendants."[60]

The case is striking in its lack of sympathy or empathy for the client. Most laypeople (and jurors) would understand that paying a lawyer to

the outlier Virginia Supreme Court case of *O'Connell v. Bean*, 556 S.E.2d 741, 742–73 (Va. 2002). *O'Connell* held that legal malpractice is based solely in contract law and thus refused a plaintiff's request for punitive damages. Virginia's doctors, in comparison, are subject to punitive damages as limited by a state statute. See *Anand v. Allison*, 55 Va. Cir. 261 (Va. Cir. Ct. 2001). The case is strange in its brisk treatment of the topic, its failure to discuss the fact that every state outside Virginia has ruled otherwise, and the incongruence of treating lawyers and other professionals differently. Nevertheless, legal malpractice has ceased to be a tort in Virginia, replaced by the much more tightly constrained doctrines that underlie contract liability.

[56] See, e.g., *Fitzgerald v. Walker*, 826 P.2d 1301, 1305 (Idaho 1992).

[57] *Douglas v. Delp*, 987 S.W.2d 879, 885 (Tex. 1999).

[58] *Long-Russell v. Hampe*, 39 P.3d 1015, 1016–17 (Wyo. 2002).

[59] Id. at 1016–17.

[60] Id. at 1017–19.

keep your home and your children and then having to lose both while the lawyer did nothing on your behalf might cause some real emotional distress. Nevertheless, the case was open-and-shut for the lawyer and recompense was limited to a relatively small actual monetary loss.

By contrast, punitive damage awards against doctors are so common that they have been described as a key aspect of the medical malpractice "crisis."[61] Damages for emotional distress are likewise regularly awarded in medical malpractice actions.[62]

One reason that courts and commentators have defended the distinction for emotional-distress damages is that medical malpractice typically includes physical injuries, so the emotional injuries are more likely to be legitimate. Nevertheless, the physical-injury rule allows plaintiffs who have *any* physical injury to collect emotional damages, so even small physical injuries can lead to large awards of emotional distress. In some medical malpractice areas this rule has been bent or simply abrogated. For example, some cases have allowed emotional-distress damages to the mother of a stillborn child, despite the fact that the mother suffered no physical injuries herself.[63]

Overall, the structure and treatment of legal malpractice further establishes that judges have analyzed and designed the tort with a unique understanding of, and sympathy for, the lawyer-defendants before them – a clear example of the lawyer–judge bias. Courts are more favorable to lawyers than to other professionals. Even in the areas in which legal malpractice has begun to catch up, it lags behind other areas of the law, and outlier courts remain.

[61] See Neil Vidmar, *Medical Malpractice and the American Jury* (Ann Arbor: University of Michigan Press, 1997), 253–54.

[62] Nicole A. Cunitz, "Mandatory Malpractice Insurance for Lawyers: Is There a Possibility of Public Protection Without Compulsion?," 8 *Geo. J. Legal Ethics* 637, 658 (1995).

[63] *Broadnax v. Gonzalez*, 809 N.E.2d 645 (N.Y. 2004); *Carey v. Lovett*, 622 A.2d 1279 (N.J. 1993). See also *Perry-Rogers v. Obasaju*, 723 N.Y.S.2d 28 (N.Y. App. Div. 2001) and *Fasano v. Nash*, 723 N.Y.S.2d 181 (N.Y. App. Div. 2001), allowing emotional distress damages for a botched in vitro fertilization.

Malicious Prosecution

The common law tort of malicious prosecution actually covers two distinct types of torts. One is for a baseless civil lawsuit and the other for a baseless criminal prosecution.[64]

There has always been concern in America over the phenomenon of baseless lawsuits; that concern has heightened in recent years as complaints about the legal system and lawyers have grown more heated.[65] The problem is somewhat blunted in other common law jurisdictions by their cost-shifting requirement. In England and most other common law jurisdictions, an unsuccessful plaintiff must pay the defendant's costs in the suit, and vice versa if the plaintiff wins.[66]

There are other options for battling this problem, however, including court sanctions or professional discipline. As we learned in Chapters 5 and 6, these tools are rarely used. Another option is the common law tort of malicious prosecution. Establishing malicious prosecution requires the proof of four elements: "(1) the initiation or continuation of a lawsuit; (2) lack of probable cause; (3) malice; and (4) favorable termination of the lawsuit."[67] Malicious prosecution is a very hard tort to prove. Indeed, courts have long held that "suits for malicious prosecution are viewed with disfavor in law and are to be carefully guarded against."[68]

Each of these elements is challenging for a plaintiff. Probable cause has quite a low standard of proof and malice is a very hard and subjective thing to prove. The "favorable termination of the lawsuit" prong is also

[64] The modern version of the civil version is called "wrongful initiation of civil proceedings." As usual, the common law name is more evocative and likable.

[65] The work of Philip K. Howard, discussed at greater length in Chapter 11, is emblematic. See Philip K. Howard, *Life Without Lawyers* (New York: W. W. Norton, 2009); Philip K. Howard, *Death of Common Sense* (New York: Warner Books, 1996).

[66] See, e.g., England's Civil Procedure Rules §44.3(2)(a) (2008).

[67] *Black's Law Dictionary*, 8th ed. (St. Paul, MN: West, 2004), 977–78.

[68] *Cottman v. Cottman*, 468 A.2d 131, 136 (Md. App. 1983); see also *Laing v. Shanberg*, 13 F.Supp.2d 1186, 1189 (D. Kan. 1998) ("[M]alicious prosecution causes of action have long been disfavored in the law because they tend to discourage individuals from seeking redress in the courts.").

quite stringent, as it states that the malicious-prosecution plaintiff must have won every aspect of the case, on the merits. Procedural victories, settlements, or a finding that one part of a lawsuit was baseless and malicious are insufficient.[69]

A suit for malicious prosecution may be brought against the original litigant and/or that litigant's lawyer. Malicious prosecution's disfavor "is particularly true when the defendant is an attorney because of the attorney's professional duty to represent his client zealously."[70] There are a series of lawyers-only modifications to the already rigorous elements listed previously that make a malicious-prosecution suit against a lawyer even harder to plead.

Although the use of the very low probable cause standard to file a suit already "allows for a liberal construction," as "applied to attorneys, the term is given an even broader interpretation because if attorneys cannot act and advise freely, parties could not obtain their legal rights."[71] The fact that the underlying plaintiff had no probable cause cannot be imputed to the lawyer. Instead, probable cause is measured by what the lawyer personally knew about the case at the time.[72] The lawyer is permitted to rely upon the statements of the client without further investigation:

> The law is well established that "an attorney is entitled to rely in good faith upon the statement of facts made to him by his client, and is not under a duty to institute an inquiry for the purpose of verifying his statement before giving advice thereon." If the client falsifies the facts, there may be a liability which attaches to the client, but the lawyer is not liable if, without more, he acts in good faith upon the facts stated by the client.[73]

[69] See, e.g., *Friedberg v. Cox*, 197 Cal.App.3d 381, 386–387 (1987).

[70] *Cottman*, 468 A.2d at 136 (Md. App. 1983).

[71] *Moffit v. Litteral*, 2002 WL 31105394, *9 (Ohio App. 2002).

[72] On the rule that probable cause is appraised on the basis of the information available to the lawyer without any requirement of investigation, see *Lucero v. Stewart*, 892 F.2d 52 (9th Cir. 1989); *Sheldon Appel Co. v. Albert & Oliker*, 765 P.2d 498 (Cal. 1989); and *Wilson v. Hayes*, 464 N.W.2d 250 (Iowa 1990).

[73] *Melksin v. Howard Hanna Co., Inc.*, 590 A.2d 1303, 1306 (Pa. Super. 1991) (quoting 52 Am. Jur. 2d Malicious Prosecution §64 (1970)).

In short, a lawyer is justified in going forward with a claim based solely on the client's word, regardless of what any further investigation might have shown.

Moreover, "even if [a lawyer] has no probable cause and is convinced that his client's claim is unfounded, he is still not liable if he acts primarily for the purpose of aiding his client in obtaining a proper adjudication of his claim."[74] This means that even if the lawyer knows that the underlying claim is legally faulty, the lawyer is allowed to go forward on the suit as long as that decision is not based on a desire to harass the opponent or to force a settlement or for another "improper" motive. Notably, a "desire to earn a contingent or other fee does not constitute an improper motive."[75] This is because an "attorney is not required or expected to prejudge his client's claim" and "although [the lawyer] is fully aware that its chances of success are comparatively slight," the lawyer's duty is to follow the client's wishes.[76] This also means that even if a claim is obviously barred by the law, a lawyer can argue that she was seeking an appropriate change in the law and escape liability. It is hard to imagine that a lay judge, as opposed to a former lawyer, would have crafted these defenses to malicious prosecution.

Note how these rationales (openness of courts and the duty of zealous representation) compare with the other rhetoric we have seen concerning lawyers' critical role as "officers of the court." Many of the previous lawyer–judge bias cases are justified as protections of the lawyer's central role as an officer of the court who guides and protects the judiciary. When it comes to malicious prosecution, however, a lawyer simply follows the wishes of the client, even if the lawyer knows the underlying case is questionable. This allowance actually works against the interests

[74] *Restatement (Second) of Torts* §674, comment d; see also *Restatement (Third) of the Law Governing Lawyers* §7, comment d; see also *Wilson v. Hayes*, 464 N.W.2d 250 (Iowa 1990); *Nelson v. Miller*, 607 P.2d 438 (Kan. 1980); *Prewitt v. Sexton*, 777 S.W.2d 891 (Ky. 1989); and *Gaar v. North Myrtle Beach Realty Co.*, 339 S.E.2d 887 (S.C. Ct. App. 1986).

[75] *Restatement (Third) of the Law Governing Lawyers* §57, comment d.

[76] *Restatement (Second) of Torts* §674, comment d.

of judges: holding lawyers to a stricter standard might shrink the number of baseless suits judges so often decry. Nevertheless, in this instance judicial self-interest is overwhelmed by a desire to protect the legal profession and judges let the parties most likely to be able to tell if a claim is legally sufficient – the lawyers – off the hook.

Absolute Immunity

The criminal version of malicious prosecution is also quite difficult to prove, with a notable additional hurdle: prosecutors are absolutely immune from suit for any and all actions taken in prosecuting cases.[77] This means that a wrongfully accused defendant who was convicted because of prosecutorial misconduct has virtually no civil recourse. Absolute immunity has been granted to prosecutors who withheld exculpatory evidence, presented fabricated or false evidence, influenced witnesses and prepared perjured testimony, breached a plea agreement, or conspired with a judge to predetermine the outcome of a case.[78]

The absolute immunity of prosecutors is based on the absolute immunity judges have when acting in their judicial capacity.[79] Like prosecutors, judges have been held immune from suit for an impressive list of activities, including ordering the sterilization of a fifteen-year old girl in an ex parte proceeding,[80] conspiring with a prosecutor to convict a defendant,[81] altering a trial transcript and docket sheet,[82] singling out

[77] *Hartman v. Moore*, 547 U.S. 250, 261–62 (2006) (citing *Imbler v. Pachtman*, 424 U.S. 409, 431 (1976)). A prosecutor receives only qualified immunity for administrative, non-case-related work. *Hartman*, 547 U.S. at 262 n. 8 (citing *Buckley v. Fitzsimmons*, 509 U.S. 259, 274–76 (1993); *Burns v. Reed*, 500 U.S. 478, 492–95 (1991)).

[78] This list and more examples can be found in Leslie E. Williams, "The Civil Regulation of Prosecutors," 67 *Ford. L. Rev.* 3441, 3457–61 (1999).

[79] Legislative officers similarly have absolute immunity when performing their jobs.

[80] *Stump v. Sparkman*, 435 U.S. 349 (1978).

[81] *Ashelman v. Pope*, 793 F.2d 1072, 1078 (9th Cir. 1986); *Dykes v. Hosemann*, 776 F.2d 942, 946 (11th Cir. 1985).

[82] *Eades v. Sterlinske*, 810 F.2d 723, 726 (7th Cir. 1987).

and yelling at a juror who refused to vote for the death penalty in a case,[83] and allegedly taking bribes.[84]

Clearly, for prosecutors and judges, immunity really is absolute. Judges have been quick to note that this is not for their own benefit, but for the benefit of the public. Consider the following statement on judicial immunity:

> [Judicial] immunity applies even when the judge is accused of acting maliciously and corruptly, and it "is not for the protection or benefit of a malicious or corrupt judge, but for the benefit of the public, whose interest it is that the judges should be at liberty to exercise their functions with independence and without fear of consequences." It is a judge's duty to decide all cases within his jurisdiction that are brought before him, including controversial cases that arouse the most intense feelings in the litigants. His errors may be corrected on appeal, but he should not have to fear that unsatisfied litigants may hound him with litigation charging malice or corruption. Imposing such a burden on judges would contribute not to principled and fearless decisionmaking but to intimidation.[85]

There is not a hint in this quote or other cases that the judges recognize their conflict of interest. These cases (by judges and for judges) decide that a judge acting as a judge can never be sued no matter what she does, so virtually all judicial behavior is free from suit.

Prosecutorial immunity receives the same treatment, for identical reasons:

> To be sure, [prosecutorial] immunity does leave the genuinely wronged defendant without civil redress against a prosecutor whose malicious or dishonest action deprives him of liberty. But the alternative of qualifying a prosecutor's immunity would disserve the broader

[83] *Emory v. Peeler*, 756 F.2d 1547 (11th Cir. 1985).

[84] *Holloway v. Walker*, 765 F.2d 517, 523 (5th Cir. 1985).

[85] *Pierson v. Ray*, 386 U.S. 547, 554 (1967) (quoting *Scott v. Stansfield*, L.R. 3 Ex. 220, 223 (1868)).

> public interest. It would prevent the vigorous and fearless performance of the prosecutor's duty that is essential to the proper functioning of the criminal justice system. Moreover, it often would prejudice defendants in criminal cases by skewing post-conviction judicial decisions that should be made with the sole purpose of insuring justice.... As is so often the case, the answer must be found in a balance between the evils inevitable in either alternative. In this instance it has been thought in the end better to leave unredressed the wrongs done by dishonest officers than to subject those who try to do their duty to the constant dread of retaliation.[86]

Although it is certainly correct that allowing absolute immunity does make the jobs of prosecutors and judges easier, it is worth considering whether the balance between "unredressed wrongs" and the working of the judicial process needs to be struck in such a one-sided manner.

Consider the veiled threat that lifting prosecutorial immunity "often would prejudice defendants in criminal cases by skewing post-conviction judicial decisions that should be made with the sole purpose of insuring justice." Here at last we have a hint of self-awareness about the lawyer–judge bias. Absolute prosecutorial immunity is necessary because if liability were a possibility, judges reviewing a faulty prosecution might be tempted to "skew" their decision to protect prosecutors. Unfortunately, this hint of awareness results in additional protection for prosecutors, rather than a judicial effort to try to call these cases fairly.

Compare these cases with the complaints of other professionals subjected to suits, such as doctors or engineers. The cries of "defensive medicine" and the constant worries over potential liability are deafening but virtually unheard by the judges. In those cases, judges are confident that the judicial process can be counted on to weed out the unfounded claims. However, when a criminal defendant wants to sue a prosecutor or a judge for conspiring to find the defendant guilty regardless of the

[86] *Imbler v. Pachtman*, 424 U.S. 409, 427–428 (1976) (quoting *Gregoire v. Biddle*, 177 F.2d 579, 581 (2nd Cir. 1949)).

evidence, it is better to leave those court officials to do their jobs unmolested by the possibility of a lawsuit.

The Litigation Privilege

We have already learned that it is quite difficult for an opposing litigant to sue a lawyer for malicious prosecution. But what about a suit for simple negligence? Anyone who has been involved in a lawsuit knows a sloppy or overzealous lawyer can impose a great deal of cost and pain on an opposing party.

That is where the "litigation privilege" comes in. Courts have uniformly held that a lawyer owes no duty whatsoever to anyone besides the client and the court:

> A defendant attorney owes no duty to the plaintiff. The attorney's paramount duty is to the trial court, as a licensed attorney and officer of the court, and to his client. No cause of action in negligence can lie because the overriding public policy guarding free access to the courts and the fact that the attorney's legal duty is to his own client demands a finding that the attorney owes no duty to an adverse party that would give rise to a claim in negligence, whether to investigate fully the client's claim prior to filing suit or to avoid filing a suit which he knew or should have known was frivolous.[87]

This privilege essentially eliminates all third-party liability for a lawyer's actions in litigation. When there is no duty, there can be no liability.

The litigation privilege also applies to any defamatory statements or questions by a lawyer before, during, or after a trial, as long as the statements are somewhat connected to the litigation.[88] This privilege means that a lawyer can make a false and defamatory statement or ask a loaded

[87] I eliminated some ellipses and brackets in this quote for ease of reading. It is from *Clark v. Druckman*, 624 S.E.2d 864, 869 (W.Va. 2005) (quoting *McKenna, Long & Aldridge, LLP v. Keller*, 598 S.E.2d 892, 894 (Ga. 2004)).

[88] See Douglas R. Richmond, "The Lawyer's Litigation Privilege," 31 *Am. J. Trial Advocacy* 281, 283–87 (2007).

question during a trial with no fear of civil reprisals. The privilege is defended as "the backbone to an effective and smoothly operating judicial system,"[89] and "is to ensure free access to the courts, promote complete and truthful testimony, encourage zealous advocacy, give finality to judgments, and avoid unending litigation."[90] The privilege is an old common law privilege from England and also extends to witnesses and parties to litigation.

The justifications are now familiar: the "overriding public policy guarding free access to the courts" and the sanctity of the lawyer–client relationship. The problems that third-party liability might cause in a professional–client relationship are not unique to lawyers, however. Certainly doctors, accountants, or architects would report that their primary responsibility is to serve their clients' interests and that worrying about third-party liability is an impediment to the fullest possible confidence in that relationship. Nevertheless, in those relationships courts credit the need to protect third parties above the desire to have an all powerful professional–client relationship.

Moreover, even though the functioning of the litigation process is important, it is worth wondering whether, given the choice, the public would balance it so heavily against punishing negligent or misbehaving lawyers. It is unclear whether the fulsome litigation privilege helps or hurts the litigation process. If lawyers were more concerned about treating opposing parties fairly, perhaps the entire process would be better run and more streamlined. Certainly, in other areas of the law, judges have expected the threat of liability to ameliorate harmful behavior. The litigation privilege is also an absolute privilege. Could the same goals be met by a conditional privilege, waived on a showing of malice, for instance?[91]

[89] *McClatchy Newspapers, Inc. v. Superior Court*, 234 Cal. Rptr. 702, 707 (Ct. App. 1987).

[90] *Wentland v. Wass*, 25 Cal. Rptr. 3d 109, 115 (Cal. Ct. App. 2005).

[91] Paul T. Hayden, "Reconsidering the Litigator's Absolute Privilege to Defame," 54 *Ohio St. L.J.* 985, 986 (1993) argues this exact point excellently.

Again, it is obvious why judges would feel that such a privilege was necessary: without it, collateral litigation from irritated litigants could become the norm. Nevertheless, note the stringency of an absolute bar to any suits based on what happens or is said in a lawsuit. Although tort liability has grown in almost every other area of American endeavor, judges have kept the operation of their own courts free from the distracting threat of possible liability.[92]

When other types of litigants argue that the threat of a lawsuit disrupts their place of business or their ability to do a job, courts are generally unsympathetic: the threat of a lawsuit is exactly what keeps these industries and professions safe for the rest of us. When this reasoning is used against lawyers or courts, however, there is an overriding public policy interest in avoiding lawsuits. Between these rules and the relative lack of judicial or disciplinary authority oversight, what is keeping us safe from incompetent or malicious lawyering?

[92] This freedom from suit arises from the litigation privilege as well as the absolute and qualified immunity discussed earlier.

8 Evidence and Civil Procedure

> More than a century of experience with the statutes has demonstrated that the [physician–patient] privilege in the main operates not as the shield of privacy but as the protector of fraud.... [The privilege] runs against the grain of justice, truth and fair dealing.
>
> – Edward W. Cleary[1]

> The lawyer-client privilege serves a salutary and important purpose: to encourage full and frank communication between attorneys and their clients and thereby promote broader public interests in the observance of law and administration of justice.
>
> – *Southern Scrap Material Co. v. Fleming*[2]

THE ATTORNEY–CLIENT PRIVILEGE GUARANTEES THAT COMmunications between an attorney and client are not admissible in court. It is the oldest and most powerful evidentiary privilege and shields communications between lawyers and clients from disclosure in almost all settings. The attorney work product doctrine covers both the discovery process and admissibility in court. It gives limited protection to documents created in anticipation of litigation and absolute protection to the thoughts, opinions, and strategies of a lawyer

[1] See Edward W. Cleary, *McCormick's Handbook of the Law of Evidence*, 2nd ed. (St. Paul, MN: West Publishing Co., 1972), §105, at 228.

[2] *Southern Scrap Material Co. v. Fleming*, 2003 WL 21783318 (E.D. La. July 30, 2003) (internal quotation marks omitted).

preparing for trial. Between these two doctrines, lawyers are able to guarantee confidentiality to clients and prepare their cases for trial with little worry about what might or might not be discoverable by the opposing party. This is obviously a substantial selling point to clients and also makes every lawyer's job much easier.

This chapter also discusses the lawyer-dominated drafting process for the various rules of evidence and procedure. The rules of procedure govern the timing and format of court activities. The rules of evidence control what evidence is admissible in court. From the original days of common law in England, courts had power to exclude certain types of evidence. Over the years, those exclusions became regularized into a loose set of principles that cover what can or cannot be said or asked in open court. The most well-known examples are the complicated rules governing hearsay. Eventually these rules were formalized. Judges and lawyers exert almost complete control over these rules and, not surprisingly, lawyer favoritism is prevalent.

Attorney–Client Privilege

One of the oldest and most ingrained examples of the lawyer–judge bias is the attorney–client privilege, which has a unique and vaunted position among all professional privileges. The primacy of the attorney–client privilege – compared with those accorded to physicians, spouses, or clergy – cannot be justified solely jurisprudentially. Instead, the difference is the result of inherent judicial sympathy for the attorney–client relationship. The special treatment of the attorney–client privilege, in conjunction with the conduct rules requiring confidentiality that were discussed in Chapters 5 and 6, make legal services much more attractive to clients.

The classic statement of the attorney–client privilege comes from Wigmore's *Evidence*. The privilege applies "(1) [w]here legal advice of any kind is sought, (2) from a professional legal adviser in his capacity as such, (3) the communications relating to that purpose, (4) made in confidence, (5) by the client, (6) are at his instance permanently protected,

(7) from disclosure by himself or by the legal adviser, (8) except the protection be waived."[3]

Courts have long treated the attorney–client privilege as the flagship evidentiary privilege. Courts frequently "wax poetic"[4] about this "most sacred of all legally recognized privileges."[5] It holds a "special position"[6] as the "oldest and most venerated of the common law privileges of confidential communications."[7] It "serves a salutary and important purpose:" the encouragement of "full and frank communication between attorneys and their clients."[8] "Thus, it is reasonable to expect that a conversation with an attorney would be private."[9] It is a "strong and absolute privilege"[10] (barring waiver and other limited exceptions) and must "receive unceasing protection."[11] It "seeks to protect 'a relationship that is a mainstay of our system of justice.'"[12]

The courts protect the attorney–client privilege by more than just rhetoric. A comparison of the treatment of lawyers and other professionals by the courts is quite instructive. Of the three longest-standing "professions," lawyers are the only ones to receive continuous common law protection. As a result, lawyers have been, and continue to be, in a much better position than their compatriots.

[3] *Cavallaro v. United States*, 284 F.3d 236, 45 (1st Cir. 2002) (quoting John Henry Wigmore, *Evidence in Trials at Common Law*, vol. 8, revised by John T. McNaughton (Boston: Little, Brown & Co., 1961), §2292.

[4] Edward J. Imwinkelried, *The New Wigmore: A Treatise on Evidence, Evidentiary Privileges* (New York: Aspen Publishers, 2002), §6.2.4.

[5] *In re Grand Jury Proceedings*, 162 F.3d 554, 556–57 (9th Cir. 1998).

[6] *In re Allen*, 106 F.3d 582, 600 (4th Cir. 1997).

[7] *United States v. Edwards*, 303 F.3d 606, 618 (2002) (citing *Upjohn Co. v. United States*, 449 U.S. 383, 389 (1981)).

[8] *Southern Scrap Material Co. v. Fleming*, 2003 WL 21783318 (E.D. La. July 30, 2003) (quoting *Swindler & Berlin v. United States*, 524 U.S. 399, 403 (1998)).

[9] *Sherbrooke v. City of Pelican Rapids*, 2006 WL 3227783 (D. Minn. November 7, 2006) (citing *Lanza v. New York*, 370 U.S. 139, 143–44 (1962)).

[10] *Fru-Con Construction Corp. v. Sacramento Municipal Utility District*, 2006 WL 2255538 (E.D. Cal. August 7, 2006).

[11] *Lanza*, 370 U.S. 139, 143–44 (1962).

[12] *Gould, Larson, Bennet, Wells and McDonnell, P.C. v. Panico*, 869 A.2d 653, 656 (Conn. 2005) (quoting *Clute v. Davenport Co.*, 118 F.R.D. 312, 314 (D. Conn. 1988)).

There has never been a common law physician–patient privilege in England or in the United States: "Notwithstanding the fact that, since the sixteenth century, the relationship of attorney and client had been sedulously protected by a privilege of non-disclosure, the courts of England resolutely refused to extend a similar privilege to members of the medical profession."[13] Although the attorney–client privilege was originally recognized during the reign of Elizabeth I and protected as a "point of honor" for lawyers,[14] the physician–patient privilege was famously rejected in 1776. The doctor at issue refused to disclose "a confidential trust...consistent with [his] professional honour." Lord Mansfield replied, "If a surgeon was voluntarily to reveal these secrets, to be sure he would be guilty of a breach of honour...but, to give that information in a court of justice, which by the law of the land he is bound to do, will never be imputed to him as any indiscretion whatsoever."[15] The court then required disclosure.

State statutes, not judge-created common law, protect physician–patient communications in this country.[16] This makes the privilege substantially less powerful than the attorney–client privilege. There is no statutory protection whatsoever in approximately one-fifth of the states.[17] The fact that the privilege was not recognized at common law means that it is generally inapplicable in federal courts applying federal law.[18]

[13] Clinton DeWitt, *Privileged Communications Between Physician and Patient* (Springfield, IL: Charles C. Thomas Press, 1958), 9–14.

[14] See Wigmore, *Evidence,* §2290.

[15] Daniel W. Shuman, "The Origins of the Physician-Patient Privilege and Professional Secret," 39 *SW. L.J.* 661, 671 (1985) (quoting *Rex. v. Duchess of Kingston*, 20 How. St. Tr. 355, 572–73 (1776)).

[16] *McCormick on Evidence*, Volume 1, ed. John W. Strong (St. Paul, MN: West Publishing, 5th ed. 1999), §98, at 397–99. One exception is the Supreme Court's recognition of a psychotherapist–patient privilege in *Jaffee v. Redmond*, 518 U.S. 1 (1998).

[17] See Arthur Best, *Wigmore on Evidence*, 2004 Cumulative Supplement (St. Paul, MN: West Publishing, 2005), §2380 at 1336–49 (listing states and statutes).

[18] *Jaffee*, 518 U.S. at 10 (distinguishing doctors from psychotherapists, and granting only psychotherapists a privilege in federal courts); Kenneth S. Broun, "The Medical Privilege in the Federal Courts – Should it Matter Whether Your Ego or Your Elbow

Even when physician–patient protections exist, the privilege suffers "significant variations and numerous exceptions."[19] For example, many state statutes require a doctor to report child abuse, regardless of confidentiality. In contrast, the judicially created confidentiality rules (both the privilege and the Rules of Professional Responsibility) do not require such reporting.[20]

For a particularly blunt comparison between the attorney–client and physician–patient privileges, it is helpful to look where the rubber hits the road: the wisdom of trial attorneys. In *Trial* magazine, the privileges are compared as follows: "All states recognize the attorney-client privilege.... On the other hand, the physician-patient privilege is weak."[21] The other privileges do not fare much better: "The psychotherapist-patient privilege (which includes counselors, psychologists, and therapists) is generally stronger than the physician-patient privilege. The parent-child and accountant-client privileges are very weak. The journalist privilege is also subject to extreme variation."[22] Many litigation strategists suggest that doctors or psychiatrists hired as experts for trial examine their patients as part of the legal team so that the more stringent protections of the attorney–client and work product privileges will attach to their work.[23]

Hurts?," 38 *Loy. L.A. L. Rev.* 657 (2004) (arguing for creation of a federal physician–patient privilege).

[19] David Weissbrodt et al., "Piercing the Confidentiality Veil: Physician Testimony in International Criminal Trials Against Perpetrators of Torture," 15 *Minn. J. Int'l L.* 43, 61 (2006).

[20] Robin A. Rosenkrantz, "Rejecting 'Hear No Evil, Speak No Evil:' Expanding the Attorney's Role in Child Abuse Reporting," 8 *Geo. J. Leg. Ethics* 327 (1995); *Arizona Department of Economic Sec. v. O'Neil*, 901 P.2d 1226, 1227 (Ariz. Ct. App. 1995) (discussing the state statute that "provides that such privileges as the physician-patient and husband-wife privilege are unavailable in cases involving dependent children, but specifically exempts the attorney-client privilege").

[21] Ashley Saunders Lipton, "Know Your Testimonial Objections," *Trial*, July, 2005.

[22] Id.

[23] See Edward J. Imwinkelried, *Evidentiary Foundations*, 6th ed. (Newark, NJ: LexisNexis/Matthew Bender, 2005), 291, 302.

The clergy–penitent privilege has a similar history. Before the Reformation, there was a common law priest–penitent privilege that protected priests from testifying.[24] Following the Reformation, however, English courts repudiated the privilege, and American courts later followed suit.[25] Similar to the physician–patient privilege, the clergy privilege has grown primarily as a result of state statutes.[26] Furthermore, although the clergy–penitent privilege is recognized in all fifty states, its statutory basis differs state by state and it is subject to many more exceptions than the attorney–client privilege.[27]

Compared with accountants, however, doctors and clergy have it good. There is no federal accountant–client privilege.[28] Most jurisdictions have refused to recognize an accountant–client privilege as a matter of statutory or common law.[29] Journalists have also had a hard time establishing a privilege for sources.[30]

Nevertheless, there is not much difference between the justifications for these other privileges and for the attorney–client privilege. Courts and commentators have generally used a utilitarian approach to defend the attorney–client privilege, arguing that the societal benefits outweigh the costs. As the Supreme Court has stated, the privilege's "purpose is to encourage full and frank communication between attorneys and their clients and thereby promote broader public interests in the observance

[24] See Mary H. Mitchell, "Must Clergy Tell? Child Abuse Reporting Requirements Versus the Clergy Privilege and Free Exercise of Religion," 71 *Minn. L. Rev.* 723, 735–36 (1987).

[25] See John J. Montone, "In Search of Forgiveness: *State v. Szemple* and the Priest-Penitent Privilege in New Jersey," 48 *Rutgers L. Rev.* 263, 267–69 (1995).

[26] An early case recognized the privilege under the First Amendment free exercise clause, but since that case the application has been through statutes. See Jacob M. Yellin, "The History and Current Status of the Clergy-Penitent Privilege," 23 *Santa Clara L. Rev.* 95, 106–10 (1983).

[27] See Montone, "In Search of Forgiveness," 283–86.

[28] See *Couch v. United States*, 409 U.S. 322, 335 (1973).

[29] See Imwinkelried, *The New Wigmore*, §6.2.4.

[30] See Jeffrey S. Nestler, "The Underprivileged Profession: The Case for Supreme Court Recognition of the Journalist's Privilege," 154 *U. Pa. L. Rev.* 201 (2005).

of law and the administration of justice. The privilege recognizes that sound legal advice or advocacy serves public ends and that such advice or advocacy depends upon the lawyer being fully informed by the client."[31]

Some of the best known historical formulations of this utilitarian justification are particularly telling in terms of the lawyer–judge bias. The 1743 case of *Annesley v. Earl of Anglesea*,[32] quoted at length in the famous common law classic, Wigmore's *Evidence*, specifically references the business interests of lawyers in the privilege: "all people and all courts have looked upon that confidence between the party and attorney to be so great that it would be destructive to all business if attornies [*sic*] were to disclose the business of their clients."[33]

Other early courts explicitly recognized the judiciary's need for a fully functioning cadre of lawyers as a justification: the privilege is necessary "out of regard to the interests of justice, which cannot be upholden, and to the administration of justice, which cannot go on without the aid of men skilled in jurisprudence, in the practice of the courts, and in those matters affecting rights and obligations which form the subject of all judicial proceedings."[34] The utilitarian defense includes two themes we have seen repeatedly: an implied concern for the welfare and business of lawyers and concern over the ease of the administration of justice.

The importance placed on the attorney–client relationship, and the relative disrespect paid to doctors and patients and other professional relationships, is striking. If candor between attorneys and clients is so critical that we should protect it in court, is candor between doctors and patients any less important? In many people's minds, health advice frequently (if not always) trumps legal advice in importance. Similarly, the relationship between a worshipper and a clergyperson seems equally worthy of societal support and protection. Under the First Amendment,

[31] See *Upjohn Co.*, 449 U.S. at 389.

[32] *Annesley v. Earl of Anglesea*, 17 How. St. Tr. 1129 (Ex. 1743).

[33] Id. at 1225, 1241 (quoted in 8 Wigmore, *Evidence*, §2291, at 546).

[34] *Greenough v. Gaskell*, 39 Eng. Rep. 618, 621 (Ch. 1833).

clergy have a much stronger constitutional argument for a privilege than lawyers do.[35]

The physician–patient privilege (among others) was scorned at common law. Wigmore's *Evidence* offers a particularly scathing rebuke. Wigmore applied a four-part test to balance the costs and benefits of all privileges: (1) The communications must originate in a confidence that they will not be disclosed. (2) This element of confidentiality must be essential to the full and satisfactory maintenance of the relation between the parties. (3) The relation must be one that, in the opinion of the community, ought to be sedulously fostered. (4) The injury that would inure to the relation by the disclosure must be greater than the benefit thereby gained for the correct disposal of litigation.[36]

Using this test, Wigmore found that only the three privileges that had been recognized at common law – husband–wife, priest–penitent, and attorney–client – satisfied all four factors.[37] Wigmore argued vociferously against the physician–patient privilege. One of his main arguments was that doctors did not really need the privilege because people would consult doctors in all candor regardless of any privilege. Wigmore argued that it is "ludicrous" to suggest that a seriously ill person would withhold vital information from a doctor out of fear of later exposure in court.[38] In this way, Wigmore used the importance of the doctor–patient relationship as support for *denying* a privilege.

Wigmore made much of the fact that states that had a physician–patient privilege, such as New York, reported no difference in usage of doctors from nonprivilege states.[39] Ironically, Wigmore said nothing about the utter lack of empirical data to support claims that the

[35] See Ronald J. Colombo, "Forgive Us Our Sins: The Inadequacies of the Clergy-Penitent Privilege," 73 *N.Y.U. L. Rev.* 225 (1998).

[36] Wigmore, *Evidence*, §2285.

[37] Id.

[38] Id. at §2380a.

[39] Id.

attorney–client privilege is critical to maintaining a functioning justice system.[40]

It is also humorous that Wigmore carped that "[t]he real support for the privilege seems to be mainly the weight of professional medical opinion pressing upon the legislature."[41] Given that the lawyer–client privilege was granted by lawyer-judges to lawyers, a claim of overweening physician influence is particularly aggressive.

Finally, the physician privilege has been criticized as fostering fraud. "More than a century of experience with the statutes has demonstrated that the [physician–patient] privilege in the main operates not as the shield of privacy but as the protector of fraud.... [The privilege] runs against the grain of justice, truth and fair dealing."[42]

The same arguments against the doctor–patient privilege fit lawyers and clients. Would lawyer–client communication truly be crippled without the privilege? Are many clients fully forthcoming with their lawyers regardless of the privilege? I do not ask these questions to argue for the abolition or curtailment of the privilege, just to note that the empirical and theoretical basis for differentiating between lawyers and doctors (or clergy or accountants) is not nearly as clear as courts have suggested. Instead, when faced with a balancing test between the importance of a professional relationship and the truth-seeking function, courts repeatedly favored the truth-seeking function – except when it came to lawyers. Although this choice has been defended on jurisprudential grounds, it is better explained by the lawyer–judge bias.

The effect of disclosures of attorney–client communications further hints at the privilege's true beneficiaries. Generally, any disclosure to a

[40] See Edward J. Imwinkelried, "Questioning the Behavioral Assumption Underlying Wigmorean Absolutism in the Law of Evidentiary Privileges," 65 *U. Pitt. L. Rev.* 145 (2004).

[41] Wigmore, *Evidence*, §2380a.

[42] See Edward W. Cleary, *McCormick's Handbook of the Law of Evidence*, 2nd ed. (St. Paul: West Publishing Co., 1972), §105, at 228.

third person outside the confidential relationship waives the privilege.[43] These rules are particularly stringent for clients: a word about a privileged matter to a friend or relative, or even a lack of care with privileged materials, can constitute a waiver. Two notable exceptions have been made for law firm practice. First, the privilege is not limited only to lawyers: any agents, secretaries, or paralegals are included.[44] Second, in a case of inadvertent disclosure during discovery, privilege may be maintained under Rule of Evidence 502 if the disclosure was inadvertent, the lawyer took reasonable steps to prevent the disclosure, and the holder promptly took reasonable steps to rectify the error.[45]

Last, although courts carefully protect these privileges in most court actions, we have already seen that disclosure is permitted to defend a malpractice action or a fee dispute. These exceptions clearly establish who the privilege benefits. When a dispute between an attorney and a client breaks out, the once inviolable protections, guaranteed by lofty language in judicial opinions and lawyer ethical codes, no longer apply.

Attorney Work Product

Unlike the attorney–client privilege, the attorney work product doctrine is of relatively recent vintage in the United States. It was created in conjunction with the adoption of the Federal Rules of Civil Procedure

[43] "The moment confidence ceases…privilege ceases." *In re San Juan Dupont Plaza Hotel Fire Litigation*, 859 F.2d 1007 (1st Cir. 1988) (quoting 8 Wigmore, *Evidence*, § 2311).

[44] Fed. R. Evid. 502. See also *United States ex rel. Edney v. Smith*, 425 F.Supp. 1038, 1046 (E.D.N.Y. 1976) ("Given the complexities of modern existence few, if any, lawyers could as a practical matter represent the interests of their clients without the assistance of a variety of trained legal associates not yet admitted to the bar, clerks, typists, messengers, and similar aides.").

[45] See *K.L. Group v. Case, Kay & Lynch*, 829 F.2d 909 (9th Cir. 1987) (inadvertent production of privileged letter, along with some 2,000 other documents during discovery, did not result in waiver of attorney–client privilege); cf. *Transamerica*, 573 F.2d at 649–50 (describing IBM's extensive privilege review procedures as "incredibl[e]" before holding no waiver).

and the change in discovery practices. Before 1938, parties were not required to disclose any particular facts, documents, or witnesses to their opponents other than the bare facts included in their pleadings. This meant that lawsuits were often a game of "blind man's bluff," with both sides hiding as much as possible about their cases until trial.[46]

The Federal Rules of Civil Procedure were an explicit effort to change that dynamic. The new rules required parties to respond to discovery requests from opposing parties via written interrogatories, depositions, and document requests. This resulted in each party knowing much more about the opponent's case. It also resulted in a series of disputes over exactly what materials could be discovered.[47]

One such dispute was whether an opposing party could demand what later came to be known as attorney work product. This question was answered in the 1947 Supreme Court case of *Hickman v. Taylor*.[48] The case dealt with a tugboat sinking. In advance of possible litigation, an attorney for the tugboat's insurance company interviewed various witnesses. Once suit was filed, the opposing party requested the witnesses' statements.[49]

The district court ordered the attorney to turn over the statements, going so far as to hold the attorney in contempt for refusing to oblige and holding him in custody.[50] The U.S. Court of Appeals for the Third Circuit reversed and the Supreme Court took the case.

Hickman is a significant lawyer–judge bias case for several reasons. First, it is not an ancient case dealing with a four-hundred-year-old privilege, so it cannot be chalked up to historical accident or seventeenth-century bias. Second, it is exactly the type of issue that really affects the legal profession. Indeed, the advisory committee in charge of amending

[46] *United States v. Procter & Gamble Co.*, 356 U.S. 677, 682 (1958).

[47] Sherman L. Cohn, "The Work-Product Doctrine: Protection, Not Privilege," 71 *Geo. L.J.* 917, 917–19 (1983).

[48] *Hickman v. Taylor*, 329 U.S. 495 (1947).

[49] Id. at 498–501.

[50] Id. at 500–01.

the rules called the handling of attorney work product during discovery its "most perplexing problem" and went so far as to "appeal to the bar" for a solution in a "tone of despair."[51] Last, although it is an issue with potentially large effects, notably encouraging the most open process of discovery possible, it is an issue that has little public salience.

In these circumstances, it is not surprising to see how things worked out. The Supreme Court granted a qualified work product privilege, for reasons that have now become quite familiar:

> Historically, a lawyer is an officer of the court and is bound to work for the advancement of justice while faithfully protecting the rightful interests of his clients. In performing his various duties, however, it is essential that a lawyer work with a certain degree of privacy, free from unnecessary intrusion by opposing parties and their counsel. Proper preparation of a client's case demands that he assemble information, sift what he considers to be the relevant from the irrelevant facts, prepare his legal theories and plan his strategy without undue and needless interference. That is the historical and the necessary way in which lawyers act within the framework of our system of jurisprudence to promote justice and to protect their clients' interests. This work is reflected, of course, in interviews, statements, memoranda, correspondence, briefs, mental impressions, personal beliefs, and countless other tangible and intangible ways – aptly though roughly termed by the Circuit Court of Appeals in this case as the "Work product of the lawyer." Were such materials open to opposing counsel on mere demand, much of what is now put down in writing would remain unwritten. An attorney's thoughts, heretofore inviolate, would not be his own. Inefficiency, unfairness and sharp practices would inevitably develop in the giving of legal advice and in the preparation of cases for trial. The effect on the legal profession would be demoralizing. And the interests of the clients and the cause of justice would be poorly served.[52]

[51] See Walter P. Armstrong, "Report of the Advisory Committee on Federal Rules of Civil Procedure Recommending Amendments," available at 5 F.R.D. 339, 354–55 (1945).

[52] *Hickman*, 329 U.S. at 510–11.

This quote covers almost every justification for the lawyer–judge bias. It starts with the oft-repeated admonishment that a lawyer is an "officer of the court," without any explanation for why this is relevant. It continues with a lengthy and exceedingly sympathetic description of how a lawyer works and what a hardship fully open discovery would be. The Court explicitly notes the "demoralizing" effect of such discovery on the profession and, at the end, throws in a line about how the interests of clients and justice would also be compromised. The Court cites no authority whatsoever for its holding or for the concept that lawyers need to work undisturbed as a "historical" matter of "jurisprudence."[53] This may be the quintessential lawyer–judge bias quote: start with the "officer of the court," continue by sympathizing and empathizing with lawyers, and end with an imagined tie-in to clients and the public interest.

This quote is not the only place in which the Court explicitly raises the concerns of the legal profession. Later, the Court notes, "We fully appreciate the wide-spread controversy among the members of the legal profession over the problem raised by this case" and refuses to interpret the rules to allow a "harsh and unwarranted" result.[54]

The work product doctrine established in *Hickman* has now been ensconced in the Federal Rules of Civil Procedure and has become the rule in every state in the union.[55] The rule comes in two forms. The absolute version protects against disclosure of "the mental impressions, conclusions, opinions, or legal theories of an attorney or other representative" concerning the litigation.[56] The qualified version protects any other arguable work product, such as witness statements or some expert reports. This sort of information is subject to disclosure on a showing

[53] In a footnote, the Court does cite to the modern English version of the attorney work product doctrine. Id. at 510 n. 9.

[54] Id. at 513–14.

[55] Steven Lubet and Cathryn Stewart, "A 'Public Assets' Theory of Lawyers' Pro Bono Obligations," 145 *U. Pa. L. Rev.* 1245, 1276–77 (1997).

[56] Fed. R. Civ. Pro. 26(b); see also Edward J. Imwinkelried, *Evidentiary Foundations*, 5th ed. (Newark, NJ: LexisNexis, 2002), 286–87.

of "substantial need" and that failing to disclose would cause "undue hardship."[57]

The post-*Hickman* history generally expands on the protection of attorney work product. One of the issues that plagued courts post-*Hickman* was whether the work product doctrine extended to the work of nonlawyers. Federal courts split on the issue until a 1970 amendment to the Federal Rules of Civil Procedure finally decided that the protection extended to a party's "representative (including the other party's attorney, consultant, surety, indemnitor, insurer, or agent)."[58] Notably the courts that presaged this rule change and extended attorney work product to non-attorneys did so as an extension of the lawyer's own prerogative, not as a free-standing privilege coming from the client or another profession's norms or duties.[59] In fact, one of the cases argued that requiring the lawyer himself to do all of the investigating "discriminate[s] in favor of the party whose lawyer himself does all the work of preparation for trial and against the one whose counsel delegates part of that task to others."[60] The privilege has also been expanded to ban disclosure before, during, or after trials.[61]

The work product protection covers a key chink in the legal profession's armor, as the attorney–client protection does not cover notes from discussions with outside parties, such as witnesses, or many trial preparation materials.[62] Although the rule does make it much easier for a lawyer to prepare a case for trial, it imposes significant costs systemwide. In the typical civil case, a party will claim that at least some of the relevant documents in its possession are protected by the privilege. The party seeking discovery then faces an unpleasant choice: either accept the

[57] Fed. R. Civ. Pro. 26(b); see also Imwinkelried, *Evidentiary Foundations*, 279–80.

[58] Fed. R. Civ. Pro. 26(b)(3) and comments (2008).

[59] See, e.g., *Alltmont v. United States*, 177 F.2d 971, 976 (3rd Cir. 1949).

[60] Id. at 976. Imagine the horrors of discrimination!

[61] Lubet and Stewart, "A 'Public Assets' Theory," 1276–77.

[62] *Hickman*, 329 U.S. at 509.

assertion of privilege and lose access to those documents or fight out the issue in collateral discovery litigation. In millions of lawsuits across the country, each of these choices imposes costs in additional litigation or lost information. Given these costs, it is hard to argue that on balance the privilege helps clients, let alone the truth-seeking function of the justice system.

Hickman never balanced these costs and never even recognized the possibility that costs might be involved. Instead, the Court addressed only the hassles for, and the concerns of, lawyers. With only these important matters in mind the Court created a new evidentiary privilege.

Rule Creation

The great bulk of the law that governs evidence and procedure in the American courts has been reduced to formal written rules. These rules are of relatively low salience to the public at large, but they have an enormous effect on the operation of the courts and the way in which a lawsuit travels from filing to completion. Insofar as American law is seen as too complicated, too expensive, and too inefficient, the rules of procedure and evidence are partly to blame.

Similar to the Rules of Professional Responsibility, these rules are written by lawyers, law professors, and judges. In the federal system, the process is governed by statute.[63] There is a separate advisory committee for each of the five types of rules: appellate, bankruptcy, civil, criminal, and evidence. The advisory committees draft the rules and are the first step to any change in the rules. The advisory committees are made up of federal judges, practicing lawyers, law professors, state chief justices, and representatives of the Department of Justice.[64]

[63] 28 U.S.C. §§2071–2077 (2008).

[64] All this information comes from the U.S. Courts' own website. See http://www.uscourts.gov/RulesAndPolicies/FederalRulemaking/RulemakingProcess/SummaryBenchBar.aspx.

If an advisory committee proposes a change, it puts the change out for public comment. But from what public are comments solicited? Mostly lawyers. The listed recipients for any proposed rule change on the U.S. Courts' website include "federal judges and other federal court officers, United States attorneys, other federal government agencies and officials, state chief justices, state attorneys general, legal publications, law schools, bar associations, and interested lawyers, individuals, and organizations requesting distribution." Moreover, "[i]n order to promote public comment, the proposed amendments are sent to points of contact that have been established with 53 state bar associations."[65] Consumer advocates have complained that the advisory committees ignored their comments.[66]

After public comment is completed, the proposed rule goes through several additional layers of review: the standing committee (also made up of lawyers and judges) must approve it, followed by the Federal Judicial Conference and then the Supreme Court. Congress does have an opportunity to weigh in, but only in a limited time frame (usually seven months). If Congress does not act within the deadline, the rules automatically go into effect.[67]

Although these rules generate out of a process that includes Congress, federal courts have repeatedly held that they have an inherent authority to create their own rules. Whether congressional involvement exists as a matter of interbranch courtesy or whether Congress actually has the final authority over the rules is an undecided question.[68] Nevertheless, cases suggest that if the Supreme Court deemed a congressional action too threatening, the inherent-authority doctrine would likely be used to overturn.[69]

[65] Id.

[66] Charles G. Geyh, "Paradise Lost, Paradigm Found: Redefining the Judiciary's Imperiled Role in Congress," 71 *N.Y.U. L. Rev.* 1165, 1211–12 (1996).

[67] See 28 USC §§2074, 2075 (2008).

[68] See Amy Coney Barrett, "Procedural Common Law," 94 *Va. L. Rev.* 813, 842–78 (2008).

[69] Id.

State rules governing procedure and evidence mirror the federal model.[70] Many state supreme courts have claimed an inherent authority to draft these rules to the exclusion of state legislatures, so there is even less possibility of outside influence.[71]

In short, at both the federal and state levels, lawyers and judges dominate almost every step of the rulemaking process. Even though the federal system allows public comment and congressional review, the relative low salience of these rules, as well as the fact that all the drafting and responding are done by lawyers and judges, makes rulemaking a particularly insular process. It also makes it much more likely that the rules themselves will primarily serve the interests of their drafters. The inclusion of other interested parties, notably litigants or jurors, might result in a different-looking court process.

Moreover, the fact that rulemaking relies largely on the main players in the current system virtually guarantees that change will be incremental. A great example is the incredibly slow adoption of the electronic filing of court papers. Although e-mail and electronic documents have been in widespread use for at least a decade, courts have resisted allowing electronic filing of papers. This is not an insignificant decision: physically filing paper copies of all legal papers means extra costs in filing and storing, and in lawyers producing and delivering the documents. Nevertheless, it took until approximately 2003 for some federal courts to start allowing electronic filing, and state courts are way behind even that slow progress.[72] Many of these jurisdictions still allow paper filing as well, which retards the change and reduces the cost savings. Even in jurisdictions in which electronic filing is allowed, a majority of lawyers report that they still file on paper.[73]

[70] See Gil Seinfeld, "Federal Courts as a Franchise: Rethinking the Justifications for Federal Question Jurisdiction, 97 *Cal. L. Rev.* 95, 134–35 (2009).

[71] See Adrian Vermeule, "The Judicial Power in the State (and Federal) Courts," 2000 *Sup. Ct. Rev.* 357, 377–81 (2000).

[72] Lynn A. Epstein, "The Technology Challenge: Lawyers Have Finally Entered the Race but Will Ethical Hurdles Slow the Pace?," 28 *Nova L. Rev.* 721, 737–38 (2004).

[73] Id.

Why did it take so long for this to change, and why is it still dragging? Judges and lawyers, as a group, are not particularly techno-savvy. The advent of mass electronic filing might also threaten the jobs of some employees in clerks' offices or, at a minimum, require a massive retraining effort. From the judicial viewpoint, each of these steps is a hassle. In reality, electronic filing does little to make a judge's job easier, and if it required the regular use of computers or electronic documents, it might make things harder. In light of the institutional incentives, it makes perfect sense that the process would drag.

Another sign of who benefits from these rules is the substantial variation in rules of procedure among different courts. Even within the relatively uniform federal system, there are great variations in procedure between different districts and even within districts. Federal Rule of Civil Procedure 83 allows individual courts to create their own local rules consistent with the federal rules as a whole, and there is substantial variation. A 1988 Judicial Conference report on the topic reported that "[t]he ninety-four district courts currently have an aggregate of approximately 5,000 local rules, not including many 'subrules,' standing orders and standard operating procedures. These rules are extraordinarily diverse and their numbers continue to grow rapidly."[74] The states provide even more radical variations, with large differences in practice common even between neighboring counties.[75]

Differences in practice and procedure between courts is a classic lawyer–judge bias problem. These differences are quite expensive for litigants, especially large companies that have a national presence and are thus required to appear in courts all over the country. Totally aside from the various licensing and admission issues, a large company could not

[74] Committee on Rules of Practice and Procedure, Judicial Conference of the United States, *Local Rules Project, Part I* (Washington, DC: Judicial Conference of the United States, 1988), 1; see also, e.g., Gregory C. Sisk, "The Balkanization of Appellate Justice: The Proliferation of Local Rules in the Federal Circuits," 68 *U. Colo. L. Rev.* 1, 61 (1997).

[75] See Seinfeld, "Federal Courts as a Franchise," 136–46.

simply hire a cadre of lawyers and expect them to appear nationally on the company's behalf. The procedural and practice dissimilarities would prove crippling.

As a result, businesses tend to hire local counsel that is familiar with the local rules and practices. Moreover, variations in practice and procedure (as well as the difficulties involved in licensing) keep outside lawyers from competing with locals. This insulates existing practitioners and creates more business for lawyers, yielding obvious benefits for the profession as a whole.

Procedural variations are also quite helpful to the judiciary, who can micro-adjust the workings of their courts to meet their own idiosyncrasies. The costs of these variations are of little concern to the judges. They rarely, if ever, have to learn the rules of another jurisdiction. With lawyers and judges united in interest, variations in the rules metastasize across the country, with little regard for the systemwide costs to litigants.

9 The Business of Law

Clients are not merchandise. Lawyers are not tradesmen. They have nothing to sell but personal service. An attempt, therefore, to barter in clients, would appear to be inconsistent with the best concepts of our professional status.

– *Cohen v. Lord, Day & Lord*[1]

[Dr. Raymundo] suggests that this case is different, because it involves the medical profession or that he is, somehow entitled to special treatment, because he is a physician and there is great need for his services. This self-serving position, however, cannot be upheld.

– *Raymundo v. Hammond Clinic Association*[2]

THIS CHAPTER COVERS A SERIES OF COURT DECISIONS THAT affect the business side of law. Because lawyers care quite a bit about the bottom line as well as their conditions of employment, the lawyer–judge bias is quite prevalent in this area. It begins with the special rules that have been applied to legal services contracts and the special court-created rights lawyers have to collect debts from clients. Next, the chapter notes that state courts have not applied (or have only partially applied) consumer protection laws to the legal profession, despite the fact that the statutes do not explicitly exempt

[1] *Cohen v. Lord, Day & Lord*, 550 N.E.2d 410, 410–11 (N.Y. 1989).
[2] *Raymundo v. Hammond Clinic Association*, 449 N.E.2d 276, 280–81 (Ind. 1983).

lawyers. Courts have likewise created different employment rules for lawyers. Lawyers are treated differently (and better) in cases dealing with noncompete agreements and when they are terminated for whistle-blowing.

Similarly, bankruptcy courts have instituted a number of practices that stretch or outright violate the law to please the bankruptcy lawyers who appear regularly before them. Last, judges have used a modified *cy pres* doctrine to use unclaimed class action awards to support legal charities and LSCs, rather than allowing those funds to escheat to the state or federal treasuries. In sum, there are a bevy of ways in which judges have supported lawyers in the business of law and in their terms and conditions of employment.

Contracts

Joseph Perillo has written an enormously helpful article called "The Law of Lawyers' Contracts Is Different."[3] Before we turn to considering some of these special doctrines, here is an aside about the tone of Professor Perillo's article. "The Law of Lawyers' Contracts Is Different" is an excellent example of law review articles covering an area of the law in which lawyers are treated differently from everyone else. First, Perillo expresses some surprise that the law is so different.[4] Then he makes an effort to rationalize the differences. By the end, Perillo has convinced himself that the "overall picture is as one might expect" and that although the treatment of lawyers is sui generis, on the whole it reflects a fair balance by the courts between the interests of clients and lawyers.[5] When writing about the lawyer–judge bias, most legal academics – lawyers themselves – just cannot bring themselves to call judges biased or to announce that the rules that govern lawyers are abnormally

[3] Joseph M. Perillo, "The Law of Lawyers' Contracts Is Different," 67 *Fordham L. Rev.* 443 (1998).

[4] Id. at 444–45.

[5] Id. at 495.

favorable. The favorable treatment is explained, defended, and eventually downplayed.

Perillo is right when he points out that the special rules for lawyers' contracts do cut both ways and in some instances lawyers are treated worse than others. These disadvantageous rules are holdovers from the common law bias against contingency fees and the entrepreneurial practice of law, however, and strike only at a historically disfavored portion of the legal profession. Insofar as lawyers are following the business model of the "upper" bar of law firms and lawyers paid by the hour, the rules are most advantageous.

For example, in a ruling that appears to be anti-lawyer, courts have strongly defended the right of a client to fire a lawyer whenever she pleases for no reason or for cause, and the courts have refused to enforce service contracts: "It is now uniformly recognized that the client-lawyer contract is terminable at will by the client. For good reasons, poor reasons, or the worst of reasons, a client may fire the lawyer."[6] In these cases, the courts put great emphasis on client autonomy.

When the relationship is terminated without cause, the lawyer can still recover fees in what is known as *quantum meruit*.[7] *Quantum meruit* measures the objective value of the lawyer's work and pays the lawyer accordingly. This means that a terminated lawyer cannot generally collect what is known as "expectancy damages." Expectancy damages measure the potential profit the lawyer would have earned if the contract had run to its conclusion. In some cases the difference between the expected profit and the *quantum meruit* measure of objective value can be quite large, so this measure of damages is relatively unfriendly to lawyers. Doctors likewise can recover only in *quantum meruit* in breach-of-contract actions with patients, but other professionals, such as engineers or accountants, have had better luck collecting expected profits.[8]

[6] Charles W. Wolfram, *Modern Legal Ethics* (St. Paul, MN: West Group, 1986), 545.
[7] Perillo, "The Law of Lawyers' Contracts," 446–47.
[8] Id.

Nevertheless, although this is one of those rules that clearly disadvantages lawyers who work on a contingency fee, it has a relatively limited effect on lawyers who are paid on an hourly basis. Contingency lawyers get paid a share of the damages from any eventual settlement or court victory, so their entire business model is based on expected profits at the end of a case. Many contingency lawyers do not even keep track of their hours on a case.[9] When the law denies these lawyers future expected profits, it is a significant loss. In contrast, lawyers who work by the hour are well compensated by *quantum meruit* damages. They already bill by the hour, so they can simply bill the client for the hours worked and argue that the objective value of their services is easy to calculate: it is the amount the client agreed to pay per hour.

One way to tell that the rule against allowing the collection of expected profits especially disfavors contingency work is to consider the rule for payment of fees after a client fires a lawyer for cause. Unlike the case with future profits, forfeiting fees after a termination for cause would directly affect lawyers who bill by the hour. Here is where the law bends in the lawyers' favor.

Under normal circumstances, a party who breaches a contract cannot collect anything under that contract.[10] Nevertheless, when a client terminates a lawyer for cause, there is still a good chance that the lawyer will be able to collect some or all of the fees in *quantum meruit*. In a section titled "Partial or Complete Forfeiture of a Lawyer's Compensation," the *Restatement (Third) of Law Governing Lawyers* states the test as follows:

> A lawyer engaging in clear and serious violation of duty to a client may be required to forfeit some or all of the lawyer's compensation for the matter. Considerations relevant to the question of forfeiture include the gravity and timing of the violation, its willfulness, its effect

[9] Herbert M. Kritzer, "Advocacy and Rhetoric vs. Scholarship and Evidence in the Debate Over Contingency Fees: A Reply to Professor Brickman," 82 *Wash. U. L.Q.* 477, 480–81 (2004).

[10] See Barry E. Adler, "Efficient Breach Theory Through the Looking Glass," 83 *N.Y.U. L. Rev.* 1679, 1681 (2008).

on the value of the lawyer's work for the client, any other threatened or actual harm to the client, and the adequacy of other remedies.[11]

Joseph Perillo noted that this section is "lawyer-friendly" and lacks "coherence" and "clarity."[12]

Indeed, this is quite a remarkable test for compensation in a breach-of-contract situation. The question presented is not the relatively straightforward question of whether the lawyer breached an employment contract through poor performance. Instead, a reviewing court is instructed to determine whether a lawyer engaged in a "clear and serious violation of duty to a client." This is a much higher burden than a mere demonstration of breach of contract.

Even if a client is able to prove a clear and serious violation, the court may grant full or partial payment based on a confusing multifactor test to determine the amount of the "forfeiture." The use of the word "forfeiture" itself is quite telling. A forfeiture is the taking away of something already earned. When a court awards damages in a breach-of-contract case against the breaching party, it does not refer to those damages as a "forfeiture," but calls those damages "restitution." Restitution damages aim to place the nonbreaching party in the position in which she would have been had the breach not occurred.[13] In general, contract law focuses on the nonbreaching party: restitution seeks to make that party whole. In contrast, the analogous law governing lawyers focuses on the breaching party – the lawyer – and asks what, if anything, the lawyer may have to "forfeit."[14]

Alex Long has noted a related issue: courts allow lawyers to collect under contracts that violate established public policy.[15] Normally, if a

[11] *Restatement (Third) of Law Governing Lawyers* §37 (2000).

[12] Perillo, "The Law of Lawyers' Contracts," 447.

[13] *Black's Law Dictionary*, 6th ed. (St. Paul, MN: West, 1990), 1313.

[14] This is a linguistic argument. A search for empirical data to support different results as a result of the different terms was unsuccessful.

[15] Alex B. Long, "Attorney-Client Fee Agreements That Offend Public Policy," 61 *S.C. L. Rev.* 287 (2009).

contract violates a clear public policy, such as a contract in restraint of trade or a contract to kill, courts refuse to enforce it.[16] This has been partially true for lawyers. If a contract violates the Rules of Professional Conduct, a court will usually not enforce it as written. Examples of violations include a contract for excessive fees or charging a contingency fee in a divorce action. Nevertheless, some courts still allow a lawyer to collect in *quantum meruit*, even if they have found the contract in violation of public policy and even if nonlawyers would not collect anything in a similar circumstance.[17]

Professor Long notes that in allowing payment through *quantum meruit* in these public policy or attorney malfeasance cases, courts do more than ratify the bad behavior of lawyers – they positively encourage it. One of the reasons that courts give in other areas in which they refuse to allow any payment on contracts that violate public policy is to discourage these contracts from ever being made. By condoning the same behavior in lawyers, courts offer misbehaving lawyers a safety net. They can either collect on the illegal contract or, in the worst case, they can collect what they would have been paid regardless, under *quantum meruit*.[18] Heads, we win; tails, you lose.

Collecting Fees

As one might imagine, the collection of fees is near and dear to every private lawyer's heart. In this regard, lawyers have been quite fortunate: on top of the generally available tools for debt collection, lawyers have two unique and extremely powerful common law liens.[19]

The first is called a "retaining lien." This lien originated in the late eighteenth century in England and migrated to the United States in the

[16] Id. at 5 and n. 27.
[17] Id. at 5–37.
[18] Id.
[19] In a minority of states these common law liens have been codified by statute.

nineteenth century.[20] Under the retaining lien, a lawyer who has not been fully paid can "retain" client papers or property in her possession until the bill is paid. Client papers can include any court filings or depositions, and the lawyer is allowed to hold these papers even if the client needs them for further litigation.[21]

As you might imagine, this lien can be extraordinarily powerful in certain types of cases, depending on the underlying papers or property. John Leubsdorf has been a prominent critic of these liens, and has collected some particularly evocative judicial quotes:

> Courts have been strikingly candid, if not gleeful, in explaining that inconveniencing clients is "the essence – the power and the bite – of the attorney's retaining lien" and that reducing the harm "would emasculate the retaining lien." It seems that biting an occasional client is a small price to pay for preserving the lien's effect. The purpose of the lien is to provide "leverage over a client," and "the effectiveness of the lien is proportionate to the inconvenience of the client in being denied access to his property." The lien is even better when it can be used to obstruct access to the truth: "[W]here the adversary has access to documents to which the client does not, the inconvenience to the client is increased, thereby enhancing the value of the lien."[22]

Considering the relative subterfuge of many other lawyer–judge bias cases, there is something refreshingly candid about these quotes. These courts do not bother to wax eloquent about the lawyer's role as an officer of the court or a pillar of the justice system, nor do they argue somehow that the retaining lien actually serves the interests of the courts or clients

[20] See *Wilkins v. Carmichael*, 99 Eng. Rep. 70, 72 (K.B. 1779); John Leubsdorf, "Against Lawyer Retaining Liens," 72 *Fordham L. Rev.* 849, 850–52 (2004).

[21] Leubsdorf, "Against Lawyer Retaining Liens," 852–53.

[22] Id. at 855 (quoting, in order, *Jenkins v. Weinshienk*, 670 F.2d 915, 920 (10th Cir. 1982); *Anthony v. Bitler*, 911 F.Supp. 341, 343 (N.D. Ill. 1996); *Brauer v. Hotel Assocs., Inc.*, 192 A.2d 831, 835 (N.J. 1963); and *Tri-Ex Enterprises v. Morgan Guaranty Trust Co.*, 583 F.Supp. 1116, 1117–18 (S.D.N.Y. 1984)).

writ large. Instead, these courts recognize the liens for what they are: a tool for inconveniencing clients and making sure that lawyers get paid.

The retaining lien is a significant caveat to the pro-client language courts have used in the context of allowing clients to terminate their lawyers. Clients have significant rights vis-à-vis their lawyers – unless they stop paying. If a client is up to date on her bills, the client can terminate a lawyer and move on. If the client is behind in payment, though, a retaining lien makes it very difficult to move to a new lawyer before the old lawyer is paid. The retaining lien is unique to the legal profession; doctors, accountants, and engineers are all barred from holding client property in a fee dispute.[23]

The second type of common law lien is called a charging lien. It allows a lawyer to place a lien on any judgment or settlement for repayment of legal fees.[24] Similar to the retaining lien, this right is afforded only to lawyers. In the case of *In re Meyer,* a New York court made this quite explicit by rejecting an accountant's request for a lien because "[i]t is a rule of universal recognition that... no one has a lien upon the property of another with whom he deals unless it is conferred by contract or by some rule of law and no statute, in this state, has been cited, creating a lien in favor of... the accountant." This is, of course, a perfectly rational response to the accountant – why should a court allow a lien unless it has been legislatively created? Nevertheless, in the very next paragraph, the court granted a charging lien for the attorneys involved, citing the judge-created common law charging lien.[25]

In a majority of jurisdictions, an attorney's charging lien has priority over an opponent's claim on the same funds. In these situations, a plaintiff wins an award, but the defendant wins a judgment via a counterclaim or separate action against the same plaintiff. The question is then whether the defendant's judgment takes priority over the charging lien in terms of payment out of the plaintiff's original judgment against the

[23] Perillo, "The Law of Lawyers' Contracts," 467.

[24] Id. at 467–72.

[25] *In re Meyer*, 106 N.Y.S.2d 688, 693 (N.Y. Sup. 1951).

defendant. Most jurisdictions choose the charging lien and the lawyers' interests.[26]

The rationale for the charging lien is that the lawyer created the judgment through her efforts, so it is only right that the lawyer have equitable interest in the funds. In a particularly aggressive version of this argument, the Florida Supreme Court noted:

> While our courts hold the members of the bar to strict accountability and fidelity to their clients, they should afford them protection and every facility in securing them their remuneration for their services. An attorney has a right to be remunerated out of the results of his industry, and his lien on these fruits is founded in equity and justice.... For this reason, proceedings at law between attorney and client for collection of fees have long been disfavored. The equitable enforcement of charging liens in the proceeding in which they arise best serves to protect the attorney's right to payment for services rendered while protecting the confidential nature of the attorney-client relationship.[27]

This court argues that the charging lien is actually a benefit to the client. Rather than facing the unpleasantness of a later lawsuit by the lawyer against the client and risking the violence to "the confidential nature of the attorney–client relationship," courts have crafted a lien that requires the client to pay the lawyer before the client can collect her own share of the damages.

Nevertheless, a client would obviously rather get paid the settlement or judgment and then face a separate lawsuit over the fee. The client would have a bird in the hand and the lawyer would face the expense and hassle of a separate lawsuit. In that new suit, the possibility of settlement, the inherent risk of any new lawsuit, and the difficulties of collecting any

[26] Jay M. Zitter, "Priority Between Attorney's Charging Lien Against Judgment and Opposing Party's Right of Setoff Against Same Judgment," 27 *A.L.R.5th* 764 (1995), §3.

[27] *Sinclair, Louis, Siegel, Heath, Nussbaum & Zavertnik, P.A. v. Baucom*, 428 So.2d 1383, 1385 (Fla. 1983).

award would all make it less likely for the lawyer to get paid. The charging lien skips all these steps. In the case of a fee dispute, it freezes the client funds until the dispute is worked out, a significant discouragement to clients pursuing fee disputes.

Fair Debt Collection Practices Act

In 1978, Congress passed the Fair Debt Collection Practices Act (FCDPA) to prevent harassment and deception in the collection of debts. Examples of harassing behavior included obscene or profane language, threats of violence, and telephone calls at unreasonable hours.[28] As originally drafted, the bill excepted lawyers from the act's coverage.[29]

Some lawyer debt collectors quickly latched onto this exception. Attorneys began to advertise to creditors that they could do with impunity what other collectors were barred from doing, including "late night telephone calls to consumers, calls to consumers' employers concerning the consumers' debts," and "disclosure of consumers' debt to third parties."[30] One advertisement actually bragged that attorneys are "exempt from the requirements of the Fair Debt Collection Practices Act of 1978, [and] you are therefore protected against judgments on counterclaims by your debtor based on unfair collection practices."[31]

In 1986, Congress responded to these abuses by amending the FDCPA to eliminate the exception for lawyers.[32] Nevertheless, the application of the FDCPA to lawyers has remained a muddle. First, the

[28] S.Rep. No. 382, 95th Cong., 1st Sess. 2, reprinted in 1977 U.S.C.C.A.N. 1695, 1696.

[29] The former 15 USC §1692a(6)(F) (1978) excluded "any attorney-at-law collecting a debt as an attorney on behalf of and in the name of a client."

[30] These quotes come from the later congressional record on an amendment to the FDCPA, H.R.Rep. No. 405, 99th Cong., 2d Sess. 3–7, reprinted in 1986 U.S.C.C.A.N. 1752, 1754–57.

[31] Id. at 1756.

[32] See P.L. 99–361, 100 Stat. 768 (1986).

federal circuits split over whether the FDCPA applied only to nonlitigation activity, such as harassing calls or letters, or whether the FDCPA covered deceptive acts by lawyers in litigation or elsewhere. The U.S. Court of Appeals for the Sixth Circuit held that there was a litigation exemption to the law, whereas various other federal circuits disagreed.[33] The Sixth Circuit rejected a "literal" reading of the statute and held that litigation was excluded because "a contrary result would produce absurd outcomes."[34] That any court would exempt so much of what lawyers do from the FDCPA after Congress explicitly amended the law to include lawyers is quite striking.

The Supreme Court reversed 9–0 in *Heintz v. Jenkins*, noting "two rather strong reasons": the plain language of the statute did not exempt litigation activities, and Congress explicitly changed the law to include lawyers without saying anything further about litigation activities.[35] This case settled the "litigation exemption," but more confusion was in store. In noting that the Act applied to lawyers, the Court limited its reach only to lawyers who were otherwise qualified as "debt collectors."[36] The FDCPA applies only to "debt collectors," and the Court left open the question of how to determine whether a lawyer was a debt collector.

This raised the new complication of determining whether an accused lawyer was a "debt collector" under the FDCPA. The FDCPA establishes two alternative definitions for "debt collector": a person or entity who engages in debt collection as the "principal purpose" of the entity's business or who "regularly" collects debts.[37]

The tests applied to lawyers are a mess. For example, in *Goldstein v. Hutton, Ingram, Yuzek, Gainen, Carroll & Bertolotti*, the U.S. Court of

[33] Compare *Green v. Hocking*, 9 F.3d 18 (6th Cir. 1993) with *Paulemon v. Tobin*, 30 F.3d 307 (2nd Cir. 1994).

[34] *Green*, 9 F.3d at 20–21.

[35] *Heintz v. Jenkins*, 514 U.S. 291, 294–95 (1995).

[36] Id.

[37] 15 USC §1692a(6) (2008).

Appeals for the Second Circuit went through a short tour of the confusion before concluding:

> We hold that the question of whether a lawyer or law firm "regularly" engages in debt collection activity within the meaning of section 1692a(6) of the FDCPA must be assessed on a case-by-case basis in light of factors bearing on the issue of regularity. None of the following factors is alone dispositive of the issue; they are illustrative rather than exclusive.
>
> Most important in the analysis is the assessment of facts closely relating to ordinary concepts of regularity, including (1) the absolute number of debt collection communications issued, and/or collection-related litigation matters pursued, over the relevant period(s), (2) the frequency of such communications and/or litigation activity, including whether any patterns of such activity are discernable, (3) whether the entity has personnel specifically assigned to work on debt collection activity, (4) whether the entity has systems or contractors in place to facilitate such activity, and (5) whether the activity is undertaken in connection with ongoing client relationships with entities that have retained the lawyer or firm to assist in the collection of outstanding consumer debt obligations. Facts relating to the role debt collection work plays in the practice as a whole should also be considered to the extent they bear on the question of regularity of debt collection activity (debt collection constituting 1% of the overall work or revenues of a very large entity may, for instance, suggest regularity, whereas such work constituting 1% of an individual lawyer's practice might not). Whether the law practice seeks debt collection business by marketing itself as having debt collection expertise may also be an indicator of the regularity of collection as a part of the practice.[38]

Any time a court lists a nonexclusive, illustrative five-factor test, plus two more unnumbered factors immediately afterward, it is a sign that the courts are flummoxed or are seeking maximum flexibility to decide as they please.

[38] *Goldstein v. Hutton, Ingram, Yuzek, Gainen, Carroll & Bertolotti*, 374 F.3d 56, 62–63 (2nd Cir. 2004).

The standard discussed previously is so pliable that it is quite likely that similar cases will be decided differently. A review of the case law in this area shows that exact result. Compare *Schroyer v. Frankel*, in which the law firm handled fifty to seventy-five collection cases a year, but that amount was less than 2 percent of the firm's practice and the lawyer was found not to be a debt collector,[39] with *Stojanovski v. Strobl and Manoogian, P.C.*, in which debt collection was only 4 percent of the firm's business, but the court held that "an attorney who engages in collection activities more than a handful of times per year must comply with the [FDCPA]."[40]

The *Schroyer* standard for finding a lawyer a debt collector is particularly stringent: "to find that an attorney or law firm 'regularly' collects debts for purposes of the FDCPA, a plaintiff must show that the attorney or law firm collects debts as a matter of course for its clients or for some clients, or collects debts as a substantial, but not principal, part of his or its general law practice."[41] This test essentially replaces the FDCPA's requirement that debt collection occurs "regularly," with a requirement that debt collection must occur either "as a matter of course" or as a "substantial" part of the practice. Courts have made a hash of a relatively uncomplicated term such as "regularly." The *Stojanovski* test – whether a lawyer or law firm collects debts "more than a handful of times a year" – is a much simpler and clearer test, but would apply the law to many more lawyers and offer the courts much less discretion in choosing which lawyers are covered. Not surprisingly, *Stojanovski* has not been widely followed.

Although the case law in the area of lawyers is a mess, there are relatively few nonlawyer cases on the issue of who is a debt collector.[42]

[39] *Schroyer v. Frankel*, 197 F.3d 1170 (6th Cir. 1999).

[40] *Stojanovski v. Strobl and Manoogian, P.C.*, 783 F.Supp. 319, 322 (E.D. Mich. 1992).

[41] *Schroyer*, 197 F.3d at 1176.

[42] For example, O. Randolph Bragg, "The Fair Debt Collection Practices Act 15 U.S.C. §§1692 Et Seq.," *1591 PLI/Corp* 437 (2007) spends four pages of his section on the definition of "debt collector" covering lawyers and one and a half on everyone else.

Courts have attempted to follow the congressional intent to apply the FDCPA to lawyers, but it has been a struggle to create clear law on the subject. The winding road of the FDCPA and lawyers and the continuing confusion suggest that the lawyer–judge bias is at work.

Consumer Protection Statutes

All fifty states have some form of consumer protection act that bars deceptive trade practices. Although these state laws vary, they all trace back (one way or another) to Section 5 of the Federal Trade Commission Act (FTCA). Section 5 bars "[u]nfair methods of competition in or affecting commerce, and unfair or deceptive acts or practices in or affecting commerce."[43] Because of their relation to Section 5 of the FTCA, these state acts are often called "little FTC Acts."[44]

The interconnection between the state acts and Section 5 of the FTCA is important, because the majority of states have held that interpretation of their consumer protection statutes should at least be influenced by the interpretation of Section 5 of the FTCA.[45] Since at least the 1970s, it has been clear that Section 5 applies to professional services, including those offered by doctors and lawyers. In 1979, the FTC sued the American Medical Association (AMA) for various restraints on trade, including limitations on advertising and solicitation. The AMA argued that it was immune. The federal courts disagreed, relying on *Goldfarb v. Virginia State Bar* and other cases that applied antitrust and consumer protection statutes to doctors and lawyers.[46] Furthermore, the FTC itself

[43] See 15 U.S.C. §45 (2000).

[44] See Mark D. Bauer, "The Licensed Professional Exemption in Consumer Protection: At Odds with Antitrust History and Precedent," 73 *Tenn. L. Rev.* 131, 144–47 (2006).

[45] Bauer, "The Licensed Professional Exemption in Consumer Protection," 148–51, has a helpful chart showing the approaches of all fifty states.

[46] *AMA v. FTC*, 638 F.2d 443, 445–46 (2nd Cir. 1980), affirmed *per curiam* by the Supreme Court, 455 U.S. 676 (1982).

has made clear that its jurisdiction includes the activities of doctors and lawyers.[47]

Despite the clarity of the federal law, the application of the state "little FTC Acts" to the "learned professions" has been a mess, with multiple approaches. A handful of states have exempted specific licensed professionals by statute.[48] Other states do the same by judicial decision. In these states, consumers can still sue for legal malpractice, but not under the consumer fraud statute, even if an attorney's advertising is deceptive or her billing is fraudulent.

The decisions exempting lawyers strain to find reasons why their states' consumer protection acts do not apply to legal services. For example, in *Frahm v. Urkovich,* an Illinois appellate court analyzed an Illinois consumer protection act that applied to "consumers" who purchase "services." The court noted that as a consumer protection statute, "the act is to be liberally construed."[49] Nevertheless, the court briskly determined that the practice of law is not a business and held that the consumer protection act does not apply to lawyers: "The interpretation urged by plaintiffs here, however, would necessarily equate the practice of law with an ordinary commercial enterprise, a proposition for which we find no support in case law or public policy."[50]

In *Cripe v. Leiter*, the Illinois Supreme Court took a different tack, holding that historically "the regulation of attorney conduct in this state has been the prerogative of this court" and that in "the exercise of this power, this court administers a comprehensive regulatory scheme governing attorney conduct."[51] Accordingly, "the attorney-client relationship in this state, unlike the ordinary merchant-consumer relationship, is

[47] Bauer, "The Licensed Professional Exemption in Consumer Protection," 165–66.

[48] See, e.g., Cal. Civ. Code §1754 (2008); Fla. Stat. Ann. §501.212 (2008); Md. Code Ann., Com. Law §13–104 (2008).

[49] *Frahm v. Urkovich*, 447 N.E.2d 1007, 1009 (Ill. Ct. App. 1983).

[50] Id. at 1010.

[51] *Cripe v. Leiter*, 703 N.E.2d 100, 197 (1998).

already subject to extensive regulation by this court."[52] Because of this extensive regulation, the court reasoned that if the legislature wanted the consumer protection act to apply to attorneys, it should have stated that "intention with specificity"[53] – all this despite the fact that the statute itself protected "consumers" who purchased "services."

In *Averill v. Cox*, the New Hampshire Supreme Court concluded that the court's own "regulation of the practice of law is comprehensive and protects consumers from the same fraud and unfair practices as" their Consumer Protection Act:

> Indeed, the rules of professional ethics that attorneys are duty-bound to observe most scrupulously are diametrically opposed to the code by which businessmen must live if they are to survive. The Rules of Professional Conduct ensure that the practice of law is not simply an occupation; it is a profession, whose members seek to avoid even the appearance of impropriety and, thus, strive to live by a higher standard of conduct than a layperson. Attorneys in this State are officers of the judicial branch of government who must secure and maintain membership in the bar association as a condition of the practice of law. The bar association was founded "to improve the administration of justice; to foster and maintain high standards of conduct, integrity, competence and public service on the part of those engaged in the practice of law."[54]

These opinions are great examples of the judicial mindset of some courts. These courts practically bristle at the suggestion that consumer protection statutes are necessary for lawyers or that the legislature could possibly have meant to include lawyers within the reach of these statutes, despite the plain, blanket language of these statutes.[55]

The New Hampshire Supreme Court's high-minded rhetoric about the role and nature of the legal profession seems particularly misplaced

[52] Id.
[53] Id.
[54] *Averill v. Cox*, 761 A.2d 1083, 1088 (2000).
[55] See also *Vort v. Hollander*, N.J. Super., 607 A.2d 1339 (1992).

in an opinion about an ugly, long-running fee dispute in a workers' compensation case. The plaintiff alleged that his lawyer "withheld $11,000 of the settlement proceeds to pay two of the plaintiff's medical bills" and in return "received $3,400 from the medical payees for collecting this money from the plaintiff" and that before the client "received the net settlement proceeds, an additional $5,193.24 was deducted from the firm's trust account to cover unenumerated 'services and expenses,'" all without the client's consent.[56] Despite these troubling facts, the former client had no opportunity to sue for consumer fraud because the bar association and the state supreme court already handle such issues. Aside from the lawyer–judge bias issues involved in a disciplinary complaint for fees, this argument ignores one quite large difference between a consumer protection claim and a regular fee dispute: victorious consumer protection plaintiffs often collect treble damages.

In *Beyers v. Richmond,* the Pennsylvania Supreme Court took an even more muscular stance, holding:

> [The] General Assembly has no authority under the Pennsylvania Constitution to regulate the conduct of lawyers in the practice of law. Thus, we conclude that any application of the [consumer protection act] to the facts of this case would purport to regulate the conduct of attorneys and would be an impermissible encroachment upon the power of this Court.[57]

Therefore, insofar as the state consumer protection act purports to regulate attorneys, it is unconstitutional and the state disciplinary rules "provide the exclusive remedy for the attorney misconduct in this case."[58]

The facts of the case well establish the relative worth of those remedies, however. The lower court held that the lawyer had collected undeserved "attorneys' fees in the amount of $68,481.91 and non-existent costs totaling $26,058.85." The court also allowed treble damages under

[56] *Averill*, 761 A.2d at 1086.
[57] *Beyers v. Richmond*, 937 A.2d 1082, 1091–93 (Pa. 2007).
[58] Id.

the consumer protection act for a total award of $467,637.20.[59] Even though the Pennsylvania Supreme Court was "extremely disturbed" by the attorney's conduct, the former client's sole remedy was under the Rules of Professional Conduct, which does not offer treble damages.[60]

The "compromise" position of other states is likewise quite protective of lawyers. In these states, a bright line is drawn between "entrepreneurial" practices, such as billing or advertising, and the practice of law. In these states the practice of law is still exempted from consumer protection acts, but the entrepreneurial aspects are covered. In Washington, for example, billing practices are covered by the consumer protection statutes, but claims challenging an attorney's legal competence or strategy are not.

The Washington Consumer Protection Act applies only to "trade or commerce."[61] In *Short v. Demopolis*, the Washington Supreme Court analyzed the meaning of that phrase and held that although the entrepreneurial aspects of law are covered by "trade or commerce," the "actual practice of law" is *not* a trade or commerce and is thus not covered.[62] The "actual practice" of law includes claims that go to the competence and strategy of lawyers, so attorney malpractice and negligence claims are exempt from Washington's Consumer Protection Act.[63]

The court's reasoning on this distinction is somewhat mysterious. On one hand, the court correctly notes that "[t]here is no statutory exemption for lawyers."[64] The court goes on to list the "entrepreneurial" complaints and then states, "These business aspects of the legal profession are legitimate concerns of the public which are properly subject to the CPA." The court then turns to the "actual practice of law" and holds, without elaboration or citation to other authority, "Since these claims

[59] *Beyers*, 937 A.2d at 1085.
[60] Id. at 1092–93 and n. 21.
[61] Wash. Rev. Code §19.86.010(2) (2005).
[62] *Short v. Demopolis*, 691 P.2d 163, 168 (Wash. 1984).
[63] Id.
[64] Id.

are directed to the competence of and strategy employed by plaintiffs' lawyers, they amount to allegations of negligence or malpractice and are exempt from the CPA."[65]

The court never explains why the practice of law should not be covered or why exactly that practice is not trade or commerce. It cannot be the existence of legal malpractice, because the court itself notes that malpractice remedies are often insufficient[66] and it is quite common to have parallel consumer protection and negligence actions in other businesses. Instead, it seems likely that the court is applying the long-standing concept that the practice of law is not a business, but rather a public service or some other, higher enterprise.

Although the reasoning of *Demopolis* is quite thin, it has proven influential. Courts in Vermont, Connecticut, Michigan, Delaware, Tennessee, and North Carolina have followed its approach.[67] Between the *Demopolis* courts and the courts that flatly exempt lawyers from consumer protection, the great majority of courts to consider the issue offer some protection to lawyers.

In a heartening development, the Colorado Supreme Court recently held that its consumer protection act applies across the board to the practice of law.[68] In doing so, the court rebuffed the "actual practice of law" exemption from *Short*, because "[t]here is no basis for making such a distinction in the plain language or the legislative history of the Act"

[65] Id.

[66] Id. at 168–69.

[67] *Kessler v. Loftus*, 994 F.Supp. 240, 242–43 (D. Vt. 1997); *Updike, Kelly and Spellacy, PC v. Beckett*, 850 A.2d 145 (Conn. 2004); *Nelson v. Ho*, 564 N.W.2d 482, 486 (Mich. Ct. App. 1997); *Jamgochian v. Prousalis*, 2000 WL 1610750 (Del. Super. Ct. 2000); *Proctor v. Chattanooga Orthopaedic Group, P.C.*, 270 S.W.3d 56 (Tenn. Ct. App. 2008); *Reid v. Ayers*, 531 S.E.2d 231, 236 (N.C. App. 2000) (citing *Short* and holding that entrepreneurial acts like advertising are outside the statutory learned profession exemption). The Texas legislature amended its consumer protection statute to explicitly include the entrepreneurial aspects of legal practice (but not the practice of law), essentially codifying the *Short* standard. Tex. Bus. & Com. Code Ann. §17.49(c) (Vernon 2008).

[68] *Crowe v. Tull*, 126 P.3d 196 (Colo. 2006).

and "application of that standard could potentially inoculate attorneys from liability when an aspect of the 'actual practice' of law contributes to a scheme to commit deceptive trade practices." The court likewise rebuffed the separation-of-powers argument and accepted the legislature's authority to regulate deceptive attorney practices.[69]

The hidden prize for the plaintiffs in each of these cases is the possibility of translating a legal malpractice action into a consumer fraud action. Most states allow different – and better – damages in consumer fraud actions. Further, compare the logistical difficulties to winning a legal malpractice action with the relatively straightforward pleading requirements for a consumer fraud case. In Colorado, for example, a consumer fraud plaintiff must prove:

> (1) that the defendant engaged in an unfair or deceptive trade practice; (2) that the challenged practice occurred in the course of defendant's business, vocation, or occupation; (3) that it significantly impacts the public as actual or potential consumers of the defendant's goods, services, or property; (4) that the plaintiff suffered injury in fact to a legally protected interest; and (5) that the challenged practice caused the plaintiff's injury.[70]

In comparison, a Colorado legal malpractice claimant must prove the case within a case, among the other difficult hurdles described more fully in Chapter 7.[71] Some other courts have explicitly warned that malpractice cases cannot be pled as consumer protection actions.[72] The reason is obvious – if clients can sue for malpractice under consumer fraud statutes, legal malpractice will become a distant second remedy for attorney misbehavior and the various protections that courts have granted lawyers will be washed away.

[69] Id. at 205–07.

[70] Id. at 201.

[71] See *Schultz v. Boston Stanton*, 198 P.3d 1253, 1256 (Colo. App. 2008).

[72] See, e.g., *James V. Mazuca and Associates v. Schumann*, 82 S.W.3d 90, 94 (Tex. App. 2002).

These cases are hard to swallow. Most of the state consumer protection statutes have no explicit exception for lawyers. The statutes are quite broad and are meant to be read broadly to suit their remedial purpose. Moreover, these "little FTC Acts" are based on a federal statute that unquestionably applies to the learned professions. However, courts all over the country have held that lawyers are either flatly immune from suit or are immune when they are practicing their profession. The courts apply several different rationales for these holdings, but the bottom line is that in these states much, if not all, lawyer behavior is exempted from state consumer protection statutes, often without any legislative or statutory support for that distinction. In a few of these states the exemption is extended to all professionals, not just lawyers.[73]

Employment Law – Lawyers as Whistle-Blowers

Courts have likewise struggled with how to treat lawsuits against employers by "whistle-blowers" – individuals who have reported illegal conduct and have subsequently been terminated. At common law in America employment has traditionally been "at will," meaning that absent a contract or some other legal protection, an employer or an employee can terminate an employment relationship at their pleasure. Over time, courts and legislatures have carved out exceptions to this rule. The various statutory and common law exceptions for whistle-blowing are an example.

States handle whistle-blowing in many different ways. Approximately forty states allow some form of the tort of wrongful discharge in violation of public policy.[74] Employees who lose their jobs for refusing to violate a law, rule, or regulation or for reporting such a violation

[73] See *Macedo v. Dello Russo*, 840 A.2d 238, 242 (N.J. 2004); *Reid v. Ayers*, 531 S.E.2d 231, 235–36 (N.C. App. 2000).

[74] Gerard Sinzdak, "An Analysis of Current Whistleblower Laws: Defending a More Flexible Approach to Reporting Requirements," 96 *Cal. L. Rev.* 1633, 1643 (2008).

can sue their employer in tort under this theory. The elements vary but generally include something like the following:

> 1. That clear public policy existed and was manifested in a state or federal constitution, statute or administrative regulation, or in the common law (the clarity element); 2. That dismissing employees under circumstances like those involved in the plaintiff's dismissal would jeopardize the public policy (the jeopardy element); 3. The plaintiff's dismissal was motivated by conduct related to the public policy (the causation element); 4. The employer lacked overriding legitimate business justification for the dismissal (the overriding justification element).[75]

In the past twenty years there has been a series of lawsuits by whistle-blowers who work as professionals and argued that they were fired for refusing to violate their profession's code of ethics. Lawyers have often received different and better treatment in these cases. Alex Long has written a masterful article on lawyers as whistle-blowers; much of the law discussed here comes from that article.[76]

For example, in states in which the tort of wrongful discharge in violation of public policy has not been adopted, lawyers have still been able to succeed in whistle-blowing actions. The New York state courts, for example, do not allow the tort of wrongful discharge for public policy at all, holding "that such a significant change in our law is best left to the Legislature."[77] Nevertheless, in *Wieder v. Skala,* a law firm associate sued after allegedly being fired for insisting that his law firm report misconduct by a fellow associate to the disciplinary authorities.[78] The court reiterated the lack of a claim for wrongful discharge but found a breach of an implied contract between the associate and the law firm. The court held that by hiring a lawyer, the law firm impliedly agreed that the lawyer

[75] *Painter v. Graley*, 639 N.E.2d 51, 57 n. 8 (Ohio 1994).

[76] Alex B. Long, "Retaliatory Discharge and the Ethical Rules Governing Lawyers," 79 *U. Colo. L. Rev.* 1043 (2008).

[77] *Murphy v. American Home Prods. Corp.*, 58 N.Y.2d 293, 300–01 (N.Y. 1983).

[78] *Wieder v. Skala*, 80 N.Y.2d 628 (N.Y. 1992).

would follow the ethics rules, so the former associate could sue the firm in contract instead of tort.[79]

The court noted that the ethical requirement to report misconduct "is critical to the unique function of self-regulation belonging to the legal profession," and that the "defendants were not only making it impossible for plaintiff to fulfill his professional obligations but placing him in the position of having to choose between continued employment and his own potential suspension and disbarment."[80] Notably, the "unique characteristics of the legal profession in respect to this core Disciplinary Rule make the relationship of an associate to a law firm employer intrinsically different from that of the financial managers to the corporate employers in *Murphy*."[81] Thus, when an accountant is terminated for reporting illegal accounting practices to the company's board of directors, as in *Murphy,* the accountant has no claim.[82] When a lawyer does the same, however, a contract is inferred and suit is allowed. New York is not alone. Delaware, likewise, does not generally allow suit for whistle-blowers, but *Shearin v. E.F. Hutton Group, Inc.* allowed a suit for an in-house attorney terminated for reporting company misconduct to the board of directors.[83]

These cases are classic lawyer–judge bias cases. On one hand, they do not want to offer wide-open protection to all whistle-blowers under the broader public policy grounds. On the other hand, the *Wieder* court notes the "unique" nature of the legal profession, and the court's sympathy for the plight of the poor associate (faced with losing a job or being disbarred) is palpable. In these circumstances, unlike the much more prosaic situation of the mere "financial managers" in the previous New York cases, a special exception is appropriate.

[79] Id. at 635–37.

[80] Id. at 636–37.

[81] Id. at 637 (citing *Murphy*, 58 N.Y. 2d 293 (N.Y. 1983), and *Sabetay v. Sterling Drug, Inc.*, 69 N.Y.2d 329 (N.Y. 1987)).

[82] *Murphy*, 58 N.Y.2d at 300–05.

[83] *Shearin v. E.F. Hutton Group, Inc.*, 652 A.2d 578, 585–89 (Del. Ch. 1994).

The development of the law in the states that allow the tort of wrongful discharge in violation of public policy has also favored lawyers. The first state supreme court case to address the issue was actually remarkably anti-lawyer and pro-client. In *Balla v. Gambro,* the Illinois Supreme Court decided that an in-house counsel could not sue for retaliatory discharge after he had been terminated for objecting to allegedly defective dialysis equipment.[84] The court reasoned that retaliatory discharge claims were meant to safeguard the public – that is, the protection is given to encourage employee whistle-blowing. In the case of a lawyer, however, no such encouragement should be necessary because of the lawyer's duty to report under the Illinois version of the Rules of Professional Conduct. "In this case, the public policy to be protected, that of protecting the lives and property of citizens, is adequately safeguarded without extending the tort of retaliatory discharge to in-house counsel. Appellee was required under the Rules of Professional Conduct to report" the potentially harmful acts.[85] The court also noted the potential harm allowing suit might cause to the special nature of the attorney–client relationship and to the corporate client's ability to choose the lawyer of its liking.[86]

The case is striking in two ways. First, the court actually seems to care more about clients and their interests. In many of the previous cases addressing the legal profession, courts naturally include clients as an add-on concern after stating what is best for the legal profession. Here we have a court choosing the side of the clients in a lawyer–client dispute.

Second, after all the language in other cases about the unique nature of the legal profession and the special role of the Rules of Professional Conduct, here the court recognizes a duty to go along with the benefits. Lawyers must report wrongdoing that might cause serious physical harm, regardless of whether they will get terminated or not.

[84] *Balla v. Gambro, Inc.*, 584 N.E.2d 104, 104–07 (Ill. 1991).
[85] Id. at 108–09.
[86] Id. at 109–11.

Nevertheless, *Balla v. Gambro* has been roundly criticized and has been rejected by every court outside Illinois. The criticism has come in legal newspapers, bar publications, and law reviews.[87] Three years later, the California Supreme Court expressly rejected *Balla* in *General Dynamics v. Superior Court*.[88] The court noted the importance of the Rules of Professional Conduct, but reached a quite different conclusion. Because the rules are "linked by their nature and goals to important values affecting the public interest at large," there is a "chain of ethical duty" for "lawyers and their work." Thus, "in-house counsel, forced to choose between the demands of the employer and the requirements of a professional code of ethics have, if anything, an even more powerful claim to judicial protection than their nonprofessional colleagues."[89] Aside from the court's confidence in the public-spirited nature of an attorney's ethical duties, the court shows a palpable sympathy for the in-house counsel at issue: "[T]he distinguishing feature of the in-house attorney is a virtually complete dependence on the good will and confidence of a single employer to provide livelihood and career success."[90]

The *General Dynamics* court did, however, note that a terminated in-house lawyer could not violate attorney–client privilege in prosecuting a wrongful termination action.[91] A few cases have followed this limitation.[92] The modern trend has been in favor of allowing the suits *and* allowing lawyers to breach the attorney–client privilege.[93] For

[87] See, e.g., S. Reisinger, "Every Lawyer's Nightmare," *Legal Times*, Oct. 20, 2003, at 25; Brett Lane, "Blowing the Whistle on *Balla v. Gambro*: The Emergence of an In-House Counsel's Cause of Action in Tort for Retaliatory Discharge," 29 *J. Legal Prof.* 235 (2005); Cullen M. Godfrey, "The Revised Role of Lawyers After Sarbanes-Oxley," 68 *Tex. B.J.* 932 (2005).

[88] *General Dynamics Corp. v. Superior Court*, 876 P.2d 487 (1994).

[89] Id. at 497–98.

[90] Id. at 498.

[91] Id. at 504–05.

[92] See Kim T. Vu, "Conscripting Attorneys to Battle Corporate Fraud Without Shields or Armor? Reconsidering Retaliatory Discharge in Light of Sarbanes-Oxley," 105 *Mich. L. Rev.* 209, 217 (2006).

[93] Id. at 217–18.

example, *Burkhart v. Semitool* included a long discussion of Rule of Professional Conduct 1.6, which allows breaches of confidence "in a controversy between the lawyer and the client." The court held, solely based on that rule, that disclosure of privileged materials was fully appropriate in a wrongful termination suit.[94] The court noted with sympathy that a lawyer "does not forfeit his rights simply because to prove them he must utilize confidential information. Nor does the client gain the right to cheat the lawyer by imparting confidences to him."[95]

Thus, an initial anti-lawyer decision was quickly turned on its head. The first cases retained a concern for clients in the form of retaining the protections of the attorney–client privilege. Later cases abandoned even these protections, leaving the attorney–client privileged materials sacrosanct against the rest of the world but further unprotected in disputes between lawyers and clients.[96]

Bankruptcy Judges and Large Bankruptcies

The next two sections cover ways in which courts have generated business or higher fees for lawyers. For the past twenty years, bankruptcy courts all over the country have engaged in a competition for the largest bankruptcies. Part of this competition has been bankruptcy court adoption of fee practices that are questionable at best and flatly illegal at worst. Lynn LoPucki has written a remarkable book called *Courting Failure: How Competition for Big Cases Is Corrupting the Bankruptcy*

[94] *Burkhart v. Semitool, Inc.*, 5 P.3d 1031, 1040–41 (Mont. 2000).

[95] Id. at 1041. For other cases allowing the breach of the attorney–client privilege, see *Spratley v. State Farm Mutual Automobile Insurance Co.*, 78 P.3d 603 (Utah 2003); *Willy v. Administrative Review Board*, 423 F.3d 483 (5th Cir. 2005); *O'Brien v. Stolt-Nielsen Transportation Group, Ltd.*, 838 A.2d 1076, 1080–82 (Conn. Super. Ct. 2003); *Crews v. Buckman Labs. Int'l, Inc.*, 78 S.W.3d 852 (Tenn. 2002); and *Heckman v. Zurich Holding Co. of America*, 242 F.R.D. 606 (D. Kan. 2007).

[96] Chapter 8 includes a fuller discussion of this exception to the attorney–client privilege.

Courts.[97] The book covers a period from the mid-1980s into the twenty-first century, in which bankruptcy courts have engaged in a competition over large bankruptcy filings by changing their court rules and even their substantive law to appeal to large companies seeking bankruptcy – and to their lawyers.[98] At the outset, it is worth considering the mystery of courts competing so hard for what essentially amounts to extra work.

The incentives of two of the three players in this competition are clear. Obviously, the executives of a company going into bankruptcy have an incentive to choose a venue that offers the most attractive law and procedure. LoPucki uses the example of the Enron bankruptcy to excellent effect. Kenneth Lay, Enron's CEO, had a strong incentive to avoid a court that would appoint an independent bankruptcy trustee to run the company because that trustee would likely investigate Lay's potentially illegal sales of Enron stock and other questionable management decisions. Enron eventually chose to file in the Southern District of New York rather than in Houston (or any other bankruptcy court in the country). The bankruptcy court chose not to appoint a trustee, and the investigation of Lay took years longer than it might have in a more aggressive bankruptcy court.[99]

Following the handling of the Enron case, the Southern District of New York received several other high-profile cases that potentially involved management misconduct: Global Crossing, Adelphia Communications, and Worldcom.[100] As part of the competition among courts, managers of failed companies have been granted large retention bonuses and creditors have had a harder time recovering money taken by those managers pre-bankruptcy.[101]

97 Lynn LoPucki, *Courting Failure: How Competition for Big Cases Is Corrupting the Bankruptcy Courts* (Ann Arbor: University of Michigan Press, 2005).

98 Id. at 9–24.

99 Id. at 13–14.

100 Id. at 9–14.

101 Id. at 143–56.

It is also clear why the bankruptcy professionals (primarily lawyers), or "case handlers" as LoPucki calls them, would care. Bankruptcy courts have competed for large filings by raising the amount they pay as an hourly rate and paying the professionals monthly, instead of at the end of the case or sporadically.[102] The courts that compete also bend over backward to satisfy the case handlers by helpfully scheduling hearings and other matters. The competition is a financial issue for lawyers. If the local bankruptcy court draws large bankruptcies, the local bankruptcy bar will receive lots of work.[103]

The financial implications go beyond the opportunity to work on these cases. LoPucki and Joseph Doherty recently published an empirical study titled "Routine Illegality in Bankruptcy Court Fee Practices."[104] The study reports:

> [bankruptcy courts] routinely authorize and tolerate professional fee practices that violate the Bankruptcy Code and Rules. Some of the practices are such clear violations that the judges must be aware of their illegality. The practices are concentrated in the largest, most visible bankruptcy cases – cases like Worldcom, Kmart, US Airways, and Delta Airlines.[105]

There are justifications for these practices, but LoPucki and Doherty present a brutal indictment of a bankruptcy court system that enriches lawyers and other professionals in clear violation of law and policy.

Likewise, George Kuney has noted that bankruptcy courts regularly approve bankruptcy plans that include a release of the bankruptcy lawyers from liability for legal malpractice. The problem with these releases is that they violate Model Rule 1.8(h) (and its state law counterparts), which bans releases of malpractice liability unless the client is

[102] Id. at 140–43.

[103] Id. at 21.

[104] Lynn LoPucki and Joseph Doherty, "Routine Illegality in Bankruptcy Court Fee Practices," available at http://online.wsj.com/public/resources/documents/lopuckistudy.pdf.

[105] Id. at 2.

separately represented by another lawyer in negotiating the release.[106] As these agreements are never "negotiated" with the bankrupt entity, let alone negotiated with separate counsel, these releases are another example of bankruptcy courts' overweening desire to please the lawyers who practice before them.

The benefit to bankruptcy judges is harder to read. Typically, American judges do not like to bend or break the law for any purpose. Thus, these actions are especially mysterious because the primary purpose of the loose payment of fees appears to be the competition for other large-scale bankruptcies – that is, extra work. Bankruptcy judges are appointed not for life, but for fourteen-year terms. Their salaries are fixed, regardless of case load, and they are not allowed to receive any direct benefits from any of the other players in the system. Under these constraints it is hard to see why judges would compete for extra work, particularly using such extreme measures. Nevertheless, LoPucki presents indisputable evidence that multiple jurisdictions all over the country have competed hard for the large-scale bankruptcies over the past twenty years or so. The judges themselves have led this competition.

LoPucki offers several explanations for this effect. First, there are some potential direct effects on the judges. If a bankruptcy judge plans to eventually leave the bench and practice law, the large case experience would likely prove helpful and obviously higher fees could eventually redound to her benefit. If the judge wants to serve another fourteen-year term, it may hurt her chances if the local bankruptcy bar is angry over the lack of big cases to litigate. Judges also like to work with the best in the profession and, like other people, often seek celebrity. Big cases offer both opportunities.[107]

[106] See George W. Kuney, "Unethical Protection? Model Rule 1.8(h) and Plan Releases of Professional Liability," draft on file with author. Model Rule 1.8(h) states that a lawyer shall not "make an agreement prospectively limiting the lawyer's liability to a client for malpractice unless the client is independently represented in making the agreement."

[107] LoPucki, *Courting Failure*, 19–24.

LoPucki sees the indirect and more subtle effects as more important. In particular, bankruptcy judges come from a community of bankruptcy lawyers. Unless they want to face possible ostracism at the local bar association meetings, they need to work to bring in these cases for their former colleagues:

> For bankruptcy professionals, bankruptcy venue is a bread-and-butter issue. If a big St. Louis company – such as TWA, Purina Mills, or Solutia – files in St. Louis, leading bankruptcy lawyers are likely to get the key roles in the case and the big fees that come with them. If the case is big enough, virtually every bankruptcy lawyer in St. Louis will have a client. If instead the company files in some other city, bankruptcy lawyers in that city will get most of the work and the money. If most cases from a city go elsewhere, the career prospects in that city may be limited. And if the lawyers in a city view their judges as the cause of that problem, things can get ugly.[108]

LoPucki follows this passage with a lengthy anecdote about the bankruptcy judges in Boston, a jurisdiction in which large bankruptcies left home, and the resulting cold reaction of the bankruptcy bar to the judges who were responsible.

LoPucki also notes a second incentive not to closely regulate professional fees in bankruptcy cases: it is a hassle. "Fee applications consist largely of time records kept in tenths of an hour. A single fee application can run hundreds and sometimes even thousands of pages. Fee reviewers are supposed to read them, but cannot possibly do so."[109] We thus have a near-perfect storm for the lawyer–judge bias – a duty that lawyers object to and judges find unpleasant.

LoPucki also demonstrates that the competition is having real and deleterious effects on the efficacy of the bankruptcy system. In particular he notes that in Delaware, the leader in the competition for large

[108] Id. at 21.

[109] LoPucki and Doherty, "Routine Illegality in Bankruptcy Court Fee Practices," 6–7.

bankruptcies, postbankruptcy companies had a much higher rate of later failure over the period marked by the competition.[110]

LoPucki's work powerfully demonstrates the influence lawyers have over judges and the tight bond that underlies the lawyer–judge bias.[111] LoPucki proves that federal bankruptcy judges would go out of their way to draw extra and harder work, at least in part to please the local bar. In order to keep the competition going, LoPucki reports that the two Delaware bankruptcy judges were doing the caseload of six judges over the relevant period.[112] Thus, in some cases, the lawyer–judge bias is so strong that judges act against what appears to be their self-interest.

Class Action *Cy Pres*

Our last example is a particular way that judges have found to support legal nonprofit entities. In the past forty years, class action lawsuits have grown exponentially in both frequency and the amount awarded. Many of the cases involve large classes of putative plaintiffs who eventually win small amounts. Because the class sizes are large and class members are often difficult to find or reach, it is quite common for some of the class action damages to go unclaimed. In these circumstances, courts are called on to determine what to do with the leftover funds. Courts have often turned to the doctrine of *cy pres* in these circumstances.[113]

Cy pres originated in the law of trusts and estates. When the original purpose of a trust had become impossible to fulfill, courts had to decide

[110] LoPucki, *Courting Failure*, 18.

[111] LoPucki's work has been (naturally) quite controversial, and some have challenged the conclusions and methodology. See Kenneth Ayotte and David A. Skeel, Jr., "An Efficiency-Based Explanation for Current Corporate Reorganization Practice," 73 *U. Chi. L. Rev.* 425, 426 (2006); and Howard B. Brownstein, "Fact or Fiction? Book Alleges Bankruptcy Court System Is Corrupt," available at https://www.turnaround.org/Publications/Articles.aspx?objectID=4803.

[112] Id. at 245–46.

[113] See *Boyle v. Giral*, 820 A.2d 561, 569 (D.C. 2003).

what to do with the trust's residual funds. Rather than have the funds go unused, the courts tried to find an "as near as possible" option that still reflected the trust's original purpose.[114]

As transplanted to class actions, however, the requirement that the award match the original purpose of the underlying lawsuit has been watered down. Some courts have disbursed unclaimed class action funds based on the judge's perception of the public good, rather than to benefit the putative class members.[115] The title of a recent article in the ABA publication *The Judges' Journal* puts it quite succinctly: "What Can a Court Do with Leftover Class Action Funds? Almost Anything!"[116]

To access these funds, courts have had to elide state and federal statutes that call for unclaimed court funds to escheat to the government. For example, in *Van Gemert v. Boeing Co.,* the U.S. Court of Appeals for the Second Circuit found that the federal statute that provides for the deposit of unclaimed funds in the U.S. Treasury "does not limit the discretion of the district court to control the unclaimed portion of a class action judgment fund."[117]

Taken together, the avoidance of escheatment and the use of *cy pres* to disburse funds is an aggressive statement of judicial prerogative. By avoiding escheatment, courts essentially claim a superior ability to spend the unclaimed funds than that of the legislature or the executive. When the requirement that the funds be used to benefit the putative class members is also eliminated, courts have usurped the legislature's prerogative to spend unclaimed damages according to its own priorities.

114 *Black's Law Dictionary*, 6th ed. (St. Paul, MN: West Publishing, 1990), 387.

115 See *Superior Beverage Co. v. Owens-Illinois*, 827 F.Supp. 477 (N.D. Ill. 1993); and *In re Infant Formula Multidistrict Litigation*, 2005 WL 2211312 (N.D. Fla. 2005).

116 Kevin M. Forde, "What Can a Court Do with Leftover Class Action Funds? Almost Anything!," *The Judges' Journal*, vol. 35, no. 3 (Summer 1996).

117 *Van Gemert v. Boeing Co.*, 739 F.2d 730, 735–36 (2nd Cir. 1984). The same result has been reached in state courts; see, e.g., *State of California v. Levi Strauss & Co.*, 715 P.2d 564, 575 (Cal. 1986).

It should come as no surprise that these grants for the general good have drifted over time toward the benefit of the legal profession. Charles Keckler has done a study of recent *cy pres* awards from class action funds and discovered that "they were predominantly directed to law-related entities such as law schools, pro bono advocacy organizations and the like."[118]

As we learned in the discussion of IOLTA funds in Chapter 4, legal services corporations (LSCs) often appeal to lawyer-dominated sources of funding, such as the IOLTA interest derived from client funds. LSCs have likewise been frequent recipients of *cy pres* class action funds. Bar associations and LSCs have actually created publications encouraging courts to donate their *cy pres* funds to legal aid organizations.[119] Law schools have likewise been the recipients of these funds.[120]

Even though these uses may be salutary (especially the potential use for law professor salary increases), such uses are very unlikely to directly or even indirectly benefit class action plaintiffs. To the contrary, law-related charitable gifts from class action funds are almost certainly a reflection of the preferences of the judiciary, not the litigants. The use of these funds also confirms one of the postulates from the study of judicial incentives in Chapter 2. Judges, as most people, like to feel important. Distributing large sums of unclaimed class action funds certainly fits the bill. In looking to curry favor with their grants, judges naturally gravitate toward the legal profession. Whether this is a result of their shared

[118] Charles Keckler, "*Cy Pres* and Its Predators" (unpublished manuscript on file with author).

[119] See New York State Bar Association, *Cy Pres for Civil Legal Services*, available at http://www.nysba.org/AM/Template.cfm?Section=Home&CONTENTID=2745&TEMPLATE=/CM/ContentDisplay.cfm; The Pennsylvania Legal Aid Network, *The Pennsylvania Legal Aid Network & Cy Pres Awards*, available at http://www.palegalservices.org/resource_development/Cy%20Pres_1010.pdf.

[120] See Colorado Law, *Clinic Receives Cy Pres Award from Alumnus*, available at http://lawweb.colorado.edu/news/showArticle.jsp?id=483. For purposes of self-disclosure, I should note that the University of Tennessee College of Law has received some class action *cy pres* funds as well.

backgrounds or the judicial vision of where the public interest lies, there is a powerful effect on judicial behavior.

This overview of the business of law demonstrates that the lawyer–judge bias is widespread and pernicious. This chapter ends the case law portion of the book. The next two chapters attempt to demonstrate that the problem has real and deleterious effects.

10 Enron's Sole Survivors

> Four years after regulators launched a task force to stamp out business corruption, numerous chief executives are on their way to prison, two of the nation's biggest accounting firms are defunct or on probation, and investment banks have shelled out billions of dollars in settlements. But lawyers serving fraud-ridden companies have emerged relatively unscathed.
>
> – Carrie Johnson[1]

THIS CHAPTER EXAMINES HOW THE LAWYER–JUDGE BIAS plays out in a high-profile, real-life scenario – the treatment of the lawyers in the Enron debacle. No doubt the Enron shareholders, along with the thousands of low-level Enron employees who lost their jobs and retirement savings, feel that the civil and criminal punishments meted out to Enron executives and accountants were light compared with the harm Enron caused. Imagine their chagrin at the fact that the Enron lawyers walked away relatively unscathed. Why did the accountants and executives face devastating financial and criminal penalties while Enron's lawyers exited with little more than a cash payment to the bankruptcy estate?

Lawyers were intimately involved in the accounting shenanigans that bankrupted Enron and destroyed approximately $68 billion in

[1] Carrie Johnson, "Look Who's Left Standing: Legal Penalties in Frauds Are Seldom Paid by Legal Advisors," *Washington Post*, August 31, 2006.

wealth. Many of the Enron executives faced criminal charges and are themselves bankrupt. Enron's primary outside auditor, Arthur Andersen, was accused of criminal fraud and eventually collapsed as an ongoing concern. In contrast, the two main law firms that helped make the Enron accounting possible are still thriving. Those lawyers have faced no criminal or bar disciplinary charges. Other than paying a cash settlement that was significantly less than the fees Enron paid them, the lawyers simply dropped the bag and walked away. This chapter explains the essential role of the lawyers in the debacle and why the lawyer–judge bias helped them escape with a comparative slap on the wrist.

It is true that much of the Enron fiasco occurred as a result of the actions of lawyers (notably prosecutors and private bankruptcy lawyers) and not judges. Nevertheless, these lawyers presumably made their decisions on the basis of what they thought would happen in court.

A Short Primer on Enron

For a time the Enron bankruptcy was the biggest financial story in America. The collapse of Enron destroyed $68 billion in wealth and cost more than 5,600 Enron employees their jobs and retirement savings.[2] It resulted in prison sentences for many Enron executives, and at least one suicide. The aftermath of the scandal destroyed Arthur Andersen, one of the world's largest and best-known accounting firms. The human, professional, and financial cost was unprecedented.

Enron is a quintessentially human story about arrogance, greed, and willful blindness. As in many of those stories, lawyers play a role. Enron began its life as a sleepy natural gas pipeline company in the days when natural gas prices were federally regulated. There was minimal competition and no market pricing. In the 1980s, the government deregulated the market and, out of a relative backwater, an energy trading company was

[2] J. Scott Dutcher, "From the Boardroom to the Cellblock: The Justifications for Harsher Punishment of White Collar Crime," 37 *Ariz. St. L.J.* 1295, 1314 (2005).

born. In the wake of deregulation natural gas prices were quite volatile, so Enron began selling "forward contracts," promising to sell gas to utilities at a set price in the future. This meant that Enron was running a risk if prices soared, but it would gain the benefit if prices fell.[3] This changed Enron's identity from an energy company to a futures company.

In 1990, Enron hired Jeffrey Skilling as CEO of Enron Finance and the transformation accelerated. Under Skilling's leadership, Enron ceased to be a traditional energy company and became a self-proclaimed new-economy company. Enron saw itself as uniquely positioned to profit off of hedging risk and finding areas of the market in which it could capture future revenue streams in the present.[4]

This business model presented Enron with two large problems. First, the creation of future revenue streams often required large outlays of cash up front to buy physical assets such as pipelines or power plants without an immediate revenue stream. This meant that Enron constantly needed to finance large transactions. Funding the new investments by issuing additional corporate debt or simply borrowing it from a bank was unattractive because of the bad effect on Enron's credit rating. If Enron's credit rating declined, the problem would be compounded because the cost of future financing would rise, creating a potentially vicious cycle.[5]

Second, it took years for Enron's projected profits to come to fruition, so under traditional accounting practices Enron would look like what it eventually turned out to be: a cash-poor company with potential future profits and massive current debt. Thus, Enron needed to hide debt and hit revenue targets to maintain both its credit rating and its stock prices.

Therefore, Enron began looking for ways to hide debt and create profit, often without regard for conventional accounting principles. Throughout this period Enron was known for aggressive accounting practices and for a relentless, no-holds-barred quest for higher earnings.

[3] Bethany McLean and Peter Elkind, *The Smartest Guys in the Room: The Amazing Rise and Scandalous Fall of Enron* (New York: Penguin, 2003), 1–44.

[4] Loren Fox, *Enron: The Rise and Fall* (Hoboken, NJ: John Wiley & Sons, 2003), 70–89.

[5] See Milton C. Regan, "Teaching Enron," 74 *Fordham L. Rev.* 1139, 1149–50 (2005).

To keep reported earnings high, Enron continually sought ways to record future profits in the present and hide or minimize losses and debts off the books. The most infamous of these methods included the creation of multiple "special purpose entities" (SPEs) to hide losses and boost perceived profits.[6] The story of these SPEs is where the lawyers come in.

Special Purpose Entities and Enron's Lawyers

The judge in Enron's bankruptcy proceedings appointed an "examiner," Neal Batson, to investigate some of Enron's questionable transactions and report on the roles of various players, including Enron's accountants, executives, bankers, and lawyers. The examiner eventually released four extremely dense, but informative, reports covering these transactions.[7] These reports underlie the explanation to come. The reports are both masterfully done and enormously confusing. The confusion arises not from the reports themselves, but from the subject matter. The Enron accounting was designed to mislead partly by being abstruse and complex.

This section addresses SPEs generally and the role of Enron's lawyers specifically. Do not worry too much if the description is overly technical or the details elusive. The takeaway point is quite simple: to accomplish its massive fraud, Enron needed a lot of help. Much of that help came from lawyers.

Publicly traded companies around the world have used SPEs quite commonly since at least the 1990s. An SPE is a separate company (sometimes a new corporation, sometimes a new limited liability corporation [LLC]) created for a variety of reasons, but usually to procure better

[6] Peter C. Fusaro and Ross M. Miller, *What Went Wrong at Enron* (Hoboken, NJ: John Wiley & Sons, 2002), 31–37.

[7] These reports are available at: http://www.enron.com/media/1st_Examiners_Report.pdf; http://www.enron.com/media/2nd_Examiners_Report.pdf; http://www.enron.com/media/3rd_Examiners_Report.pdf; and http://www.enron.com/media/Final_Report_Neal_Batson.pdf. Henceforth I refer to these four reports, respectively, as First Report, Second Report, Third Report, and Final Report.

loan terms. Typically a company will create a new company and transfer a significant asset to that new company. For example, a company might transfer one of its office towers into an SPE. The new entity now has one asset and no liabilities. As such, it will be easier to find good terms of credit for the new company. If more than 3 percent of the new entity is owned by an outsider to the original company that has true ownership of the risks and rewards associated with the underlying asset, the new loans taken out are "off book" for the original company. Thus, in the case of a new office building, a company could transfer the building to an SPE, lease it back from the SPE, and have the SPE borrow money for a second building, all the while keeping the entire transaction (and, most important, the amount of the loans to the new SPE) off the original company's books. Assuming a true sale to the new company, this is fair enough. The new company can rise or fall on the worth of its assets. It is only if the accounting and legal rules of SPEs are abused that real trouble arises.[8]

The abuse of SPEs was at the heart of the Enron meltdown. Enron did several things that flouted the usual accounting treatment of SPEs. Enron retained the rights to profits derived from the assets in the SPEs and retained a contractual right to buy the assets back in the future. Further, Enron regularly guaranteed the debts of its SPEs. These two activities utterly destroyed the fiction that the Enron SPEs were separate or that the transactions were anything other than liabilities that should have been included on Enron's books.[9]

Enron's use of SPEs had a major effect on its reported profits. In 2000, for instance, SPE transactions increased Enron's net income by $351.6 million, increased cash flow from operations by $1.2 billion, and kept $1.4 billion in debt off Enron's balance sheet.[10]

One of the tests for whether an SPE can be treated as "off book" for accounting purposes is whether the asset is transferred according

[8] Neal Newman, "Enron and the Special Purpose Entities – Use or Abuse? – The Real Problem – The Real Focus," 13 *Law & Bus. R. of the Americas* 97 (2007).

[9] See Newman, "Enron and the Special Purpose Entities," 115–18.

[10] Second Report at 38.

to a "true sale." The purpose of the true sale requirement is to avoid exactly the situation Enron created. An SPE's liabilities can be off book only if the underlying asset was part of a true sale, in which control of the asset was transferred from the parent company to the SPE. Generally accepted accounting principles require a true sale letter from a reputable lawyer or law firm to establish that the parent company has actually transferred the assets underlying the new SPE. The true sale letter sounds like what it is: a lawyer opines in writing that the parent has actually sold the asset to the SPE.

Of course, the true sale letter is really just the tip of the iceberg for a lawyer's involvement in the creation of an SPE. As a general rule, lawyers draft all the underlying paperwork creating an SPE. Creating an SPE is like incorporating a brand-new company, and the lawyers are in charge of all of the legalities of the creation. In fact, even though Enron's SPEs have regularly been described as accounting tricks, the nuts and bolts of creating each of them fell primarily to the lawyers, not the accountants.[11]

Vinson and Elkins (V&E) was Enron's primary outside law firm. Founded in 1917, V&E is one of the largest, oldest, and most prestigious law firms in Texas and the United States. Enron was one of the firm's biggest clients.[12] Enron paid V&E $18.6 million in 1997, $26.6 million in 1998, $37.8 million in 1999, $42.8 million in 2000, and $36.4 million in 2001. V&E represented Enron on approximately sixty-six SPE matters between 1997 and 2001, many of which turned out to be questionable.[13]

From 1998 to 2001, Andrews & Kurth (A&K) provided legal services for twenty-eight SPE transactions. A&K is another large, old, and prestigious Houston law firm.[14] Enron paid A&K $29 million in fees over this

[11] Regan, "Teaching Enron," 58–62.

[12] Jim Yardley, "Enron's Collapse: The Law Firm," *N.Y. Times*, January 16, 2002.

[13] Final Report at 48.

[14] See Andrews & Kurth, "Firm History," available at http://www.akllp.com/about-history.html.

period.[15] Both A&K and V&E were well-known, politically connected Houston firms. It is important to remember how much of the success of Enron's sleight of hand relied on the reputations of its lawyers and accountants. From the outside, Enron looked like a thriving, ingenious concern backed by the best of the best.

V&E and A&K both drafted true sale or true issuance letters for Enron in its SPE transactions. As noted above, Enron needed these true sale letters to keep the SPE transactions off book. This requirement posed a challenge, naturally, because the transfers it was making were not in fact true sales.

Enron navigated this roadblock in two ways. First, it sometimes asked for the wrong type of letter from the lawyers, and Arthur Andersen accepted these letters regardless. A true sale letter indicates that the parent company has truly sold the asset to the SPE. In comparison, a "true issuance" opinion dealt with how the asset would be treated in a later bankruptcy and has much looser transfer-of-ownership requirements. According to the lawyers at V&E, they knew this was the wrong type of letter, but they wrote the letters anyway after raising concerns with Arthur Andersen and Enron's general counsel.[16] Second, in some instances V&E and A&K simply issued true sale opinion letters in transactions that later turned out not to have been sales at all.

Moreover, even on the transactions for which V&E was not the primary counsel, it was the primary counsel on Enron's various SEC filings showing profits, losses and, most importantly, indebtedness.[17] Thus, even if V&E was confused somehow by the individual SPE transactions, it was intimately involved in creating an extremely misleading public and regulatory picture of Enron's finances.

The opinion letters issued by the lawyers, the legal work in the creation of the SPEs, and the SEC filings were all absolutely critical to

[15] Final Report at 50.

[16] See Regan, "Teaching Enron," at 1162–66.

[17] R. T. McNamar, "Lawyers as Corporate Monitors," in *After Enron: Lessons for Public Policy*, ed. William A. Niskanen (Lanham, MD: Rowman & Littlefield, 2005), 186.

Enron's massive fraud. None of it could have happened without the work of the lawyers.

The Aftermath

Three main groups contributed to Enron's financial architecture: Enron executives, Arthur Andersen, and Enron's lawyers. In the wake of the scandal, significant attention was paid to each of these groups and there was much speculation about how Enron's demise would play out for each. In hindsight, two of the three groups paid a substantial price, whereas the third, the lawyers, got off relatively easy.

The executives who ran Enron into the ground have been financially ruined; many have been convicted of crimes and spent time in jail. In total, at least nineteen Enron executives pled guilty or were convicted of crimes.[18] In 2006, the *New York Times* did a "where are they now" update on ten different Enron players. Many of the former executives are disgraced and are serving or facing jail time and substantial fines.[19]

On May 25, 2006, Kenneth Lay and Jeffrey Skilling, the two top Enron executives, were convicted of multiple counts of fraud, conspiracy, and insider trading. Lay died shortly thereafter, but Skilling reported to jail December 13, 2006, to serve a twenty-four-year sentence.[20] The lower-profile executives who were not indicted have also paid a heavy price, from the total loss of their Enron-related retirement savings to the black marks on their résumés.

In some ways, Arthur Andersen suffered the worst punishment. Arthur Andersen was founded in 1913, as Andersen, DeLany, & Co. Until 2002, Andersen was a $9 billion "Big Five" accounting firm with

[18] Shaheen Pasha and Jessica Seid, "Lay and Skilling's Day of Reckoning," available at http://money.cnn.com/2006/05/25/news/newsmakers/enron_verdict/index.htm.

[19] Jonathan D. Glater, "10 Enron Players: Where They Ended After the Fall," *New York Times*, January 29, 2006.

[20] Associated Press, "Ex-Enron CEO Skilling Reports to Prison," available at http://www.msnbc.msn.com/id/16189124/.

hundreds of partners and more than 28,000 U.S. employees and 85,000 global employees. By any measure it was one of the best-known accounting firms in the world.[21]

Post-Enron, Arthur Andersen was destroyed almost overnight. David Duncan and Michael Odom were two of the leaders of Arthur Andersen's Enron team. In August 2001, they were informed that things were about to go south for Enron and its accounting. By mid-September, a "crisis response team" had been created, including general counsel Nancy Temple. From October through November, Arthur Andersen and Enron began an aggressive campaign of document shredding. Temple and Odom regularly reminded employees about Enron's document retention policy and basically encouraged the shredding of potentially incriminating documents. The government brought an obstruction-of-justice charge against the firm itself, accusing Arthur Andersen of violating 18 USC §§1512(b)(2)(A) and (B), alleging that between October 10 and November 9, 2001, Arthur Andersen persuaded others to withhold documents from use in regulatory and criminal proceedings and investigations.[22] Arthur Andersen was found guilty and lost its license to audit companies before the SEC, which essentially doomed it as a company. The case was later reversed on appeal to the Supreme Court,[23] but by then there was no way to reconstitute Arthur Andersen.

The Arthur Andersen charges were unusual in several respects. First, it is atypical for the government to bring criminal charges against an entity rather than an individual. The choice to indict a company, rather than people, has grave consequences for the company as a whole. Commentators have noted that Arthur Andersen was effectively convicted and punished within weeks of its indictment because partners and clients

[21] Jeffrey S. Kinsler, "Arthur Andersen and the Temple of Doom," 37 *SW. U. L. Rev.* 97, 99–100 (2008).

[22] *Arthur Andersen LLP v. United States*, 544 U.S. 696, 698–702 (2005).

[23] Id. The reversal was because of faulty jury instructions on the requirement that Arthur Andersen employees knew their actions were illegal.

began fleeing the company as soon as the news broke.[24] By the time the Supreme Court eventually reversed the conviction, the company was already destroyed.

Second, the government did not charge Arthur Andersen directly with obstruction of justice for the destruction of documents in advance of an SEC investigation. At the time, destroying documents in advance of an anticipated SEC investigation was not a crime. Instead, the government charged Arthur Andersen with witness tampering, a roundabout way of getting at the allegedly wrongful behavior.[25] In the aftermath, there has been significant criticism of what is now seen as government overreaching on both the law and on the decision to essentially seek the death penalty against a huge company employing thousands of people who had nothing to do with Enron or document shredding.[26]

Third, the federal prosecutors pursued criminal charges against only a single individual from Arthur Andersen, the accountant David Duncan. Duncan pled guilty to the charge, but the guilty plea was later withdrawn in the wake of the Supreme Court's reversal of the charges against the company.[27]

The decision not to pursue charges against the general counsel, Nancy Temple, is particularly striking. Temple was at least as aware as Duncan was of an impending SEC investigation. On October 8, her notes from a meeting with other Arthur Andersen lawyers called an SEC investigation "highly probable."[28] Temple encouraged document shredding at least as much as Duncan did, if not more. On October 12, she encouraged Enron head accountant Michael Odom to "remind the engagement team of our documentation and retention policy." On

[24] Assaf Hamdani and Alon Klement, "Corporate Crime and Deterrence," 61 *Stan. L. Rev.* 271 (2007).

[25] John Hasnas, "The Significant Meaninglessness of *Arthur Andersen LLP v. United States*," 2005 *Cato Sup. Ct. Rev.* 187, 192 and n. 31 (2005).

[26] Lisa L. Casey, "Class Action Criminality," *J. Corp. L.* 153, 236–37 (2008).

[27] "Charges Dropped Against Andersen Accountant," *Houston Chronicle*, December 16, 2005.

[28] *Arthur Andersen LLP v. United States*, 544 U.S. 696, 699 (2005).

October 16, she redistributed a copy of the document retention policy to the accountants. During a conference call on October 20, Temple orally reminded them to follow the policy. It was not until an SEC subpoena arrived on November 8 that Duncan, not Temple, ordered an end to the shredding.[29] In short, Temple was an instigator of the shredding, if not the leader of it. She certainly does not appear to be less blameworthy than Duncan. In interviews following the trial, the Arthur Andersen jury singled out Temple, not Duncan or Odom, as the employee responsible for the destruction of the documents and the conviction.[30] A congressional committee specifically asked the Justice Department to investigate Temple's actions in the shredding and whether she had testified truthfully about them afterward.[31] She has become the "poster child" for illegal shredding and is "infamous" in legal ethics circles.[32]

Somehow, though, Temple faced no individual criminal charges, nor has she faced any punishment whatsoever from any lawyer disciplinary authority. Instead, she returned to Chicago and resumed her law practice.[33] In comparison, Michael Odom received a two-year ban on practicing as an accountant before the SEC.[34] David Duncan received a lifetime ban.[35] For big-firm accountants, losing the right to practice before the SEC is essentially a loss of the right to work in high-end accounting at all.

Nancy Temple is not the only lawyer breathing a sigh of relief. The third column of Enron's cooked books, the law firms, paid a settlement to the bankruptcy estate and still face some lingering civil lawsuits, but have

[29] Id. at 699–702.

[30] "Attorney Defends Andersen Lawyer Crucial to Verdict," *Houston Chronicle*, June 16, 2002.

[31] Richard A. Oppel, Jr., "Inquiry on Andersen Lawyer Is Urged by House Committee," *New York Times*, December 18, 2002.

[32] Kinsler, "Arthur Andersen and the Temple of Doom" at 97 and n. 1.

[33] Glater, "10 Enron Players: Where They Landed After the Fall." At the time of this writing, Temple's website was available at http://www.kattentemplelaw.com/nan.html.

[34] The SEC order is available at http://www.sec.gov/litigation/admin/2008/34–57209.pdf.

[35] The SEC announcement is available at http://sec.gov/litigation/litreleases/2008/lr20441.htm.

survived and even thrived. As this book goes to press, no lawyer involved in the Enron case has been disbarred or has even faced public sanction from a licensing body. Likewise, no lawyer involved in the matter has faced charges or been convicted of any crime.

Vinson and Elkins, Enron's primary outside law firm, not only continues to exist and practice, but it is also thriving. V&E's "About the Firm" website states:

> V&E cut its teeth on oil and gas matters, and today remains one of the world's leading energy law firms, with offices in Abu Dhabi, Austin, Dallas, Houston, New York, Washington, Beijing, Dubai, Hong Kong, London, Moscow, Shanghai and Tokyo. Influenced by the strong personalities of its founding partners, V&E's early hallmarks were stability, adaptability and a congenial informality among its lawyers. Those traits are still in evidence today, even as Vinson & Elkins has grown into a worldwide operation with over 700 lawyers in 13 offices across the globe.

In 2008, V&E ranked fifty-fifth in the world on the *American Lawyer*'s "global 100" list for gross law firm revenue, forty-fifth on the "AmLaw 200" list of American law firms for gross revenue, and sixty-second in average profits per partner, at $585,000 per partner.[36] Similarly, A&K has bettered its position since the fall of Enron.[37]

V&E did pay $30 million to the Enron bankruptcy estate to settle what were essentially malpractice claims,[38] but in light of the $800 million paid by banks that were less involved, and the fact that V&E billed Enron $36 million in 2001 alone, $30 million is a fairly light penalty.

[36] The three charts are available at http://www.datacert.com/Customers/AmLaw200.asp, http://www.datacert.com/Customers/AmLawGlobal100.asp, and http://www.law.com/special/professionals/amlaw/amlaw200/amlaw200_ppp.html.

[37] The same charts show that Andrews & Kurth is also one of the top 100 American firms in gross revenue and profits per partner.

[38] Kristen Hays, "Law Firm's Settlement Is $18.5 Million," *Houston Chronicle*, January 19, 2007.

Likewise, A&K paid an $18.5 million malpractice settlement, which was also substantially less than the $29 million in fees A&K collected from Enron between 1998 and 2001.[39]

The individual lawyers involved have also fared well. No attorney for Enron, Arthur Andersen, or any outside firm has faced public sanction from any bar disciplinary authority. Joseph Dilg was the V&E billing partner in charge of the Enron account throughout the period in question and was heavily involved with everything the firm did for Enron.[40] Far from suffering repercussions, Dilg has remained at V&E and was the managing partner of the firm in 2008.[41] David Barbour was the lead A&K lawyer on the Enron account.[42] He likewise remains a partner at the firm and was named a "Texas Super Lawyer" in 2008, according to the firm's website.[43] James Derrick was Enron's general counsel and, as of 2008, he was the head partner of the Houston office of the law firm Kelly, Hart & Hartman. Derrick's website notes that he was general counsel at Enron from 1991 "until his retirement in 2002."[44]

Why?

How did the lawyers walk away from a vortex that completely swallowed the accountants and the executives involved? Why have none of the lawyers been sanctioned? This is where the cumulative effects of the lawyer–judge bias come to the fore.

39 Id.

40 Reagan, "Teaching Enron," 1155.

41 Joseph Dilg's website is available at http://www.vinson-elkins.com/lawyers/showpdf.aspx?page=http://www.vinson-elkins.com/lawyers/lawyer_detail_fb_print.aspx?id=322.

42 Reagan, "Teaching Enron," 1155.

43 See http://www.andrewskurth.com/lawyers-DavidBarbour.html and http://www.andrewskurth.com/pressroom-197.html.

44 See http://www.khh.com/default.asp?NodeId=233. The website also notes, "Mr. Derrick and his wife, Carrin Patman, are captivated daily by the shenanigans of Lord Wellington S.S. Derrick, Q.C., their much loved Cavalier King Charles Spaniel."

Remember that malpractice is very difficult to prove and requires a plaintiff to jump through multiple hoops. In a case such as Enron's, the bankrupt estate would have to prove the existence of faulty advice and that things would have turned out differently if proper advice were given. This is obviously a difficult burden to prove.

Remember the structure of the attorney disciplinary system. The rules themselves are drafted narrowly and generally focus on lawyers and clients, not anyone outside that relationship. Incredibly, it is not clear that any of the lawyers involved in the Enron fiasco violated *any* disciplinary rule whatsoever.[45] Commentators have suggested possible changes to the rules to address this situation[46] and the SEC has drafted some preliminary rules of its own (over the strong objections of the ABA).[47] The fact that lawyers could be intimately involved in one of the worst accounting scandals ever and their actions would not violate any disciplinary rules is a clear sign of whom those rules are meant to benefit.

Finally, remember that even if the rules did apply, the lawyer disciplinary authorities rarely enforce anything but the most egregious violations. These agencies are often underfunded and backlogged with cases, so they are generally not in the business of seeking out violations, even in a high-profile case such as Enron.

As the *Washington Post* and others have noted, Enron is not sui generis. Although lawyers have been intimately involved in all the most famous accounting fraud cases of the past ten years, they have faced almost no consequences for their actions.[48]

[45] Roger C. Crampton, "Enron and the Corporate Lawyer: A Primer on Legal and Ethical Issues," 58 *Bus. Lawyer* 143 (2002).

[46] See Deborah L. Rhode and Paul D. Paton, "Lawyers, Ethics, and Enron," 8 *Stan. J.L. Bus. & Finance* 9 (2002).

[47] Brent J. Horton, "How Corporate Lawyers Escape Sarbanes-Oxley: Disparate Treatment in the Legislative Process," 60 *S. Car. L. Rev.* 149, 175–78 (2008).

[48] Carrie Johnson, "Look Who's Left Standing: Legal Penalties in Frauds Are Seldom Paid by Legal Advisors," *Washington Post*, August 31, 2006.

Clearly, the lawyer–judge bias has real-world consequences. In a case such as Enron's, the lawyers were relatively unscathed in comparison with the other actors. From the outside, the closed world of lawyers and judges can seem abstruse and relatively unimportant, so it is crucial to remember how a self-regulated bar protected by the judiciary affects us all.

11 Complexity and the Lawyer–Judge Bias

> The broadest judicial bias I see . . . is the bias in favor of legal complexity. The volumes of the third edition of the Federal Reporter spread themselves like Kudzu vine over the shelves of law libraries.
>
> – Dennis Jacobs, Chief Judge, U.S. Court of Appeals for the Second Circuit[1]

> The multiplication of rules and standards, carrying in its train as it does endless debate over boundaries, is one of the banes of the American legal system, a source of its appalling complexity.
>
> – *Holmes v. Buss*[2]

EARLIER CHAPTERS OFFER MULTIPLE EXAMPLES OF THE lawyer–judge bias in case law. Chapter 10 discusses Enron as a recent real-world example of the way in which the lawyer–judge bias has important and deleterious consequences. In this chapter, we consider a more diffuse, but equally insidious, consequence of the lawyer–judge bias: how the lawyer–judge interrelation leads to the overweening legal complexity described by the judges at the start of this chapter.

Before defining legal complexity, let me start with a caveat. I have presented parts of this book at law schools and conferences all over the

[1] Dennis Jacobs, "The Secret Life of Judges," 75 *Fordham L. Rev.* 2855 (2007).

[2] *Holmes v. Buss*, 506 F.3d 576 (7th Cir. 2007, Posner, J.).

country and I have had multiple colleagues read it in draft. This chapter is invariably their least favorite. Law professors, judges, and lawyers have a very hard time seeing what seems obvious to outsiders – the American legal system is hopelessly and miserably complex and much more complicated than it needs to be. In fact, George Wright has argued vociferously that American law is optimally complex as is, and that it would be impossible to simplify.[3]

In deference to Professor Wright and my other colleagues, complexity is indeed difficult to measure and, to a certain extent, complexity rests in the eyes of the beholder. Some legal issues are themselves complicated, so some complexity in the law is unavoidable. Nevertheless, as I have practiced and taught law for years, the main tenets of this chapter strike me as painfully obvious: (1) American law is more complex than it needs to be; and (2) one major reason for this is that complexity behooves two of the main players in the system – judges and lawyers.

For those who consider the first proposition controversial, consider the following. Robert Kagan has collected and digested various empirical studies that show American law to be unusually expensive, expansive, complex, and uncertain. He terms this American "exceptionalism" and argues that these studies describe a legal system that is uniquely complex and unwieldy:

> For one social problem after another, the studies show, the American system for making and implementing public policy and resolving disputes is distinctive. It generally entails (1) more complex bodies of rules; (2) more formal, adversarial procedures for resolving political and scientific disputes; (3) more costly forms of legal contestation; (4) stronger, more punitive legal sanctions; (5) more frequent judicial review of and intervention into administrative decisions and processes; (6) more political controversy about legal rules and

[3] R. George Wright, "The Illusion of Simplicity: An Explanation of Why the Law Can't Just Be Less Complex," 27 *Fla. St. U. L. Rev.* 715 (2000).

institutions; (7) more politically fragmented, less closely coordinated decisionmaking systems; and (8) more legal uncertainty and instability.[4]

In short, American law is especially prone to complexity, more pervasive in more areas of our lives, and more suffused with uncertainty.

Moreover, judges, lawyers, law professors, economists, and the public have noticed an ever-growing and unhealthy complexity in American law.[5] The opacity of the legal system, much of which is a result of the natural indeterminacy that comes from complexity, is a main source of public distrust and unhappiness with the legal system.[6]

This drift toward indeterminate complexity is harmful.[7] The most obvious expense is in transaction costs. When the law is complicated, individuals need to hire lawyers to help decode it. When the law is complicated *and* indeterminate, consumers receive the worst of all worlds – the expense of seeking legal advice without any clear answer about how to proceed. Evidence of the drift into indeterminate complexity is all around us. The past forty years have seen a huge uptick in the number

[4] Robert A. Kagan, *Adversarial Legalism: The American Way of Law* (Cambridge, MA: Harvard University Press, 2001), 6–9 and Table 1.

[5] Judges: Dennis Jacobs, "The Secret Life of Judges"; *Holmes v. Buss*. Lawyers: Philip K. Howard, *The Death of Common Sense – How Law Is Suffocating America* (New York: Warner Books, 1994). Law professors: Richard A. Epstein, *Simple Rules For A Complex World* (Cambridge, MA: Harvard University Press, 1995); Peter H. Schuck, "Legal Complexity: Some Causes, Consequences, and Cures," in Peter H. Schuck, *The Limits of Law: Essays on Democratic Governance* (Boulder, CO: Westview, 2000), 3–46. Economists: Gillian K. Hadfield, "The Many Legal Institutions that Support Contractual Commitments," in *Handbook of New Institutional Economics*, eds. Claude Menard and Mary M. Shirley (Dordrecht, Netherlands: Springer, 2005), 191–92. The public: Perhaps the most famous example is the web site "Overlawyered," available at http://overlawyered.com/ as a website, or in Twitter format: http://twitter.com/overlawyered.

[6] Jose Juan Toharia, "Evaluating Systems of Justice Through Public Opinion: Why, What, Who, How, and What For?," in *Beyond Common Knowledge*, eds. Erik G. Jensen and Thomas C. Heller (Stanford, CA: Stanford University Press, 2003), 21–31.

[7] See, e.g., Gillian Hadfield, "The Price of Law: How the Market for Lawyers Distorts the Justice System," 98 *Mich. L. Rev.* 101 (2000).

of lawyers per capita, the money spent on lawyers, and the number and pages of reported judicial decisions.[8]

Three Views of American Legal Complexity

Legal complexity is a difficult thing to define. As the blind men in a room did with an elephant, it is often helpful to consider several different perspectives on an amorphous subject. As an introduction, I offer a brief discussion of three different books that well capture some of the "appalling complexity" referred to previously: Paul Campos' *Jurismania*, Philip K. Howard's *Life Without Lawyers*, and Robert A. Kagan's *Adversarial Legalism*. These authors come from very different perspectives: Campos is a distinguished law professor and nationally known (and relatively liberal) newspaper columnist. Howard is a lawyer and well-known conservative activist and has been on the forefront of the tort reform movement. Kagan is a professor of political science at Berkeley. The books range from Kagan's relatively dry and scholarly work to Howard's populist call for a legal system without lawyers. The diversity in approach and authors shows that a concern about legal complexity cuts across ideology.

Campos' *Jurismania* suggests that Americans suffer from a collective mental illness caused by the extension of the legal system into every corner of our lives. Campos describes the process as a change in our national psychology: law has become a default filter for most areas of life.[9] Moreover, law is growing ever more complex. Campos attributes this to an overbearing desire to get every case exactly right and an overconfidence in the powers of human reason. These instincts lead judges to add complexity in legal tests and case results. Although the results may be better in individual cases (which is debatable), the results

[8] Epstein, *Simple Rules*, 3–12.

[9] Paul F. Campos, *Jurismania: The Madness of American Law* (Oxford: Oxford University Press, 1998), 3–15.

systemwide are disastrous.[10] *Jurismania* paints an evocative portrait of the problem and explains many of the causes, but misses the key influence of the lawyer–judge bias.

Howard argues that lawyers and law run amok are choking the country. Howard has argued that lawyers are killing American businesses,[11] restricting our freedom[12] and destroying our common sense.[13] His most recent book invites us to imagine an almost-utopian world without lawyers.[14] I have disagreed with Howard's work in the past,[15] but his visceral description of the crippling effects of legal complexity is an invaluable addition to the topic.

Howard misses the point when he focuses on a life without lawyers, however. In legal complexity, judges are more the problem than lawyers. Disputants will always have an incentive to hire lawyers to navigate a dispute through a government's dispute resolution processes. Those helpers (whether they are called lawyers or not) will always have an incentive to do whatever it takes to achieve a successful result, including making ever more complex arguments parsing any law to fit their case. The key to reducing complexity is to control the incentives of the judges, because the incentives of the lawyers and their clients will always center on individual victories.

Last, political scientist Kagan notes that American law is unique in its focus on adversarial legalism. Kagan does an excellent job of boiling American exceptionalism down to two broad factors: the

[10] Id. at 64–80.

[11] Philip K. Howard, *The Collapse of the Common Good: How America's Lawsuit Culture Undermines Our Freedom* (New York: Ballantine Books, 2002).

[12] Philip K. Howard, "Is Civil Litigation a Threat to Freedom?," 28 *Harv. J.L. & Pub. Pol'y* 97 (2004).

[13] Howard, *The Death of Common Sense*.

[14] Philip K. Howard, *Life Without Lawyers: Liberating Americans From Too Much Law* (New York: W. W. Norton, 2009).

[15] See Benjamin H. Barton, "Tort Reform, Innovation, and Playground Design," 57 *Fla. L. Rev.* 265, 270 n. 19 (2006).

uniquely adversarial nature of our courts and their costly and complex "legalism."[16]

Kagan argues that adversarial legalism really took off as a reaction to the social upheaval of the 1960s and the desire for a society marked by "total justice." Courts greatly expanded their reach in an effort to bring justice to more people in more circumstances. The result was a massive expansion of the role of the courts in American life and the crippling complexity Campos described as "jurismania": courts were continually trying to calibrate their rules and decisions to maximize justice. On a micro level, this may have helped in individual cases. On the macro level, it has resulted in endless, costly, and damaging adversarial legalism.[17] Kagan includes a good section describing how the American legal profession contributes to, and profits from, adversarial legalism, but he also misses the special role and incentives of judges in the system.[18]

Legal Complexity Defined

Now we turn to a definition of legal complexity. This chapter addresses only judge-made legal complexity – that is, the complexity of the rules created in judicial opinions. Much of the complexity in American law comes as a result of legislation or regulation that is outside the realm of the lawyer–judge bias. Nevertheless, there is a persuasive argument to be made that the creeping "legalization" of all areas of American life is itself a reaction to judge-made complexity, as private entities, regulators, and legislatures try to craft rules that will stand up in court. As the legal system increasingly pervades American life, some of the most damaging aspects of the shared lawyer–judge proclivities have crossed over:

[16] Kagan offers an overview of the argument in the book's introduction, Kagan, *Adversarial Legalism*, 9–16. Kagan's full argument covering the American criminal and civil law systems is exceptional and extremely persuasive. Id. at 61–155.

[17] Id. at 34–58.

[18] Id. at 55–58.

treating every disagreement as an opportunity for a formal adversary process and the overuse of technical language in endless sentences. Thus, the complexity that first seemed only the domain of the legal system has leaked out, transforming institutions and social interactions far beyond the courthouse walls.

Many definitions of legal complexity are themselves quite convoluted. For example, Peter Schuck describes legal complexity across four axes – density, complexity, institutional differentiation, and indeterminacy.[19] Richard Epstein offers a definition that defines complexity in terms of the public and private costs of compliance with any rule.[20] In comparison, consider Louis Kaplow's relatively straightforward statement that "the relative complexity of legal rules refers to the number and difficulty of distinctions the rules make."[21] This simpler definition will work fine for our purposes.

Critics have gravely objected to this definition as hopelessly amorphous and nonspecific. I offer the following retort. Complexity, like pornography, is usually obvious to the eye of the beholder and, by any definition, American law is extremely complex. One reason is the lawyers' obsession with precise definitions and continual worry about gray areas, rather than black and white areas of general agreement. I submit this overspecificity as a key source of complexity and will not re-create it in the very definition of complexity.

Not all complexity is bad, and complex systems are not necessarily indeterminate.[22] Complexity will sometimes add granularity and certainty. If an area of law is one in which it is critical to have very precise calibration, complexity is often necessary, even if it is not efficient.

[19] Schuck, "Legal Complexity," 4.

[20] Epstein, *Simple Rules*, 25–26.

[21] Louis Kaplow, "A Model of the Optimal Complexity of Legal Rules," 11 *J.L. Econ. & Org.* 150, 150 (1995). This definition jibes nicely with nonlegal definitions, such as John Casti's definition that "the complexity of an object is directly proportional to the length of its shortest possible description." John L. Casti, *Complexification* (New York: Harper Collins, 1995), 9.

[22] Kaplow, 151–52.

The tax code is an example of an area in which the drafters have clearly attempted to be complex, yet as precise as possible.

That said, much of the judge-made complexity drifts into what I call "indeterminate complexity." In these situations, legal complexity offers the worst of both worlds: it is complicated and it makes predicting the outcomes of cases more difficult. In determining whether complexity is helpful or not, consider two separate continuums for judge-created law. One continuum considers whether the law is simple or complex; the second considers whether the law is relatively determinate or indeterminate.

Being at an extreme of one continuum does not necessarily affect placement on the other. For example, simple rules can be determinate or indeterminate. Our courts could operate based on a single statement: "All disputes will be decided fairly." This statement is simple, but would be woefully indeterminate in practice. In comparison, rules stating a speed limit or the legal age for drinking are simple and determinate.

Similarly, complex systems can be determinate or indeterminate. Many IRS and EPA regulations are attempts to use complexity to increase determinacy.[23] The end of this chapter argues that the law of standing is complex and indeterminate. We have already seen some good examples of indeterminate complexity. One hallmark of indeterminate complexity is the multifactor test in which it is unclear which factor weighs the most – or even that every factor needs to be considered. Remember the test for the forfeiture of a legal fee when the lawyer has breached an employment contract through poor performance:

> A lawyer engaging in clear and serious violation of duty to a client may be required to forfeit some or all of the lawyer's compensation for the matter. Considerations relevant to the question of forfeiture include the gravity and timing of the violation, its willfulness, its effect

[23] The relative failure of this effort, however, may be evidence that it is harder than one might think to increase determinacy with complexity. Consider Edward McCaffery's discussion of indeterminacy, taxpayer behavior and "dynamic complexity" in the creation of IRS regulations. Edward J. McCaffery, "The Holy Grail of Tax Simplification," 1990 *Wis. L. Rev.* 1267 (1990).

> on the value of the lawyer's work for the client, any other threatened or actual harm to the client, and the adequacy of other remedies.[24]

The seven-pronged test for determining who is a debt collector under the Fair Debt Collection Practices Act quoted in Chapter 9 is another great example.[25]

Most would agree that these tests are confusing and will prove difficult to apply, and that predicting an outcome in any close case will be impossible. Litigants facing these tests must hire a lawyer to gather information and argue all the different factors with little clue as to how the case will come out at trial.

Another hallmark of indeterminate complexity is case law that applies to only one set of facts. *Bush v. Gore* is a great example of a case in which the Supreme Court attempted to limit the decision to the facts at hand.[26] The Fair Labor Standards Act case of *Sahyers v. Prugh, Holliday & Karatinos, P.C.* that began Chapter 1 is another such case.[27] These

[24] *Restatement (Third) of Law Governing Lawyers* §37 (2000).

[25] "Most important in the analysis is the assessment of facts closely relating to ordinary concepts of regularity, including (1) the absolute number of debt collection communications issued, and/or collection-related litigation matters pursued, over the relevant period(s), (2) the frequency of such communications and/or litigation activity, including whether any patterns of such activity are discernable, (3) whether the entity has personnel specifically assigned to work on debt collection activity, (4) whether the entity has systems or contractors in place to facilitate such activity, and (5) whether the activity is undertaken in connection with ongoing client relationships with entities that have retained the lawyer or firm to assist in the collection of outstanding consumer debt obligations. Facts relating to the role debt collection work plays in the practice as a whole should also be considered to the extent they bear on the question of regularity of debt collection activity (debt collection constituting 1% of the overall work or revenues of a very large entity may, for instance, suggest regularity, whereas such work constituting 1% of an individual lawyer's practice might not). Whether the law practice seeks debt collection business by marketing itself as having debt collection expertise may also be an indicator of the regularity of collection as a part of the practice." *Goldstein v. Hutton, Ingram, Yuzek, Gainen, Carroll & Bertolotti*, 374 F.3d 56, 62–63 (2nd Cir. 2004).

[26] *Bush v. Gore*, 531 U.S. 98 (2000).

[27] As discussed in Chapter 4, the cases approving limits on in-person solicitation by lawyers and allowing IOLTA programs to gather client interest are now essentially limited to their facts as well.

cases create indeterminate complexity because litigants will still try to use them as precedents, regardless of an opinion's disclaimer. Despite the Supreme Court's limiting language in *Bush v. Gore*, litigants, courts, and scholars have tried to find future uses for the precedent.[28] Moreover, the existence of case-specific, nonrecurring decisions causes uncertainty in forecasting cases because these limited decisions suggest that judges may attempt to decide a case regardless of the precedential effect of the decision, upsetting any calculation of how a controversial case might be decided.

What explains the existence of these indeterminately complex decisions? Lawyers and appellate judges love complexity. This chapter focuses on the appellate, lawmaking courts in comparison with law-applying district courts. The classic lawmaking courts are the U.S. and state supreme courts.[29] The various federal and state courts of appeal also regularly make law. Trial courts at the federal and state level are considered law-applying courts. This is not to say that these courts do not have substantial (and, in some cases, largely unfettered) discretion to make law in any given case or that these courts do not add to the overall complexity of the system. Instead, it is the nature of precedent and the likelihood that a written, published decision by a court will affect existing law or create new law that separates the lawmaking from the law-applying courts. In analyzing legal complexity, it is critical to separate out these different types of courts, because their incentives and responsibilities differ greatly. Notably, district courts bear the brunt of the costs of complexity, whereas appellate courts reap the benefits.

Complexity and Lawyers

We begin with lawyers, rather than judges, for two reasons: all judges were lawyers first and, as earlier chapters have established, the legal

[28] See Edward B. Foley, "The Future of *Bush v. Gore*," 68 *Ohio St. L.J.* 925 (2007).

[29] Richard Posner has gone so far as to argue recently that the U.S. Supreme Court's caseload and approach makes the Court an essentially legislative body. Richard A. Posner, "Foreword: A Political Court," 119 *Harv. L. Rev.* 31 (2005).

profession exercises a mighty sway over the judiciary. Lawyers have multiple reasons to favor complexity. First, lawyers sell a single good: technical expertise of the legal system. The more complicated that system is (and that includes procedural and substantive complexity), the more business there will be for lawyers.[30]

If the system were to grow simpler, usage of lawyers would decline. Consider the push toward nonlawyered mediation (whether electronic systems such as eBay's or in-person mediation) as a less expensive and simpler form of dispute resolution. Litigants have moved toward these less formal dispute resolution mechanisms to avoid the expense and complexity of traditional court proceedings. The eBay online dispute resolution system is particularly on point. Because of issues of personal service and jurisdiction, it is very complicated for a citizen in one state to sue a citizen in another state, especially if that state is far away and the amount at issue is relatively small. The eBay system circumvents that complexity in favor of simple, effective, and cheap online mediation.[31]

Seen in this light, legal complexity is an expected result of public choice theory. Lawyers are a well-organized interest group that pushes for beneficial law (in this case, complicated law and procedure) at the expense of the public. Public debates over legal complexity bear this out. Whenever nonlawyers complain about the legal system, lawyers fall back to claims of unique institutional knowledge: "Of course the legal system is complicated. If you were a lawyer you would understand why it must be so." This is true even in relatively simple and straightforward areas of the law, such as divorce and bankruptcy. At the low end, most of this law and procedure is very simple, but most jurisdictions nonetheless require lawyers to file the paperwork and prosecute the cases, even when a lay advocate or paralegal could serve adequately.

[30] Gillian Hadfield has been particularly persuasive on this point. See Hadfield, "The Price of Law."

[31] See Colin Rule, *Online Dispute Resolution for Business: B2B, ECommerce, Consumer, Employment, Insurance, and Other Commercial Conflicts* (New York: Jossey-Bass, 2002).

Lawyers also add legal value to litigation by finding applicable precedents, statutes, or regulations and then either distinguishing or applying them through a process of case law synthesis. Regardless of whether precedents are to be distinguished or embraced, overall complexity assists. Having multiple overlapping precedents or multifactor tests always allows a lawyer room to find good precedent and distinguish bad precedent. This is especially so because a lawyer can almost always distinguish a case on the facts. In this regard lawyers build snowflakes: they are trying to make each case unique and sui generis.

Gillian Hadfield has likewise argued that the American lawyer's dedication to zealous advocacy on behalf of individual clients virtually guarantees complexity and ignores the broader benefits of simplicity.[32] If a more complex solution will best suit a lawyer's client that is the rule the lawyer will suggest, regardless of the overall effect on the law. The sum total of each of these individual case decisions in favor of complexity results in a system heading toward entropy.[33]

Complexity is not good for legal clients or for society as a whole. Nevertheless, because of informational asymmetry (which means that the lawyers have much better information than their clients about any given case and the system as a whole) and agency costs, clients are not usually in a position to advocate for a simpler result over more complexity in any given case, let alone across the law in general. A great example of this gap is the tort reform efforts. As a general rule, these reforms have focused on damages caps or jurisdictional controls and not on fundamental reform of the underlying law.[34] Damage caps and jurisdictional changes limit the overall losses in litigation, but they do little to rein in indeterminacy or complexity, which remains untouched. In this way, the defense lawyers are still quite necessary to defend these cases.

[32] Gillian Hadfield, "Legal Barriers to Innovation: The Growing Economic Cost of Professional Control Over Corporate Legal Markets," 60 *Stan. L. Rev.* 1689, 1694–95 (2008).

[33] Id.

[34] Margo Schlanger, "Second Best Damage Action Deterrence," 55 *DePaul L. Rev.* 517, 535 n. 66 (2006).

On the whole, complexity is a great detriment to the purchasers of legal services. On an individual basis, however, complexity can be a client's best friend, especially if an able lawyer uses that complexity toward a better individual case result. Thus, unlike the typical collective action problem, it is not just the cost of organizing that puts the large group at a disadvantage. In legal complexity, the individual choice in favor of complexity actually carries benefits to each individual client in the short term. This phenomenon is also reflected in surveys that show that the public has a generally unfavorable impression of the legal profession as a whole, but a favorable impression of any individual lawyer who worked for them.[35]

Complexity and Judges

How does complexity benefit judges? Complex systems are harder to administer, so one might think that judges would seek simplicity – but they rarely do. A study of judicial incentives and behavior helps explain why.

There are multiple reasons for judges, like lawyers, to favor complexity. The first is that the courts most affected by complexity – trial courts – are not the courts generally responsible for its creation. Lawmaking appellate courts are in charge of creating precedential complexity, and complexity affects them only the next time that issue appears on appeal. These courts are not on the front line of deciphering or applying complexity.[36] It is quite common to hear district courts grousing about the complexity of the law they must apply.

Second, judges tend to favor lawyers because lawyers and judges are the system's repeat players. One of the critical lessons of game theory is that players in iterated games have a strong incentive to cooperate,

[35] Steven K. Berenson, "Institutional Professionalism for Lawyers: Realizing the Virtues of Civic Professionalism," 109 *W. Va. L. Rev.* 67, 67–68 (2006).

[36] For a particularly evocative description of this effect by a federal judge, see Jacobs, "The Secret Life of Judges."

whereas one-time games, such as the classic prisoner's dilemma, discourage cooperation.[37] Lawyers and judges will naturally want to work together; judges and litigants, not so much.

Third, just as complexity has benefits for the legal profession as a whole, it carries great benefits for the lawmaking judiciary as well. Complexity makes it easier to decide almost any case in line with the judge's other preferences.[38] Complexity is a powerful tool for any part of the government. Complex rules allow more latitude and less accountability throughout the government because it is costly for the public to decipher or lobby against complex systems. Complexity allows any government official to pursue her individual goals under cover of an opaque legal system that the public cannot disentangle. The standing law discussed later in this chapter is a perfect example. The law is a confusing mess, so a judge can allow or disallow a plaintiff standing in what appears to be a neutral process governed by precedent.

If an aggrieved member of the public wishes to change an overly complex area of the law, she must first decipher it, try to understand exactly which government actor or actors are responsible for the situation at hand, and then lobby for change. This lobbying process will be especially difficult if the opponent is the "independent" judiciary. Moreover, a hallmark of indeterminately complex judge-made law is the impenetrable opinion, written as if it is compelled by previous precedent and obviously correct.

Fourth, complexity does have costs, but lawyers do a great deal of every judge's work. As noted in Chapter 2, in the advocacy system judges rely on lawyers to do the bulk of the work in trying, briefing, researching, and investigating cases. When the system is working properly, the judges sit back and decide cases based on the legal and factual work presented by the lawyers.

[37] Eric Rasmusen, *Games And Information: An Introduction to Game Theory* (London: Blackwell, 1994), 16–19; Robert Axelrod, *The Evolution of Cooperation* (New York: Basic Books, 1984), 68–69.

[38] Eric J. Miller, "Judicial Preference," 44 *Hous. L. Rev.* 1275 (2008).

On appeal, the lawyers generally find and research the law, place it in written briefs, and then apply it to the facts at hand for the judges. As such, complexity arrives for the judge hand-wrapped by the litigants. Judges can, of course, disregard the lawyers' legal research and theories of the case. But insofar as that requires independent research or a novel legal outcome (and, in most cases, a simplification of the law would be novel), substantial additional work is required and the judge risks the opprobrium of other judges and the legal profession. Thus, paradoxically, a judge seeking simplicity will have to work much harder than a judge who applies the complex theories and law presented by the lawyers in the case.

Fifth, although innovation in almost all areas of legal practice and judging has been painfully slow, one area of a judge's work – writing opinions – has been greatly streamlined by word processing technology. One hundred years ago it took substantial physical effort to write or edit a legal document. Even forty years ago, judges worked through multiple drafts, writing their changes by hand in an effort to reach a final edit. Word processors have revolutionized this process, so a practical barrier to complexity (the hassle of committing it to paper) has been removed.

Finally, lawmaking judges like complexity. It is likely that they were good at complexity as lawyers and this is quite possibly why they sought a job as a judge in the first place. Remember the discussion in Chapter 2 of legal thought as an "institution," a group of thoughts and behaviors that tightly bind a group. Legal analysis itself is a powerful and constraining institution. In considering a judicial and lawyerly taste for complexity, it is critical to understand *how* the institution of legal thought is developed and passed on within the legal profession and the judiciary.

The first stop is law school. Justice Felix Frankfurter once opined that "the law is what the lawyers are. And the law and lawyers are what the law schools make them."[39] The stated goal of American law school, to

[39] Letter from Felix Frankfurter to Mr. Rosenwald (May 13, 1927) (on file with the Harvard Law School Library).

teach law students to "think like a lawyer," is an explicit attempt to pass along the rules of an institution. American law schools are aimed at the study (and celebration) of indeterminacy. In class and exams, students are repeatedly presented with an unclear area of the law and asked to argue both sides of the issue. "Thinking like a lawyer" requires a student to see each issue as multifaceted and to recognize that the law likely does not have a clear answer for the questions raised in class or on the exams.

Students are instructed that the important point is not to find the "right" answer, because there likely is no right answer. Instead, students are taught and graded on their thinking processes: Did they spot all the potential issues? Once they spotted the issues, did they correctly analyze them and note the different ways in which the law could apply? I have previously called this approach to teaching law "the siren song of indeterminacy."[40] Law school's continual focus on gray areas is a specialized training in complexity. The students who are best at it end up with the best grades and the highest credentials when they exit law school.

Law schools are not irrational to focus on indeterminacy, however. The next stop for almost every lawmaking judge is practice. As noted earlier, coping with, and often creating, complexity and indeterminacy is much of what lawyers are paid to do.

The lawyers who are selected to be lawmaking (i.e., appellate) judges come from the elite of the profession.[41] As members of this elite, these lawyers have mastered the skills involved in the creation and understanding of legal complexity. Furthermore, it is likely that they actually quite enjoy the entire process. When lawyers, judges, or law professors talk about a "true love of the law," they are talking about this exact process of digesting and generating complexity.

In addition to the sorting process of law school and practice, consider the power of self-selection for lawmaking judges. Many, if not most, of

[40] Benjamin H. Barton, "The Emperor of Ocean Park: The Quintessence of Legal Academia," 92 *Cal. L. Rev.* 585 (2004).

[41] For example, graduates of elite law schools are disproportionately represented on the federal bench. *Grutter v. Bollinger*, 539 U.S. 306, 322 (2003).

these judges have not taken their jobs for the money. Most could earn more in private practice. It is likely that some chose the work for prestige or job security (for judges appointed for life) or for a lighter workload, but there is another substantial nonpecuniary benefit to becoming a lawmaking judge: the work itself.

American judges who hear appeals have jobs that are radically distinct from the jobs of most lawyers or even trial court judges. Lawmaking judges spend the vast majority of their time reading briefs, researching the law, and writing opinions. They hear oral arguments, but for only a small fraction of their time. They have very little contact with the public. As much as possible, they delegate unpleasant or managerial tasks to staff or clerks and focus on the "fun" part of their job: legal reasoning and deciding cases.[42] The delegation of most of their regulatory authority over the legal profession is a great example of this phenomenon. By choice, most lawmaking judges spend almost all their time engaged in the hermetic pursuit of legal complexity, a true "life of the law."

Every lawyer who becomes a judge knows what the job entails, and it is thus quite likely that they expect to enjoy it. A big part of the nonpecuniary benefit of the lawmaking judge is the pleasure (or "craft value," to use Peter Schuck's terminology) that lawyers gain from legal complexity.[43]

This helps explain why the "costs" of complexity do not deter lawmaking judges. To lawmaking judges, complexity is not a bug; it is a feature. If complexity means that later interesting appeals, raising new and different legal questions in the same complex area, will arise in the future, that is sauce for the goose.[44]

[42] Paul D. Carrington, "A Critical Assessment of the Cultural and Institutional Roles of Appellate Courts," 9 *J. App. Prac. & Process* 231 (2007).

[43] Peter H. Schuck, "Legal Complexity: Some Causes, Consequences, and Cures," 42 *Duke L.J.* 1, 7, 31–38 (1992).

[44] This helps explain the competition among bankruptcy judges for complex cases discussed in Chapter 9. These judges are literally seeking out complexity.

Many lawyers became appellate judges specifically to hear, think about, and decide complex constitutional cases. When those former lawyers get their chance to decide these cases, reducing complexity is the last thing on their mind. The Supreme Court's cases on First Amendment freedom of speech or the religion clauses can actually be rationalized under this analysis. The best way to understand them is to assume that judges decide them according to their preferences (usually liberal versus conservative) and then a combination of a desire to cover their preferences and to enjoy the writing process leads to decisions that often further cloud the law.

It is also worth noting the ways in which complexity fits the judicial interest in "prestige," which generally means the way in which judges are perceived among lawyers and other legal elites.[45] Lawyers, legal academics, and other judges hold complex thinking and writing in high esteem. The more a judge is able to display a mastery of those skills, the higher her prestige.

Paul Campos has also noted that the human instinct to get each case right results in crippling complexity: "The emphasis on getting it right, and the agonized struggle to define just what that might entail, produce a distinctive vision of law that is totalizing, relentless, and most oblivious to such crass considerations as time, money, and possible limits to the powers of human reason."[46] Richard Epstein and Robert Kagan likewise note the problem of seeking perfect or total justice in individual cases.[47] As a psychological matter, this quest to decide each case justly and correctly helps explain the desire to add exceptions to codicils under subrules in multifactor tests. Again, the damage from these cases is the cumulative effect systemwide. In trying to get each case perfect and trying to write down reasons for that perfection, complexity multiplies exponentially.

[45] Frederick Schauer, "Incentives, Reputation, and the Inglorious Determinants of Judicial Behavior," 68 *U. Cin. L. Rev.* 615, 627–31 (2000).

[46] Campos, *Jurismania*, 20.

[47] Kagan, *Adversarial Legalism*, 37–40; Epstein, *Simple Rules*, 37–42.

As a matter of practice and custom, judges rarely write judicial decisions as if the cases were tricky or close. To the contrary, judicial opinions are often full of the reasons that the decision is correct and an opposing decision would be flawed. In individual cases this may add to the comfort of the litigants or the confidence in that opinion. Nevertheless, treating hard cases as if they were obviously easy cases is itself a cause of complexity, because writing convincing opinions in hard cases often requires multiple reasons for the result or adding dicta, which creates later confusion in applying the precedent.

A brief review of the backgrounds, incentives, and proclivities of lawyers and lawmaking judges establishes a strong, systemic bias toward complexity. This is not to suggest that there is a one-sided drift toward complexity or that reform efforts are impossible. The reform of civil pleading requirements embodied by the current Federal Rules of Civil Procedure establishes that legal complexity has boundaries and that if the situation grows sufficiently grave, complexity can be rolled back.[48]

A Brief Case Study in Complexity

In my third year of law school, I was fortunate enough to be selected for a clerkship on the U.S. Court of Appeals for the Fourth Circuit. When I received the clerkship, one of my professors advised, "Take our Federal Courts course in the spring. It is the hardest class in law school, but you'll need it for the clerkship." I asked around the law school, and this was indeed the scuttlebutt – everyone who had a clerkship was going to take the class, and it consisted of extremely difficult material. The Federal

[48] Stephen N. Subrin, "How Equity Conquered Common Law: The Federal Rules of Civil Procedure in Historical Perspective," 135 *U. Pa. L. Rev.* 909 (1987). Of course, in American law simplification revolutions are often short-lived. Christopher Fairman and others have persuasively argued that notice pleading (the main simplification effort of the Federal Rules of Civil Procedure) is currently dead for all practical purposes. Christopher M. Fairman, "The Myth of Notice Pleading," 45 *Ariz. L. Rev.* 987 (2003).

Courts course thus embodied my complexity theory. It was filled with the future "elite" lawyers, some likely to be judges themselves one day, all involved the study of some of the most complex law in America.

The Federal Courts course covers the role of the federal courts in the federal system, with a particular focus "on standing and other justiciability questions; power of Congress to define the scope of federal court jurisdiction; state sovereign immunity; abstention; interjurisdictional preclusion and injunctions; and appellate and collateral review, including habeas corpus."[49]

The course was as advertised and the cases were quite difficult to digest. Nonetheless, I found I had quite a different reaction to the material than did my classmates and the professor, who seemed enthralled by the onionlike layers of complexity. It struck me as odd that a set of cases drafted by the finest judges in the land (U.S. Supreme Court Justices), based on law almost wholly within the Court's control (i.e., constitutional or federal common law), would be so convoluted and complicated. I had a true "emperor's new clothes" moment that semester as I came to realize that smart people working on hard problems do not always reach simple, or even good, solutions. Often, smart people working on hard problems produce a vast quantity of unnecessary complexity.

The law of standing was one of the prime offenders in Federal Courts and, as such, it is a good case study. Standing governs when an individual may sue in court. Article III of the U.S. Constitution limits the federal judicial power to hearing "cases" or "controversies." Standing – along with ripeness, mootness, and the political question doctrine – helps define when a plaintiff may bring suit in federal court.[50] I offer a brief

[49] This quote comes from the Vanderbilt Law School catalogue. Vanderbilt University Law School, LAW 744: Federal Courts and the Federal System, available at http://law.vanderbilt.edu/academics/curriculum/index.aspx.

[50] Ripeness asks whether the case is ready to be tried. Mootness asks whether the plaintiff still has an interest in the case at issue. The political question doctrine asks whether the case raises issues better resolved by nonjudicial actors, either because the Constitution requires it or because other branches are better situated to resolve the issues.

overview of standing not in an effort to explain it – I sincerely doubt that anyone could do that – but to show how the tests and subtests create a system so confused as to be fully indeterminate.

The Supreme Court has announced:

> [T]hree requirements . . . constitute the irreducible constitutional minimum of standing. First, a plaintiff must demonstrate an injury in fact, which is concrete, distinct and palpable, and actual or imminent. Second, a plaintiff must establish a causal connection between the injury and the conduct complained of – the injury has to be fairly traceable to the challenged action of the defendant, and not the result of some third party not before the court. Third, a plaintiff must show the substantial likelihood that the requested relief will remedy the alleged injury in fact.[51]

In addition to the constitutional requirements, there are a series of prudential standing principles: "The general prohibition on a litigant's raising another person's legal rights, the rule barring adjudication of generalized grievances more appropriately addressed in the representative branches, and the requirement that a plaintiff's complaint fall within the zone of interests protected by the law invoked."[52] In many of the standing cases the Court does not explicitly state whether its decision was prudential or constitutional.[53] Because prudential standing can be overridden by Congress but constitutional standing cannot, the distinction is, nevertheless, quite important.[54]

Each of the six tests listed above has subtests, and some have competing tests that are used in some cases, but not in others. Take the very first of the three constitutional prongs, injury. Erwin Chemerinsky separates the "injury-in-fact" requirement into two related questions – whether the

[51] *McConnell v. Federal Election Commission*, 540 U.S. 93, 225–26 (2003).

[52] *Allen v. Wright,* 468 U.S. 737, 751 (1984).

[53] Craig R. Gottlieb, "How Standing Has Fallen: The Need to Separate Constitutional and Prudential Concerns," 142 *U. Pa. L. Rev.* 1063 (1994).

[54] Erwin Chemerinsky, *Federal Jurisdiction,* 2nd ed. (St. Paul, MN: West, 1994), 57–58.

plaintiff personally suffered the injury, and whether the injury was sufficiently concrete.[55]

Even this division does not capture the multifaceted nature of the "injury-in-fact" determination, because everything tends to bleed together. For example, in *Lujan v. National Wildlife Federation,* the plaintiff, National Wildlife Foundation, lost because no individual member of the organization alleged that she had traveled to the specific government land at issue.[56] Justice Antonin Scalia wrote *Lujan* and, in addition to the narrow holding requiring a visit to the affected land, he announced a quite firm requirement that environmental plaintiffs state a "concrete and particularized" injury. This, in turn, requires "specific facts" to support the plaintiffs' claims, not just generalized harm from environmental degradation.[57] Thus *Lujan* had both a "personal" injury aspect (did the plaintiff personally visit the affected land) and a "concreteness" aspect (was the alleged injury concrete and particularized enough).

The concreteness portion of *Lujan*, however, was later overruled, or substantially watered down, by *Friends of the Earth, Inc. v. Laidlaw Environmental Services*.[58] *Friends of the Earth* found standing when a plaintiff alleged visiting the actual polluted river at issue but could not allege any injury concrete enough to satisfy Justice Scalia, who wrote a scathing dissent.[59] As such, *Friends of the Earth* upheld the "personal" aspect of *Lujan*, but allowed a lesser showing on the concreteness question, all without explicitly overruling anything that came before.

The funny thing about this very brief description of one small corner of standing law is that even this black-letter and bare-bones description of the law is bewildering, and I have made almost no effort whatsoever to describe or synthesize the cases themselves. I have not done this

[55] Id. at 58–65.

[56] *Lujan v. National Wildlife Federation,* 497 U.S. 871 (1990).

[57] *Lujan*, 497 U.S. at 560–65.

[58] *Friends of the Earth, Inc. v. Laidlaw Environmental Services,* 528 U.S. 167 (2000).

[59] Id. at 198–215.

because standing cases have been called "notoriously inconsistent,"[60] a "jumbled mess,"[61] "a quagmire,"[62] a "chaotic collection of rules and standards,"[63] "confused,"[64] and "incoherent."[65] As a further example, a Westlaw search of all law reviews for the term "standing" in the same sentence as "complex" or "complexity" results in 1,299 documents.[66]

There are several reasons that standing law is a great case study for the complexity theory laid out earlier. First, even though standing may be virtually unknown outside the legal profession, it is critically important to litigants. If a person is willing to suffer the expense and hassle of bringing a lawsuit in federal court, it is of tremendous importance that she not get bounced for lack of standing.

Second, standing, ripeness, mootness, and the political question doctrine are all fully within the control of the Supreme Court and, to a lesser extent, the lower federal courts. None of the complexity in this law comes from congressional actions or bad legislative drafting or bureaucratic overenthusiasm. Standing is a purely judicial doctrine, created as a gloss on two words, "case" and "controversy." This means that the judges involved have no one to blame but themselves for complexity and indeterminacy.

Third, standing is one of those areas of the law in which it is obvious that the complexity involved is not the kind that leads to clearer application of the law on a more individual basis – in other words, standing complexity is not of the sort that might confer a benefit along with its

[60] *Hein v. Freedom From Religion Foundation, Inc.*, 127 S.Ct. 2553, 2574 (2007) (Scalia, J., concurring).

[61] John A. Ferejohn and Larry D. Kramer, "Independent Judges, Dependent Judiciary: Institutionalizing Judicial Restraint," 77 *N.Y.U. L. Rev.* 962, 1010 (2002).

[62] Kathleen C. Engel, "Do Cities Have Standing? Redressing the Externalities of Predatory Lending," 38 *Conn. L. Rev.* 355, 389 (2006).

[63] Nancy Staudt, "Modeling Standing," 79 *N.Y.U. L. Rev.* 612, 671 (2004).

[64] Michael A. Cohen, "Plaintiffs' Standing in *Lee v. Oregon*: The Judicially Assisted Demise of the Oregon Death with Dignity Act," 74 *Or. L. Rev.* 741, 743 (1995).

[65] Andrew F. Hessick, "Standing, Injury in Fact, and Private Rights," 93 *Cornell L. Rev.* 275, 276 (2008).

[66] I searched for "standing /s complex complexity" in the JLR database.

costs. To the contrary, as standing law has grown more complicated, its application has grown increasingly cumbersome and its applicability to any given set of facts has grown even harder to predict.

As noted previously, this makes standing a valuable area of the law for lawyers. For any given case involving environmental law or group rights, there is the strong possibility of a challenge to standing. Because of the confusion in the law, this challenge will require a substantial amount of legal work for all the litigants. It will allow clever lawyers to craft and recraft highly technical arguments on either side of the issue, all before the merits are even reached.

Fourth, standing law well establishes the value of complexity for judges. Standing and related doctrines are an easy route for judges to get rid of cases they do not like, either because of political preferences or a distaste for the litigants or the subject area. Richard Pierce argues that lawyers can predict standing decisions "with much greater accuracy if they ignore doctrine and rely entirely on a simple description of the law of standing that is rooted in political science: judges provide access to the courts to individuals who seek to further the political and ideological agendas of judges."[67] Standing is the perfect example for the complexity theory because the law is sufficiently complex that a judge has great discretion to decide whether to find standing and yet still has plenty of

[67] Richard J. Pierce, "Is Standing Law or Politics?," 77 *N.C. L. Rev.* 1741, 1742–43 (1999). Pierce establishes this argument as follows: "Five Supreme Court decisions issued between 1991 and 1998 illustrate the accuracy of the political scientist's description of the law of standing. In those cases, the Court resolved standing disputes applicable to environmentalists (two cases), employees, prisoners, and banks. In each case, the Justices divided either five-to-four or six-to-three on the standing issue. In each case, the 'votes' of the Justices were as easy to predict as the votes of their ideological counterparts in the legislature. Liberals voted to grant access to the courts to environmentalists, employees, and prisoners, but not to banks. Conservatives voted to grant access to banks, but not to environmentalists, employees, or prisoners. Of course, in each case, all the Justices claimed to reach their politically preferred result through objective application of legal doctrines. The applicable doctrines are so malleable, however, that it is impossible to avoid the inference that the Justices manipulated the doctrines to rationalize their politically preferred results." Id. at 1743.

complexity to cover her hindquarters in a learned written opinion either denying or granting the right to sue.

Fifth, standing shows how judges are drawn to and enjoy complexity. The Supreme Court has returned again and again to standing in the past thirty years, with each new foray further muddying the waters. The cases are often split. They frequently involve lengthy dissents and multiple concurrences. In short, there is little to suggest that the Justices dislike standing law or that they see any particular need to clarify, avoid, or scrap it. To the contrary, the standing cases look like the work of legal technicians and theorists who are enjoying themselves.

In conclusion, a combination of institutional factors leads both lawyers and lawmaking judges to favor complexity in law creation. The question of what, if anything, can or should be done about the problem, as the question of what should be done about the lawyer–judge bias, however, is harder to tackle. One hope is that judges will recognize the costs of complexity and adjust their behavior accordingly. Given the judicial taste for multifactor balancing tests and complicated procedures, this result seems rather unlikely. There is an old adage that "hard cases make bad law." A corollary might be that interesting cases make unnecessarily complex law. The next chapter turns to what we might do about all this.

12 Rays of Hope, Ramifications, and Possible Solutions

I would like to see more people from outside the judicial monastery, somebody who has had some real-life experience, not just as a judge.
– Senator Patrick Leahy on Supreme Court appointments[1]

BEFORE I TURN TO RAMIFICATIONS AND SOLUTIONS, I discuss a trio of recent Supreme Court cases that suggest a growing awareness of, and resistance to, the lawyer–judge bias. First, consider *Montejo v. Louisiana*,[2] which I briefly discussed in Chapter 3. *Montejo* overruled *Michigan v. Jackson*,[3] which was a criminal procedure case that held that the police could not question a suspect after she had requested the appointment of a lawyer at an arraignment unless the lawyer was present.[4] *Jackson* stated a strict rule to ensure that questioning under these circumstances would not occur; even if the suspect waived the presence of counsel, any statement in response to lawyerless police questioning must be suppressed.[5] This rule was helpful and deferential to lawyers. As soon as a lawyer was appointed, the lawyer could

[1] Douglas K. Daniel, "Senators: Next Justice Should Have Wide Experience," *Yahoo News*, May 3, 2009, available at http://news.yahoo.com/s/ap/20090503/ap_on_go_su_co/us_scotus_senate.

[2] *Montejo v. Louisiana*, 129 S.Ct. 2079 (2009).

[3] *Michigan v. Jackson*, 475 U.S. 625 (1986).

[4] Id. at 636.

[5] Id.

count on the police to leave the client alone when the lawyer was not present.

Montejo eliminated *Jackson*'s prophylactic rule. After *Montejo*, the police can question a represented defendant, and if that defendant waives the presence of a lawyer, the defendant's statements are now admissible.[6] Notably, the Court explicitly rejected an appeal to the Model Rules of Professional Conduct:

> [*Jackson*'s] rule appears to have its theoretical roots in codes of legal ethics, not the Sixth Amendment. The American Bar Association's Model Rules of Professional Conduct (which nearly all States have adopted into law in whole or in part) mandate that "a lawyer shall not communicate about the subject of [a] representation with a party the lawyer knows to be represented by another lawyer in the matter, unless the lawyer has the consent of the other lawyer or is authorized to do so by law or a court order." Model Rule 4.2 (2008). But the Constitution does not codify the ABA's Model Rules, and does not make investigating police officers lawyers.[7]

Admittedly, *Montejo* may say more about the current Court's hostility to criminal defendants than about its feelings on the Model Rules, but the preceding quote is still remarkably strident. Further, the overruled case, *Michigan v. Jackson*, was from 1986, not 1966, so *Jackson* itself was a pro-lawyer and pro-defendant decision during a time when the Court was otherwise retracting constitutional protections for criminal defendants. *Montejo*'s explicit rejection of the Model Rules, to the disadvantage of defendants represented by counsel, is thus an explicit step away from the lawyer–judge bias.

Second, *Milavetz, Gallop & Milavetz v. United States*[8] held that the Bankruptcy Abuse Prevention and Consumer Protection Act (BAPCPA) could limit the advice that lawyers give to clients, despite the

[6] *Montejo*, 129 S.Ct. at 2085–91.

[7] Id. at 287.

[8] *Milavetz, Gallop & Milavetz v. United States*, 130 S.Ct. 1324 (2010).

First Amendment. BAPCPA applies to "debt relief agencies" and bans certain types of advice, notably advice to incur more debt in contemplation of bankruptcy.[9] A "debt relief agency" includes "any person who provides any bankruptcy assistance to an assisted person in return for payment or who is a bankruptcy petition preparer."[10]

The lower court opinions in *Milavetz* are actually terrific lawyer–judge bias cases. Despite the broad definition of "debt relief agency," the district court in *Milavetz* held that lawyers were not included and were "relieved of any duties relating to BAPCPA."[11] The U.S. Court of Appeals for the Eighth Circuit reversed on that ground, but held that the BAPCPA provisions that covered attorney advice to clients were impermissible under the First Amendment.[12]

The Supreme Court held that BAPCPA applied to lawyers and that the restriction on advice was allowable under the First Amendment. The Court did so by reading BAPCPA narrowly to prohibit a lawyer "from advising a debtor to incur more debt because the debtor is filing for bankruptcy, rather than for a valid purpose."[13] This meant that BAPCPA barred lawyers only from giving a client advice to break the law, which even the Model Rules suggest is appropriate, and the Court cites and quotes Model Rule 1.2(d).[14] Nevertheless, applying BAPCPA to lawyers and enforcing its strictures despite the imposition on the lawyer–client relationship is progress.

Last, *Jerman v. Carlisle, McNellie, Rini, Kramer & Ulrich LPA*[15] refused to grant a "mistake-of-law" defense under the Fair Debt

[9] Id. at 1330.

[10] Id. (ellipses and other punctuation omitted).

[11] *Milavetz, Gallop & Milavetz P.A. v. United States*, 2007 WL 1227598 (D. Minn. 2007).

[12] *Milavetz, Gallop & Milavetz P.A. v. United States*, 541 F.3d 785 (8th Cir. 2008).

[13] *Milavetz*, 130 S.Ct. at 1336.

[14] Id. at 1337–38 (quoting ABA Model Rule of Professional Conduct 1.2(d) (2009) ("A lawyer shall not counsel a client to engage, or assist a client, in conduct that the lawyer knows is criminal or fraudulent").

[15] *Jerman v. Carlisle, McNellie, Rini, Kramer & Ulrich LPA*, 130 S.Ct. 1605 (2010).

Collection Practices Act (FDCPA) to lawyers. The law firm in *Jerman* argued that enforcing the FDCPA against lawyers without a mistake-of-law defense would create "an irreconcilable conflict between an attorney's personal financial interest and her ethical obligation of zealous advocacy on behalf of a client," because the lawyer would be so worried about FDCPA liability that she would act against her client's interests.[16]

The Court explicitly rejected this claim of lawyer exceptionalism and held that "[t]o the extent the FDCPA imposes some constraints on a lawyer's advocacy on behalf of a client, it is hardly unique in our law."[17] Taken together, these three cases evince a dawning understanding that not every reference to the sanctity of the lawyer–client bond should result in special exemptions for the legal profession. It is too soon to say that these cases mark a new trend; furthermore, the U.S. Supreme Court hears so few cases that such a trend would trickle down slowly, if at all. These cases are a helpful counterpoint, however, and offer some hope that the lawyer–judge bias may recede over time.

Ramifications

Notwithstanding these recent developments, I hope that I have convinced you that the lawyer–judge bias is real and that it explains a diverse subset of cases and doctrines that affect the legal profession. The variety of case areas and situations in which the lawyer–judge bias appears are part of what made this topic sufficiently interesting to write a whole book about. As I was writing, new examples appeared and colleagues continuously recommended new avenues of exploration. I have little doubt I could fill a second volume if need be.

The sources of this bias are legion but can be divided into two broad categories. The first is that judges have every possible incentive to favor the legal profession. These incentives run from the venal – judges count

[16] Id. at 1620.
[17] Id. at 1622.

on lawyers to get and keep their jobs – to the social – judges' friends and colleagues are often lawyers – to a simple interest in hassle-free relations with the main repeat players in their job, the lawyers.

The second category is more subtle, but perhaps more powerful – the effect of years of training and socialization as members of the legal profession. Judges have learned more than how to "think like a lawyer" over the course of their distinguished legal careers. They have internalized the norms and behaviors of the legal profession. As noted in Chapter 2, to say that all judges were lawyers first is both temporally and spiritually accurate.

These two basic reasons also track two economic theories. The first is public choice theory. Judges (like everyone else) are assumed to be rational and self-interested. Thus, their actions will be based on what most closely tracks their incentives, and it is clear that keeping lawyers happy is in every judge's interest.

The socialization of lawyer-judges is also a compelling example of "institutions" in action. Judges are driven by the institution of legal thought. For their entire careers, they have learned a very specialized way of seeing the world and analyzing legal disputes. It is unrealistic to expect these former lawyers to abandon the very thought processes that led them to the bench. To the contrary, judges lean on the institution of legal thought even more as judges than as lawyers. It is thus quite predictable that these same judges would decide cases that affect the legal profession as lawyers; it would be impossible for them to apply a different mindset.

The results in the Enron case establish that the systematic bias in favor of the legal profession has real-world consequences. It is not clear whether stricter oversight of the profession or harsher criminal or civil penalties would have affected the Enron lawyers ex ante (it did not apparently affect the accountants or the executives), but the lack of punishment certainly will not deter future lawyers, and it leaves an uncomfortable asymmetry in the treatment of the main Enron players.

Chapter 11 establishes that the lawyer–judge bias has contributed to the "appalling complexity" of American law. I recognize that any claim about legal complexity and its causes will prove controversial, and I realize that Chapter 11's argument is the hardest to prove or swallow. That said, in many ways Chapter 11 is the most important chapter in the book, because it purports that the lawyer–judge bias has played a major role in the complex mess that American law and procedure have become. It is also a major source of the legal system's grave expenses of time, energy, and money (all with little accompanying return in terms of consistency or clarity). These problems have contributed to waning public confidence in lawyers, judges, and the entire system. In short, if one gives credence to the argument in Chapter 11, it substantially raises the stakes on the effects (and possible necessary cures) of the lawyer–judge bias.

If you are unconvinced by Chapter 11, but do believe the lawyer–judge bias is real, you might still ask, "So what?" It may be that judges treat lawyers differently and better, but maybe this treatment is justified. Maybe lawyers are, in fact, special. Lawyers do play an important role in our society, which may justify certain latitudes. Certainly, the judicial language in many of these cases suggests that judges believe so: lawyers are officers of the court, critical to the administration of justice, and deserve to be treated differently.

I have two responses to this argument. First, it strikes me as self-evidently insalubrious to have the judiciary favor one group of persons over others. If the legal profession is so critical, let the judges lobby along with the lawyers before legislatures, as everyone else does. Given the unique position of the judiciary in a common law system within a democracy, it is clearly inappropriate for judges to create special benefits for lawyers, even if they are truly deserving. Legislatures should make those decisions.

Further, even if it is true that lawyers play a special role in the adjudicatory process, many of the examples in this book have nothing to do with the inner workings of the court system. To the contrary, judges have used this justification to defend everything from *cy pres* gifts to legal groups to the common law lawyers' liens. These case law examples clearly do nothing to make the judicial process any easier. They do, however, make life better for lawyers.

Small-Scale Solutions

If you concede that the lawyer–judge bias exists, you still may not see the need for any radical changes. After all, the American justice system is, on the whole, one of the very best and most just systems in the world. That may be damning with faint praise, but sometimes choosing the least bad option is a wise choice.

Drawing attention to the lawyer–judge bias is, in and of itself, a partial solution. Gathering the cases, making the argument, and shedding light on the trend may be enough to shift the law in some of these areas. As the discussion of the underlying theory in Chapter 2 noted, some or most of the bias results from unconscious judicial favoritism toward lawyers based on the judges' own experiences and naturally increased empathy for litigants who share similar backgrounds and experiences. Perhaps pointing out the cumulative effects of these unconscious decisions will lead to more self-awareness and some reform. Public choice theory also predicts that insofar as public awareness of the issue grows, there will be pressure on the judiciary to rein any bias in a bit.

One possible solution, therefore, is to bang the drum and hope that the judiciary is paying attention and reacts appropriately. This solution has the advantage of not upsetting other aspects of the American justice system. Nevertheless, given the recalcitrance and long history of the lawyer–judge bias, increased awareness may have little effect.

Large-Scale Solutions

This leads to the potential larger solutions. Drawing attention to the lawyer–judge bias allows for a frank discussion of the costs and benefits of the American model for selecting judges. It is certainly not the case that the current system should be abandoned because it tends to favor lawyers without a much deeper evaluation of the strengths and weaknesses of alternatives. Over the years commentators have debated the merits of the common law judicial selection process versus civil law procedures.[18] The advantage to recognizing the lawyer–judge bias is that the judges' sympathy for lawyers can be balanced along with the various other strengths and weaknesses of each system.

At a minimum, the recognition of the lawyer–judge bias calls for some thinking about the hows and whys of our current model of judicial selection. Most people assume that all judges should be former lawyers because that is how it has been done for years.

The next part of this chapter argues that it is not obvious that all, or even any, judges should be former lawyers. To the contrary, the history of this country and the model of civil law judiciaries around the world demonstrates that a workable system could be organized around lay judges or professionally trained judges who have never been lawyers.

Recall the discussion in Chapter 5 of how lawyer-judges came into being in fourteenth-century England. The selection of lawyer-judges to run the new, centralized courts was as much a result of happenstance as any careful forethought of the alternatives. Over time this structure ossified into a tradition. The fact that the traditions have endured is obviously a sign of strength. Nevertheless, endurance should never be mistaken for eternal endorsement.

Lay judges have always been common in the United Kingdom, America, and around the world.[19] The current lawyer-centric structure of the American justice system – in which the vast majority of all judges are lawyers, lay representation is explicitly barred by law, and pro se

[18] See, e.g., Charles H. Koch, Jr., "The Advantages of the Civil Law Judicial Design as the Model For Emerging Legal Systems," 11 *Ind. J. Global Legal Stud.* 139 (2004).

[19] Doris Marie Provine, "Lay Judiciaries," in *Legal Systems of the World: A Political, Social and Cultural Encyclopedia, Vol. II*, ed. Herbert M. Kritzer (Santa Barbara, CA: ABC-CLIO, 2002), 867–70.

appearances are frowned on by judges and clerk's offices – is relatively new.

The office of the justice of the peace originated in England and was traditionally staffed by nonlawyers. From the fifteenth century on, justices of the peace were quite important. They generally supervised the criminal process, and their powers included summary arrest.[20] Furthermore, until 1834, lords with no legal training heard appeals in the House of Lords.[21] Currently, British justices of the peace (also known as magistrates) are laypersons who receive training before assuming office and require continuing education every three years.[22] They hear certain classes of civil and criminal cases and adjudicate 90 percent of all criminal cases in England.[23]

The history of lay judges in America is even richer. Colonial America had practically no lawyer-judges.[24] Until the late 1700s, many justices of the newly established state supreme courts had never studied or practiced law themselves.[25] For example, in 1798 two of the three justices on the New Hampshire Supreme Court were ministers, not lawyers.[26]

Moreover, the British justice of the peace was basically transplanted to America, with lay judges running courts of limited jurisdiction.[27] Such courts were established in colonial times and went westward with the

[20] John P. Dawson, *A History of Lay Judges* (Cambridge, MA: Harvard University Press, 1960), 138–39.

[21] Adrian Vermeule, "Should We Have Lay Justices?," 59 *Stan. L. Rev.* 1569, 1573 (2007).

[22] Maria Dakolias, "A Strategy for Judicial Reform: The Experience in Latin America," 36 *Va. J. Int'l L.* 167, 205 & n. 162 (1995).

[23] Vermeule, "Should We Have Lay Justices?," 1573; Dakolias, "A Strategy for Judicial Reform," 204 and n. 159.

[24] Doris Marie Provine, *Judging Credentials: Nonlawyer Judges and the Politics of Professionalism* (Chicago: University of Chicago Press, 1986), 1.

[25] Cathy Lesser Mansfield, "Disorder in the People's Court: Rethinking the Role of Non-Lawyer Judges in Limited Jurisdiction Court Civil Cases," 29 *N.M. L. Rev.* 119, 134 (1999).

[26] John Phillip Reid, "Controlling the Law: Legal Politics," in John Phillip Reid, *Early National New Hampshire* (DeKalb: Northern Illinois University Press, 2004), 22.

[27] Provine, *Judging Credentials*, xii.

pioneers.[28] In the eighteenth, nineteenth, and early twentieth centuries, many judges and justices of the peace were not lawyers. Even today, some American justices of the peace are not lawyers.[29]

Predictably, bar associations were at the forefront of the (largely successful) effort to eliminate lay judges.[30] There are some great old articles and books by scions of the bar denouncing justices of the peace. For example, in 1927, Professor Chester H. Smith called lay judges an "anachronism in our jurisprudence the perpetuation of which cannot be justified."[31] In 1905, Simeon Baldwin derided "the vesting of jurisdiction of small civil causes in justices of the peace" as the "weakest point" in the American judiciary.[32]

Lay judges are quite common in other countries. In Germany, lay judges staff criminal courts of first instance. In the *Amtsgericht*, which hears civil and less serious criminal cases, one professional judge sits with two lay judges. Likewise, in the *Landgericht*, which hears all serious criminal cases, three professional judges sit with two lay judges. Japan recently introduced lay judges into its criminal justice system by creating hearing panels composed of three career judges and six lay judges. Austria, the Czech Republic, France, Italy, Sweden, Latvia, Cuba, and Kosovo all use nonlawyer judges on appellate courts or courts that hear serious criminal charges.[33]

Further, as noted in Chapter 5, in the nineteenth century lay representation was quite common all over the United States. Many states had no restrictions on the practice of law. Currently the United Kingdom

[28] Julia Lamber and Mary Lee Luskin, "City and Town Courts: Mapping Their Dimensions," 67 *Ind. L.J.* 59, 59 and n. 1 (1991).

[29] Vermeule, "Should We Have Lay Justices," 1573; *Goodson v. State*, 991 P.2d 472, 444–45 (Nev. 1999) (holding that a misdemeanor trial before a nonlawyer justice of the peace was constitutional).

[30] Provine, *Judging Credentials*, 1–60.

[31] Chester H. Smith, "The Justice of the Peace System in the United States," 15 *Cal. L. Rev.* 118, 140–41 (1927).

[32] Simeon Baldwin, *The American Judiciary* (New York: The Century Co., 1905), 129.

[33] Vermeule, "Should We Have Lay Justices?," 1573–74.

has largely eliminated restrictions on the unauthorized practice of law, essentially deregulating large swaths of its legal profession.[34]

Last, although selecting former lawyers as judges seems natural and obvious in this country, the opposite is true in civil law countries, which train their judges separately. Civil law systems are those based on Roman law and often have commercial laws based on the French Napoleonic Commercial Code.[35]

The training and selection of judges is a key distinction between civil law and common law systems. Civil law judges are educated and apprenticed as judges, not lawyers, and usually serve that role throughout their career. Existing judges train the new judges and they also control promotions and career advancement. These are merit systems and, in theory, the very best judges rise to the highest judicial offices.[36] The fact that so many countries select and train judges differently and still have functioning rules of law suggests that the common law lawyer-judge model is not the only route to success.

As noted in Chapter 2, American judges are not ever really trained to be judges. Practice offers future judges a chance to observe a judge's job from the lawyer's point of view and provides training in advocacy and legal reasoning. Nevertheless, a judge's job is quite distinct from a lawyer's.

[34] Gillian K. Hadfield, "Legal Barriers To Innovation: The Growing Economic Cost of Professional Control Over Corporate Legal Markets," 60 *Stan. L. Rev.* 1689, 1731 (2008).

[35] *Introduction to Foreign Legal Systems*, eds. Richard A. Danner and Marie-Louise H. Bernal (New York: Oceana, 1994), 47–48. See generally id. at 47–55 for more on the differences between common and civil law systems. Civil law systems can be further subdivided into two main categories: the Romanist-Latin group (Belgium, Italy, France, the Netherlands, Portugal, Spain, former colonies of the same, countries of Central and South America, Egypt and several other Arab countries, Puerto Rico, Louisiana, and Quebec); and the Germanic group (Austria, Germany, Switzerland, Denmark, Finland, Iceland, Norway, Sweden, several Central and Eastern European countries, Greece, Turkey, and Japan). *Introduction to Foreign Legal Systems*, 49–50.

[36] Koch, "The Advantages of the Civil Law Judicial Design," 142–46.

The large-scale solutions to the problem are clear, but radical: move to more nonlawyer judges, train judges separately, or both. A full argument about the relative merits of lay judges versus separately trained judges versus lawyer-judges is beyond the scope of this book. Nevertheless, I will offer some general thoughts on the issue here.

Either measure would reduce or eliminate the lawyer–judge bias. Some of the institutional problems of capture would remain, because lawyers and judges (however selected) will always be the repeat players in the game and have certain shared incentives. Moreover, under any system, lawyers will have a great deal of interest in who becomes a judge and will likely play an active role in selecting judges, so the odds that any judge will owe her job to support from lawyers would likely remain high.

Nevertheless, nonlawyer judges would not share the experiences, thought processes, social contacts, and general fraternity with the legal profession. This alone would make a large difference. Assuming the nonlawyer judges came from a populace that is usually wary and distrustful of lawyers, that effect may well be multiplied. The fact that lawyers have spent years lobbying courts to take over their regulation is a sign that bar associations well understand that lawyer-judges will be more favorable than the public on these issues.

A hybrid solution is certainly possible. As noted earlier, Japan and Germany (among other countries) have hybrid judicial panels consisting of professional and lay judges for certain types of cases. Adrian Vermeule has recently argued that there should be at least one nonlawyer Justice of the U.S. Supreme Court, and possibly more.[37] The U.S. Constitution prescribes minimum age and citizenship qualifications for members of Congress, senators, and presidents, but imposes no particular qualifications for federal judges.[38] Vermeule argues that because

[37] Vermeule, "Should We Have Lay Justices?"

[38] U.S. Const. art. I, §2, cl. 2 (Representatives); id. §3, cl. 3 (Senators); id. art. II, §1, cl. 4 (Presidents).

nonlawyers would bring different expertise to deciding cases, the overall quality of the judgments would rise.[39]

Vermeule's argument does not need to be limited to the Supreme Court, however, and a mixed model of lay and professional judges could work at any level of the judiciary. This might satisfy those who cannot imagine a judiciary that included nonlawyers, because it would blend different types of expertise and perspectives. It might also naturally lessen the conscious and unconscious factors that lead to the lawyer–judge bias.

A mixed model could also allow for more public participation and legitimacy in the judiciary, as well as more transparency. One of the key factors in the creation of both the lawyer–judge bias cases and, more generally, indeterminate complexity is the attempt by judges and lawyers to work within a very specialized type of legal reasoning and language. In some cases this intricate reasoning and language is consciously or unconsciously obfuscatory; nonlawyer judges could curtail this habit.

This idea is not without American precedent. Greg Sergienko has done a great study of New York's 1821 state constitution. Under the 1821 constitution, the state's highest court included a majority of state senators to counteract the appointed judges. Conceptually, the constitution sought to give elected legislators control of the court in the hope that senatorial judges would abolish legal technicalities and promote justice.[40]

The lay senator-judges voted against the professional judges many times and occasionally reversed the decisions of lower courts over the complaints of the professional judges. Many rejected precedent and relied instead on principles of morality, common sense, and justice.[41]

Sergienko notes that the lay senator-judges adopted some reforms that disfavored lawyers over the objection of the professional judges,

[39] Vermeule, "Should We Have Lay Justices?," 1581–97.

[40] Greg Sergienko, "A Body of Sound Practical Common Sense: Law Reform Through Lay Judges, Public Choice Theory, and the Transformation of American Law," 41 *Am. J. Legal Hist.* 175, 177–85 (1997).

[41] Id. at 185–205.

suggesting that the "judges themselves constituted a special interest, against which lay judges provided an appropriate guard."[42] For example, some New York statutes required losing plaintiffs to pay double costs to a party (such as a sheriff) deemed likely to suffer harassment through lawsuits. Under prior practice the additional costs were paid to the defendant's lawyer. The senator-judges overruled one of these cases and awarded the costs to the defendant himself.[43]

A second example is less sanguine. Lois Harrison was the lone nonlawyer involved in drafting the ABA Model Rules of Professional Conduct. Ted Schneyer reports that she advocated for a single change to the rules: requiring all lawyer fee agreements to be written.[44] This suggestion survived the drafting process but was voted out by the ABA House of Delegates.[45] To this day, the Model Rules do not require written fee agreements.[46] These examples, along with the international experience, show that a hybrid judiciary is workable. It also shows that token lay involvement will likely change little.

Another possibility is a separate track for training judges. The job of a judge is quite distinct from that of a lawyer, and a separate track for training might accomplish two critical reforms. The training could emphasize the importance of simplicity and clarity in the law and would lessen the tendency to favor lawyers.

A middle-ground alternative is a more extensive training break between exiting practice and becoming a judge. Although it is not clear that an institution such as legal thought or years of membership in the legal profession can (or even should) be unlearned, a training period that forced new judges to internalize and strongly consider the very different role they were undertaking would likely prove helpful.

[42] Id. at 178–79.

[43] Id. at 202–03.

[44] Theodore Schneyer, "Professionalism as Politics: The Making of a Modern Legal Ethics Code," in *Lawyers' Ideals/Lawyers' Practices*, eds. Robert Nelson et al. (Ithaca, NY: Cornell University Press, 1992), 95–109.

[45] Id.

[46] Model Rule of Professional Responsibility 1.5(b) (2008).

Frankly, though, the likeliest reform is also the easiest reform. Current judges must become more aware of the lawyer–judge bias, and the public must also complain when these cases arise. It is not acceptable to have one of the three branches of government systematically favor a profession. Hopefully, sunshine can prove the best disinfectant.

Index